THE

FATE

OF

WONDER

THE

FATE

OF

WONDER

Wittgenstein's Critique
of Metaphysics
and Modernity

KEVIN M. CAHILL

COLUMBIA UNIVERSITY PRESS

NEW YORK

COLUMBIA UNIVERSITY PRESS
Publishers Since 1893
New York   Chichester, West Sussex

Copyright © 2011 Columbia University Press

Library of Congress Cataloging-in-Publication Data
Cahill, Kevin (Kevin M.)
The Fate of Wonder : Wittgenstein's critique of metaphysics and modernity /
Kevin M. Cahill.
p. cm. — (Columbia themes in philosophy)
Includes bibliographical references (p.   ) and index.
ISBN 978-0-231-15800-8 (cloth : alk. paper) — ISBN 978-0-231-52811-5 (e-book)
1. Wittgenstein, Ludwig, 1889–1951. I. Title.

B3376.W564C32 2011
192—dc22   2011005422

Columbia University Press books are printed on permanent
and durable acid-free paper.
This book is printed on paper with recycled content.
Printed in the United States of America

c 10 9 8 7 6 5 4 3 2 1

References to Internet Web sites (URLs) were accurate at the time of writing.
Neither the author nor Columbia University Press is responsible for URLs that
may have expired or changed since the manuscript was prepared.

To my earliest fellows in wonder,

my pals from St. Gabriel Parish, San Francisco,

wherever they may be

CONTENTS

2. The Ethical Purpose of the *Tractatus*   42

3. A Resolute Failure   88

Conclusion to Part I   99

PART II

4. The Concept of Progress in Wittgenstein's Thought   107

5. The Truly Apocalyptic View 125

6. The Fate of Metaphysics 151

PREFACE AND ACKNOWLEDGMENTS

Abrief word on the text: I expect that some readers will find the many long endnotes tedious and perhaps a sign of limited powers of expression. My apology for this is only partial, however, because provided in the endnotes are many important qualifications and explanations, which, while they might have been distractions if given in the main text, contain what I believe to be much useful information. I therefore ask for the reader's patience and encourage him or her to take the time to read them.

There are two people in particular who deserve special thanks here. The first is Hubert Dreyfus, who more than anyone else fostered my interest in the sorts of problems that are important for this book. Over the course of nearly thirty years, from when I was an undergraduate knocking on his door during office hours to the 2005–2006 academic year, which I spent as a visiting scholar at Berkeley, Dreyfus has been both very generous with his time and an inspirational teacher. The second person to deserve special thanks is my dissertation advisor at the University of Virginia, Cora Diamond. A better advisor or teacher of Wittgenstein is simply unimaginable to me. Both during my years in graduate school and later, Diamond's careful reading and insightful comments greatly helped me to improve most of what, in one form or another, eventually became the final text. In no way should it be assumed, however, that either Dreyfus or Diamond has given his or her imprimatur to this book. I am solely responsible for its content.

Thanks also to the following institutions and persons for making possible two research stays that were essential to finishing the book: the Department of Philosophy at the University of California, Berkeley, where I was a visiting scholar for the 2005–2006 academic year; the Department of Philosophy at the University of Trondheim, for helping to make this stay in Berkeley possible; and the Department of Philosophy at the University of Bergen, for granting me permission to spend the spring semester of 2009 in California. Finally, thanks to Professor Carla Frecerro, director of the Center for Cultural Studies at the University of California–Santa Cruz, for her hospitality during my stay as a resident scholar for winter and spring quarters, 2009. It was here that I put the text into its nearly completed form.

Portions of chapter 2 have appeared as "The *Tractatus*, Ethics, and Authenticity," *Journal of Philosophical Research* 29 (2004): 267–288; "Explanation, Wonder, and the Cultural Point of the *Tractatus*," *Norsk Filosofisk Tidsskrift* 44, no. 3–4 (2009): 206–217; and "30. Dezember 1929, Zu Heidegger: Was Konnte Wittgenstein sich Denken?" proceedings from the conference "To Be or Not to Be Influenced: Wittgenstein and His Treatment of Other Thinkers" (forthcoming in German from Parerga Verlag, Berlin). Much of chapter 3 has appeared as "Ethics and the *Tractatus*: A Resolute Failure," *Philosophy* 79, no. 1 (January 2004): 33–55. Much of chapter 4 has appeared as "The Concept of Progress in Wittgenstein's Thought," *Review of Metaphysics* 40, no. 1 (September 2006): 71–100. Portions of chapter 5 have appeared as "*Bildung* and Decline," *Philosophical Investigations* 32, no. 1 (January 2009): 23–43. Much of chapter 6 has appeared as "Wittgenstein and the Fate of Metaphysics," *Sats: Nordic Journal of Philosophy* 9, no. 2 (2008): 61–73. I am grateful to the publishers concerned for permission to reprint this material.

THE
FATE
OF
WONDER

INTRODUCTION

I.1

Stephen Toulmin has described how, as students of Wittgenstein, he and his class-mates tended to make a sharp distinction between Wittgenstein the philosopher, who worked on technical problems in logic and language that were central in contemporary British philosophy, and Wittgenstein the man of eccentric cultural and moral views. Toulmin adds, however, "We would have done better to see him as an integral and authentically Viennese genius who exercised his talents and personality on philosophy among other things, and just happened to be living and working in England."[1] In a related vein, Maurice Drury, another former student as well as close friend, wrote in 1966:

> The number of introductions to and commentaries on Wittgenstein's philosophy is steadily increasing. Yet to one of his former pupils something that was central in his thinking is not being said.
>
> Kierkegaard told a bitter parable about the effects of his writings. He said he felt like the theatre manager who runs on stage to warn the audience of a fire. But they take his appearance as all part of the farce they are enjoying, and the louder he shouts the more they applaud.
>
> Forty years ago Wittgenstein's teaching came to me as a warning against certain intellectual and spiritual dangers by which I was strongly tempted. These dangers still surround us. It would be a tragedy if well-meaning commentators should make it appear that his writings were now easily assimilable into the very intellectual milieu they were largely a warning against.[2]

Drury does not speak here of the technical competence (or incompetence) of the many commentaries already by then produced on Wittgenstein. Instead, he suggests that they remain strangely silent about central aspects of his former teacher's thought, aspects concerned with present intellectual and spiritual dangers that "still surround us" and make the assimilation of Wittgenstein's thought into our current intellectual milieu problematic.

My earliest encounter with Wittgenstein produced in me a fairly inchoate notion that something like this was the case. My graduate studies and subsequent research solidified my initial impression into the three main ideas that inform this book. The first idea is that Wittgenstein saw it as one of his philosophy's central tasks to reawaken a sense of wonder for what he felt was the deeply mysterious place of human life in the world. His thought and work in philosophy cannot be fully understood out of relation to this idea. The second idea is that because the task of philosophy as Wittgenstein understood it embodied a profoundly untimely sensibility, that task could only be carried through as a form of cultural criticism. Specifically, Wittgenstein's critical relation to Western metaphysics must be understood in its critical relation to Western modernity. The third idea is that from the *Tractatus* onward, Wittgenstein believed that only a way of practicing philosophy that both avoided and undermined traditional philosophy's reliance on theory was suited to accomplishing this task.

Wittgenstein's philosophy never addresses itself *merely* to technical problems in philosophical logic, the philosophy of mathematics, the philosophy of language, the philosophy of psychology, and so on. Instead, his work must also be understood as always attempting to effect a particular kind of change in his readers' relationship to language, a specific kind of shift in how they envisage their lives with language, and thereby how they think about themselves and the particular contexts in which philosophical problems arise.[3] I believe one of the main animating forces of Wittgenstein's philosophical activity was the ambition to loosen, if not break, the hold that metaphysical conceptions of necessity can exercise on our imagination. More than once, he described his work as depending on something like this idea: "One of the most important methods I use is to imagine a historical development for our ideas different from what has actually occurred. If we do that the problem shows us a quite new side."[4] "Nothing is more important though than the construction of fictional concepts, which will teach us at last to understand our own."[5] Our sense that we need such conceptions of necessity and our belief that they should guide our thinking in philosophy can come from a (collective or personal) failure to face the contingency that characterizes human life as well as from a failure to make genuine commitments in the face of (collective or personal) uncertainty. Thus, one of the most important changes that Wittgenstein hoped to bring about through his philosophy was a newfound willingness on the part of his readers or students to let their thought be shaped, at least in part, by contingencies of human life from which they formerly sought to escape with the aid of a theory, whether a theory of ethics, logic, epistemology, metaphysics, or aesthetics. It is in large measure because this willingness can only be sustained through sensitivity, honest self-reflection, courage, and integrity that, for example, in a 1919 letter to the publisher Ludwig Ficker, Wittgenstein described the point of the *Tractatus* as an "ethical one." Understanding what Wittgenstein might have even roughly meant by this remark and reading the book in a way that takes account of it have proven to be challenging tasks for interpreters of the *Tractatus*. I will have much to say about this issue as it relates both to the *Tractatus* and to how we can find a closely connected "ethical point" integral to his later work. But in pointing out that Wittgenstein's philosophical activity has an essential ethical dimension, I do not mean to suggest that we ought to be looking for something that can be easily connected to ethics as that subject is ordinarily treated in philosophy departments. Friedrich Waismann recorded Wittgenstein as once remarking, "I think it is definitely important to put an end to all the claptrap about ethics—whether intuitive knowledge exists, whether values exist, whether the good is definable."[6] This is from Waismann's notes of a conversation that took place in December 1929, and Wittgenstein's immediate target is very likely G. E. Moore's *Principia Ethica*. Nevertheless, the words reflect an attitude that Wittgenstein held from before the *Tractatus* to the end of his life. In particular, there is nothing in Wittgenstein's thought like an ethical theory or even a theory of linguistic meaning that would place him on one side or another in debates in metaethics.[7] Stanley Cavell has stressed this point in relation to *Philosophical Investigations*: "Granted the intuitive pervasiveness of something that may express itself as a moral or religious demand in the *Investigations*, the demand is not the subject of a separate study within it, call it Ethics."[8] Indeed, I will show that what Wittgenstein means by "ethical" in his letter to Ficker is best understood as modulated by a critique of metaphysics-*cum*-critique of culture, all moving through his concern for the fate of wonder. Finally, because Wittgenstein's understanding of the nature of philosophy obviously changed substantially between his writing the *Tractatus* and composing his later work, it is important for me to show how these concepts are essential for understanding this transition. Consequently, much of this book fleshes out *how* this dimension is present in Wittgenstein's early and later philosophical work. Specifically, I argue that one can read the *Tractatus* as containing a critique of metaphysics-*cum*-critique of culture in one sense and read *Philosophical Investigations* as containing such a critique in a sense both quite different yet recognizably continuous with the first.

Something interesting about this last claim in particular is that while there has certainly been fine work done on the subject of Wittgenstein's cultural and spiritual concerns, as these can be gleaned from his biography and as they get expressed, for example, in some of the remarks collected in *Culture and Value*, relatively little energy has been expended in investigating what role those concerns might play in our overall understanding and evaluation of his thought and its development. As a result, there tends to be a gulf between researchers interested in these aspects of Wittgenstein's outlook and what seems to be the majority of students and commentators, for whom he is a seminal figure in twentieth-century analytic philosophy of language, logic, mathematics, and psychology. There is a conspicuous and troubling lack of integration here. G. H. von Wright, one of Wittgenstein's literary executors and close friends, comments:

> It is surely part of Wittgenstein's achievement to have made concern for language central to philosophy. But few only of those who shared Wittgenstein's concern for language also shared the peculiar motivation which aroused his concern for it. *One* aspect of Wittgenstein's all too obvious alienation from his times is his feeling that not even those who professed to follow him were really engaged in the same spiritual endeavor as he.[9]

Certainly there have been notable efforts to document the many sources of Wittgenstein's intellectual and spiritual formation. Janik and Toulmin's *Wittgenstein's Vienna* (1973) certainly made important early contributions in this regard. Yet this work devotes very little space to Wittgenstein's later work, and the interpretation it offers of the *Tractatus* is among those that I would argue should be resisted. Stanley Cavell's *The Claim of Reason* (1979) contains many valuable insights on relevant themes. Yet, presumably because Cavell's interests in that work are quite different from mine here, his suggestions remain mostly undeveloped. Moreover, his discussion treats *Philosophical Investigations* in near isolation from Wittgenstein's other work. A later essay by Cavell, "Declining Decline: Wittgenstein as a Philosopher of Culture" (1989), does focus on relevant themes. It, too, however, also deals exclusively with the *Investigations*. More importantly, it gives a very misleading picture there of the importance of practices in Wittgenstein's later thought. There has of course been valuable work done whose goal has been a keener insight into the man, Ludwig Wittgenstein. A recurring claim of such work has been that we do not understand the philosophy unless we understand the man. Brian McGuinness's (1989) and Ray Monk's (1990) excellent biographies both fall into this category. Yet Monk's focus in particular is largely psychological, emphasizing Wittgenstein's internal moral struggles. Relatively little attention is paid to the conceptual interplay between Wittgenstein's philosophy and his views on cultural matters. Where Monk does consider those views, it is often with horror and embarrassment.[10] Stephen S. Hilmy's *The Later Wittgenstein: The Emergence of a New Philosophical Method* (1987) was one of the first important works that explicitly tied the method of Wittgenstein's later work to its relation to cultural factors. Hilmy's book, however, reinforces the standard interpretation that there is a sharp distinction between Wittgenstein's early and later philosophy. It also ascribes to Wittgenstein a much more systematic, constructive view of philosophy than is warranted. More recently, in his *Ludwig Wittgenstein* (2007), Edward Kanterian has tried to integrate many of these elements into his interpretation of Wittgenstein's philosophy. But this attempt, too, is vitiated by Kanterian's traditional ascription to Wittgenstein of theoretical ambitions.[11]

So while it has long been recognized that Wittgenstein's intellectual formation included influences from many thinkers concerned with cultural questions, little has been written that sees Wittgenstein as a philosopher on whose thought such concerns exert a steady pressure on the thoroughgoing nontheoretical ambitions of his work. Thus, we have works that examine various aspects of Wittgenstein's philosophy and others that focus on his moral and spiritual concern for himself and culture, but there is surprisingly little on what I believe is the spiritually charged cultural critique running through all of his philosophy. One reason for this might be that for many years the study of Wittgenstein's writings was largely confined to the analytic tradition, for which the kind of issues that I shall take up here have not been generally recognized as philosophical issues at all.[12] A second, possibly related reason is the distaste with which many of the writers who are relevant here have often been received in the English-speaking philosophical world.[13] There is thus a great need for an investigation carried out with the aim of understanding Wittgenstein's remarks and views on cultural and spiritual questions as part of a coherent intellectual framework. I attempt to address this gap in our understanding of Wittgenstein's philosophy, and I argue that by closing it we can come to see an essential dimension of his thought that most commentaries tend to bypass altogether.

I.2

This and the next section deal with methodological questions that I want to bring out into the open right at the beginning of the book. I hope this will help to frame both the book's ambitions and limitations. This section deals briefly with a number of such questions, and the next section discusses only one issue at greater length.

First, and certainly not least, I assume as correct the core ideas of resolute approaches to the *Tractatus*, therapeutic (or "quietist") approaches to reading *Philosophical Investigations* (and the later work more generally), and, without denying the strong contrasts between those two works, I agree, too, with the strong continuity between them that those two approaches have been taken to imply.[14] This means that I agree with those who read Wittgenstein as having eschewed constructive, theoretical ambitions from the *Tractatus* until the end of his life. I realize that putting this book on such a controversial basis runs the risk of making it uninteresting to those who find the relevant debates far from resolved. I came to feel, however, that it was pointless for me to enter substantively into these debates here, let alone to attempt any definitive contribution to them, because I found that nothing I could say hadn't already been said better by those who had convinced me of the rightness of their readings. Being convinced at one point in time doesn't necessarily preclude the possibility of changing one's mind in the future, but being convinced of something is no sin in philosophy. You can't argue for everything everywhere, and I have tried to make my interpretative commitments clear enough throughout the book.

Nevertheless, despite my intention to avoid directly participating in these debates, I have included a chapter that introduces (in a sympathetic light, obviously) the basic parameters of one of the resolute approaches to the *Tractatus*. I have done this in part because this chapter sets much of the tone for the remainder of the book but also out of my sense that the issues involved in this debate are especially difficult and less likely to be familiar to many readers than are parallel discussions surrounding Wittgenstein's later work. It is not, however, as though the remainder of the book is argumentatively inert regarding these debates over how to read Wittgenstein. It remains a legitimate and substantial hermeneutic point that if assuming the basic correctness of these ways of understanding Wittgenstein's texts allows me to make better sense of much else that he said and wrote than do other ways of approaching those texts, then this speaks well for making these assumptions in the first place. Further, regardless of how large such assumptions may seem, making them is very far from giving away the whole game, as it were. There is clearly much left for me to argue for here. In the cases of several of the very commentators on whose work I draw, ideas only hinted at in their writings are extended into regions where they may not have naturally taken them of their own accord. In other cases, I mark my strong disagreements with them over important questions.

Next, I allow what strike me as some fairly standard, if not wholly uncontroversial, divisions to guide what I call the "early" and "later" Wittgenstein. In doing so, I certainly do not wish to contribute to the unintentional reification of these categories. But this is not a question that I explore here. By the "early" Wittgenstein, I mean his work up to the *Tractatus*, naturally giving pride of place to the book itself. By the "later" Wittgenstein, I mean everything from the *Brown Book* on (perhaps also including the *Blue Book*), where *Philosophical Investigations* is given a privileged position. I do not deal directly very much with the texts that form the core of Wittgenstein's so-called transitional or middle phase of the late 1920s through the early 1930s. These include the posthumously published *Philosophical Remarks* and *Philosophical Grammar* (excerpted, of course, from the "Big Typescript"). I *do*, however, sometimes put some material from this period to important uses. I accord great weight, for instance, to the "Lecture on Ethics" and to Friedrich Waismann's recorded conversations in my discussion of the ethical point of the *Tractatus*. It certainly seems as though the view of ethics that Wittgenstein is elucidating in these places is useful for understanding the one that he held in 1918. I also employ certain other writings stemming from this period, specifically some portions of "Remarks on Frazer's *Golden Bough*," most of which date from 1931, and various remarks from this time found in *Culture and Value* and elsewhere in the *Nachlass*, when I find these helpful for understanding Wittgenstein's philosophy, early or late.

These considerations in turn indicate several additional points that bear mentioning. First, although the book certainly makes some quite substantial claims, it does not pretend to give anything like an exhaustive interpretation of Wittgenstein's philosophy. There is simply too much material, published and unpublished, that I do not discuss for that to be plausible. The book tries to develop and offer a coherent framework for understanding the material that it does address and it suggests this as a framework for interpreting much of the material that it does not address. Its success or failure depends on whether it fulfills the first task here and withstands the test of the second over time. This latter point is especially pertinent because, specifically regarding Wittgenstein's later thought, the book focuses heavily on the remarks on rule-following in *Philosophical Investigations* for developing its interpretation. This means that not only will that interpretation have to stand the test of confronting other material of various types but that it will have to be able to shed further light on other parts of *Philosophical Investigations* itself. Of course, the remarks on rule-following themselves, and so any interpretation of them, have to be taken against the background of what precedes them and what they precede in the text of the *Investigations*.[15] So, in fact, focusing on them is not as insulating as it might appear. At any rate, my reading will not only have to accommodate other parts of this text, but it will have to accommodate other *aspects* of the *Philosophical Investigations* that it does not take up, including other aspects of the rule-following remarks themselves. I do not, for example, discuss the multiplicity of voices in the *Investigations*, its frequent dialogic nature. So-called polyphonic readings emphasize the significance of the multiplicity of voices in the text, specifically how these are essential to grasping its overall therapeutic, nontheoretical aims. This can refer to, among other things, the way in which different voices in the book give expression to Wittgenstein's own struggles with certain philosophical temptations. On the other hand, while I do not discuss these issues here, this aspect of the text plays an important role in the writings of a number of the commentators on whose work I rely.

Next, there is an assumption I make about what I think of as the *constancy* of Wittgenstein's cultural views, as these are germane for understanding the cultural dimension of his philosophical projects. If someone finds what I mean by "constancy" overly obscure, I am tempted simply to respond with something like "Read *Culture and Value*, recorded conversations, and his letters, and you will see what I mean." This is because I find the strong continuity displayed openly in these places. While following this suggestion is not likely to make the idea clearer for everyone, or even for every sympathetic reader, I will not say more about this. Of course, because Wittgenstein's views on the nature of philosophy changed, it stands to reason that his understanding of philosophy's place in history and its relation to culture changed—and so too how the cultural project of reawakening wonder à la cultural criticism had to be carried out (including being carried out in opposition in several respects to his own early work). Nevertheless, I still think we get the best understanding of his carrying out that cultural project if we regard his views on the state of Western culture as a relatively stable element or *Leitfaden* in this constellation.

Next, I want to say a few words about the role of Heidegger's thought in my interpretation of Wittgenstein. His mere presence in my interpretation should not, I hope, strike too many as dubious or eccentric. Charles Taylor, for example, has drawn out some of the possible connections between the work of the later Heidegger and the later Wittgenstein in a way relevant here:

> There are therefore good reasons for mentioning Wittgenstein and Heidegger in the same breath, as there are for going back again and again to their arguments. What makes the latter so necessary is the hold of the disengaged view on our thought and culture, which has a lot to do, of course, with the hegemony of institutions and practices that require and entrench a disengaged stance: science, technology, rationalized forms of production, bureaucratic administration, a civilization committed to growth, and the like. The kind of thinking of which both are variants has a certain counter-cultural significance, and inherent thrust against the hegemonic forms of our time.[16]

Nevertheless, although certain Heideggerian themes are relevant (and occasionally indicated) throughout the book, I do not make the type of explicit, comparative use of Heidegger's later work in the chapters dealing with the later Wittgenstein as I do of his early work in my discussions of the *Tractatus* in the second and third chapters. This may seem surprising, both because comparing *Being and Time* with the *Tractatus* in the way I do may strike many as too unconventional to be right and because of how much of Heidegger's later work is explicitly devoted to the subject of cultural critique in ways that line up with much of what I say about the later Wittgenstein. The explanation for this is simply that I found an explicit comparison with early Heidegger to be useful for my exposition of the early Wittgenstein, but when it came to possible connections between their later works, I preferred not to foreground but only to gesture occasionally at this possibility in footnotes or a turn of phrase. And this underscores an important point about the book. Even though the mere fact of the comparability of important themes in their work suggests to me the validity of taking a point of view from which both of these philosophers are seen as sharing a common place in the history of Western thought, and even if on occasion I devote attention to the comparison in a way that makes it seem as though that comparison is the point of my exposition, and even if sometimes I find it necessary to explicate Heidegger for some of my readers, it is, in the end, in the service of understanding Wittgenstein that the comparison is made at all.[17]

The above paragraph indicates a final point that I should mention here, namely, the significance of the work of Charles Taylor for the intellectual framework of this book. As is evident from the quoted passage, Taylor regards Wittgenstein as relevant to my concerns, and, indeed, he invokes Wittgenstein at numerous junctures of his authorship, particularly when dealing with "the hold of the disengaged view on our thought and culture" (a central topic for this book). Still, for the most part, Wittgenstein plays a helpful but decidedly supporting role in most of Taylor's discussions of what he sees as the crises of modernity. My sense is that Taylor would likely be open to giving Wittgenstein a larger place alongside the many other figures from the history of Western thought who populate his narratives of modernity but that perhaps the style of Wittgenstein's writing combined with his scattered treatment of relevant themes have made this difficult. At any rate, Taylor's importance does not lie in my agreeing with everything he says about Wittgenstein[18] or even with his entire diagnosis of our modern predicament. Rather, it is that for over three decades, in his *Hegel* (1975), *Sources of the Self* (1989), *The Ethics of Authenticity* (1992), and on to *Modern Social Imaginaries* (2003) and most recently *A Secular Age* (2007), Taylor, as much as any other contemporary public thinker I know of, has grappled with the network of overarching themes concerning philosophy, religion, culture, politics, and modernity central to the conception of and motivation for this book. An additional aspiration, then, of the current project is that it might contribute to making Wittgenstein's thought a much more available, perhaps even integral, resource for those involved in the kinds of discussions of contemporary issues that have been at the center of Taylor's well-known engagement in the public sphere.

I.3

Assuming one thinks that the main questions I will discuss here are good and interesting ones, it may seem most natural to set about trying to address them by referring to those places where Wittgenstein makes explicit statements of his views on the nature of philosophy. In addition to consulting what are standardly taken to be his philosophical works, this might also suggest checking "extratextual" sources such as the various volumes of recorded conversations, diaries, students' lecture notes, *Culture and Value*, and, of course, the *Nachlass*. While the rest of this book makes it clear that I find nothing wrong with this practice, there may be those in whom it may give rise to a certain kind of anxiety, if that practice appears to be coupled with a dogma about authorial intentions that maintains that extratextual sources are not only *appropriate* places to look for answers but that they are the *unquestionably best* places to look for answers.[19] The dogma would be something like this: authorial intentions can never really be discerned from a piece of work; there is an inevitable epistemological gap.[20] Because I don't find this dogma at all compelling, I imagine that when a question like "How did Wittgenstein conceive of our cultural relation to metaphysics?" is posed, *one* adequate response could be "Read and reflect on *Philosophical Investigations*."[21]

But I worry that such a laconic response is itself liable to be motivated by its own dogma, according to which consulting the extratextual sources I mention above is *itself* superfluous, because whatever Wittgenstein thought about the nature of philosophical questions can only be found from a careful reading of his philosophical work. This sort of view may even seem to be one to which Wittgenstein lends his support in the following remarks, which occur at the end of a sketch for the foreword to *Philosophical Remarks*:

> The danger in a long foreword is that the spirit of a book has to be evident in the book itself and cannot be described. For if a book has been written for just a few readers that will be clear just from the fact that only a few understand it. The

book must automatically separate those who understand it and those who do not. Even the foreword is written just for such as understand the book.

It is a great temptation to want to make the spirit explicit.[22]

What Wittgenstein says here might be taken as weighing against the sort of approach that I adopt in this book. This is because in some cases my explication moves between Wittgenstein's "strictly philosophical texts" and other sources, and this practice might make it look as though I am succumbing to something like the temptation against which Wittgenstein is warning us, rather than letting the reader find any relevant implications of the texts for herself.

In order to set this issue aside, I will first make two obvious points. First, what Wittgenstein writes in the passage above leaves undetermined just what it would be to try to make the spirit of a work explicit, and so it also leaves undetermined whether that is a temptation to which I succumb here. Second, as Wittgenstein himself surely realized, if a foreword gives a reader *no* assistance in understanding a book, then it is utterly useless as a foreword. Both Wittgenstein's sketch for a foreword as well as what eventually came to be the actual foreword to *Philosophical Remarks* try to guide the reader by telling her that the spirit of the book "is different from the one that informs the vast stream of European and American civilization in which all of us stand."[23] The motto to *Philosophical Investigations* is a line concerning progress taken from Nestroy's play *Der Schützling*, and in the preface Wittgenstein shares his doubt about his book's power "to bring light into one brain or another" in "the darkness of this time."[24] However cryptic one may find the words of these paratexts, one of their main functions must be to orient the reader by inviting her to examine the relevance of the cultural context for understanding their respective main texts. Yet it is far from obvious that in providing such clues Wittgenstein aims to describe or to make explicit the spirit of his books. Finding that spirit is still left for the reader to do for herself. After having embarked on that search, she may hopefully also come to a fuller understanding of the significance of the paratext, and so on.

I am not denying that for various purposes there may be a relevant difference in the relation that, on the one hand, a foreword bears to its text and, on the other, the bearing that the kinds of remarks one finds, say, in *Culture and Value* may have on our grasp of some region of Wittgenstein's thought. But I am arguing that, as with a foreword to a text, for certain purposes these remarks can orient us to that thought in interesting ways and that there is no telling in advance whether a practice that tries to elucidate this orienting is justified in advance of a determination of how intelligently and convincingly that elucidation is carried out.[25] In the preface to *Culture and Value*, von Wright remarks that "these notes can be properly understood and appreciated only against the background of Wittgenstein's philosophy and, furthermore, that they make a contribution to our understanding of that philosophy."[26] My way of heeding this wise advice in this book is to take it to mean that there ought to be something like a reflective equilibrium between Wittgenstein's extratextual remarks about our relation to the problems of philosophy and whatever view one can discern from a careful reading of what are customarily taken to be his philosophical texts. The way in which I proceed here, then, represents neither the assumption that we can never discern an author's intentions in a text nor the equally problematic insistence that there is only one respectable place to look. It reflects, rather, a refusal to accept any dogma that says that two ways of understanding a text and a thinker are necessarily mutually exclusive and exhaustive.

I.4

Chapter 1 begins with an introduction to the closely related problems of the role of nonsense in the *Tractatus* and what Wittgenstein called the "ethical point" of the book. I then provide an overview of the widely held "ineffabilist" reading of the book, according to which Wittgenstein thought that nonsense could be used to help us grasp ineffable truths of logic, ontology, and ethics. There follows a short discussion of the way in which Schopenhauer's influence on the early Wittgenstein can be understood as supporting ineffabilist readings. Next, I present Cora Diamond's and James Conant's "resolute" approach to reading the *Tractatus*, making clear its advantages over ineffabilist readings. Because the interpretation articulated by Diamond and Conant makes the question of Wittgenstein's method of the *Tractatus* into an issue that touches on his entire authorship, my taking on their overall framework for understanding his early work has important consequences for much of the remainder of this book. This is especially true for the question of the relation between the method of the *Tractatus* and ethics. Chapter 1 thus not only has strong implications for the interpretation I give in chapter 2 of the *Tractatus*' purported "ethical aim," but it also frames my discussion of the book's weaknesses in chapter 3. Moreover, these implications are also felt in chapters 4 and 5, where related themes in Wittgenstein's later work are taken up.

Chapter 2 is the longest and most ambitious chapter in the book. While resolute readings provide a framework for how the relation between ethics and the *Tractatus* should be understood, as of yet none of those readings, including Diamond's and Conant's, have offered a detailed explanation of this relation. I begin with a brief discussion about the problem of conveying an intention in the context of reading the *Tractatus* resolutely. I then give an overview of the concepts of anxiety, the "they" (*Das Man*), and authenticity in Heidegger's early work *Being and Time*. The next several sections elaborate how the ethical point of the *Tractatus* can be found in the book's attempt to reawaken a sense of wonder in its reader and how this in turn depends on the way in which the book embodies a kind of cultural critique, specifically, a critique of what Wittgenstein regarded as a widespread and incoherent "scientific worldview." In the 1929 "Lecture on Ethics," Wittgenstein describes our predicament in relation to the propositions of natural science when he spoke of a "basic tendency of the human mind" to express wonder, even if the inevitable result of trying to do so is nonsense. Central to the *Tractatus* is precisely the attempt to clarify and distinguish this impulse from the ordinary intentions expressed through meaningful speech. I show how Heidegger's description of an authentic stance toward anxiety and the "they" helps to clarify Wittgenstein's own position and thus the strategy of the *Tractatus*. My discussion turns next to what might seem to be a difficulty for juxtaposing wonder and anxiety. I argue that not only is there no genuine problem here but that in fact deep conceptual resonances between wonder and anxiety shed light on passages in the *Tractatus* dealing with the self and solipsism. Next, I bring out how the early Heidegger's understanding of the relation between authenticity and truth can help to solve another apparent problem for Conant's and Diamond's resolute reading, namely, that it cannot account for what Wittgenstein says about truth in the preface to the *Tractatus*. There follows a brief discussion of the significance of Wittgenstein's reference to Heidegger in conversation with members of the Vienna Circle from late 1929. I close the chapter by pointing to an important difference between the ethical point of the *Tractatus* and authenticity in *Being and Time*. Based on this difference, I then point out a problem for the way that Michael Kremer has interpreted the ethical aim of the *Tractatus* in relation to the writings of St. Paul and St. Augustine and for the similar way that James Conant has compared the *Tractatus* to the work of Kierkegaard.

Chapter 3 is the shortest chapter in the book and deals with one question: why, on the interpretation laid out in chapter 2, the *Tractatus* cannot fulfill its ethical aim. I try to bring out the way in which the method of the book, rather than helping the reader to achieve the change in his relationship to language and self-understanding that is key to fulfilling its ethical purpose, actually hinders this change from taking place. Using some of Wittgenstein's own later criticisms of his early work, I show that the failure here is due to a fundamentally metaphysical, essentialist view of language that inadvertently underlies the method of clarification that the *Tractatus* employs.

A central aim of chapter 4 is to show how it broadens our perspective on the nature and significance of Wittgenstein's later philosophy when we see how two ways of thinking about progress in his thought are actually woven together in his work. I begin by addressing some textual and literary-critical questions that bear on the motto of *Philosophical Investigations* and on the interpretative use of source materials that fall outside of Wittgenstein's "strictly philosophical" texts. Next, I show how the motto of the *Investigations*, a quotation about the nature of progress taken from a work by the Austrian playwright Nestroy, can be understood to refer both to certain features of the development of Wittgenstein's thought and to the concept of progress when it is connected to certain value judgments one makes when comparing, for example, different features of earlier and later historical periods. The motto can thus be seen as orienting the reader toward the remainder of the text, specifically prefiguring how the concept of progress is relevant for grasping some of its central philosophical objectives. Finally, I make clear how the remarks on rule-following, particularly as they have been interpreted by John McDowell, can be taken as an example of Wittgenstein trying to lead his reader to a perspective on language that prepares the way for a distinctive kind of cultural critique.

Chapter 5 deepens the line of inquiry into Wittgenstein's later thought begun in chapter 4. I show how numerous contexts in which he addresses cultural-historical topics help to bring out the quite specific connections he saw between the philosophical problems with which he grappled in his later philosophy and the cultural setting in which those problems arose. I first sketch how Wittgenstein's development of certain themes he found in Spengler are an important connecting link between his critique of metaphysics and his concerns with cultural decline. Next, by elaborating some ideas broached by Stanley Cavell, I show how *Philosophical Investigations* can be read as substantially continuous with the *Tractatus*, both in the way it attempts to embody a nontheoretical conception of philosophy and in the way in which this conception is in the service of what can be seen as an attempt to fulfill something like the earlier work's ethical purpose. However, my discussion also points to an essential difference between the early and later Wittgenstein's philosophical activity, namely, that the earlier work's aim of reawakening a sense of wonder in the reader has receded to the background, having instead been largely taken over by the essential preliminary task of foregrounding what I believe Wittgenstein regarded as the virtues essential for this kind of reverence. My way of articulating these connections has the further result of making clear the genuine significance of the connection in Wittgenstein's later thought between his philosophical activity and his views about cultural decline and the modern West. I then take up briefly the question of how these issues intersect with Wittgenstein's attitude toward and engagement with religion. Finally, I address a concern that Wittgenstein's perspective on cultural progress and decline entails a kind of political conservatism. I show that this concern is unfounded because it fails to take into account the nature of Wittgenstein's critique of metaphysics.

In the last chapter, I discuss two different suggestions, one by John McDowell and the other by Stanley Cavell, to the effect that Wittgenstein believed that the sources of metaphysical confusion were so fundamentally rooted in human beings that any freedom from philosophical quandaries one may enjoy could at best be temporary. My goal is not to offer a competing diagnosis of our relation to metaphysics but rather simply to present some reasons for doubting the positions of McDowell and Cavell and for thinking instead that Wittgenstein believed it possible to abandon metaphysics. After providing an overview of McDowell's and Cavell's respective views on this issue, including a separate discussion of what I think are the latter's failure to understand the significance of practices in Wittgenstein's later thought, I try to make a case for thinking that Wittgenstein envisioned the possibility of letting go of the Western metaphysical tradition as one perhaps necessary step in a process of a cultural transformation that was deeply important to him.

PART
I

I

INTERPRETING THE *TRACTATUS*

1.1

In a 1919 letter to *Der Brenner*'s publisher Ludwig von Ficker, sent in the hopes of getting the *Tractatus* published, Wittgenstein writes:

> You see, I am quite sure that you won't get all that much out of reading it. Because you won't understand it; its subject-matter will seem quite alien to you. But it isn't really alien to you, because the book's point [*der Sinn des Buches*] is an ethical one. I once meant to include in the preface a sentence which is not in fact there now but which I will write out for you here, because it will perhaps be a key to the work for you. What I meant to write, then, was this: My work consists of two parts: the one presented here plus all that I have *not* written. And it is precisely this second part that is the important one. My book draws limits to the sphere of the ethical from the inside as it were, and I am convinced that this is the ONLY *rigorous* way of drawing those limits. In short, I believe that where *many* others today are just *gassing*, I have managed in my book to put everything firmly into place by being silent about it.[1]

Shortly after this remarkable passage, in which he says that his book has an ethical point and in which he claims to have delimited the ethical precisely through what he does not say in the book, Wittgenstein tries to give Ficker more help in understanding the *Tractatus* by offering the following advice: "I would recommend you to read the *preface* and the *conclusion*, because they contain the most direct expression of the point of the book."[2] The preface to the *Tractatus* begins as follows:

Perhaps this book will be understood only by someone who has himself already had the thoughts that are expressed in it—or at least similar thoughts.— So it is not a textbook.—Its purpose would be achieved if it gave pleasure to one person who read it with understanding.

The book deals with the problems of philosophy, and shows, I believe, that the reason why these problems are posed is that the logic of our language is misunderstood. The whole sense of the book might be summed up in the following words: what can be said at all can be said clearly, and what we cannot talk about we must remain silent about.[3]

Thus the aim of the book is to set a limit to thought, or rather—not to thought, but to the expression of thoughts: for in order to be able to set a limit to thought, we should have to find both sides of the limit thinkable (i.e. we should have to be able to think what cannot be thought).

It will therefore only be in language that the limit can be drawn, and what lies on the other side of the limit will simply be nonsense.[4]

The preface concludes with these remarks:

If this work has any value, it consists in two things: the first is that thoughts are expressed in it, and on this score the better the thoughts are expressed—the more the nail has been hit on the head—the greater will be its value.—Here I am conscious of having fallen a long way short of what is possible. Simply because my powers are too slight for the accomplishment of the task.—May others come and do it better.

On the other hand the *truth* of the thoughts that are here set forth seems to me unassailable and definitive. I therefore believe myself to have found, on all essential points, the final solution of the problems. And if I am not mistaken in this belief, then the second thing in which the value of the work consists is that it shows how little is achieved when these problems are solved.[5]

Turning now to the concluding three remarks of the *Tractatus*, Wittgenstein writes,

§6.53 The correct method in philosophy would really be the following: to say nothing except what can be said, i.e. propositions of natural science—i.e. something that has nothing to do with philosophy—and then, whenever someone else wanted to say something metaphysical, to demonstrate to him that he had failed to give a meaning to certain signs in his propositions.

§6.54 My propositions serve as elucidations in the following way: anyone who understands me eventually recognizes them as nonsensical, when he has used them—as steps—to climb up beyond them. (He must, so to speak, throw away the ladder after he has climbed up it.)

He must overcome these propositions, and then he will see the world aright.

§7 What we cannot talk about we must remain silent about.[6]

Taken together, what Wittgenstein writes in the letter to Ficker, in the preface, and in the conclusion sets any interpreter of the *Tractatus* a formidable exegetical challenge. For in them Wittgenstein tells us, among other things, that his book has an ethical point, that the truth of the thoughts expressed in it is definitive, and that anyone who understands him will recognize the propositions of the book as nonsense. This chapter will lay out an interpretative framework for understanding the *Tractatus* and what followed it, and this will shape my discussion for the remainder of this book.

1.2

I begin by presenting two lines of interpretation that, in various forms, have been adopted by some well-known interpreters of the *Tractatus*. The second line in particular relies on a certain way of understanding the distinction between saying and showing in the *Tractatus*. One place where this distinction is prominent is in the remarks that run from §4.12 to §4.124.[7]

§4.12 Propositions can represent the whole reality, but they cannot represent what they must have in common with reality in order to be able to represent it—logical form.

In order to be able to represent logical form, we should have to be able to station ourselves with propositions somewhere outside logic, that is to say outside the world.

§4.121 Propositions cannot represent logical form: it is mirrored in them.

What finds its reflection in language, language cannot represent.

What expresses *itself* in language, *we* cannot express by means of language.

Propositions *show* the logical form of reality. They display it.

§4.1212 What *can* be shown, *cannot* be said.

§4.122 In a certain sense we can talk of formal properties of objects and states of affairs, or, in the case of facts, about structural properties: and in the same sense about formal relations and structural relations.

(Instead of "structural property" I also say "internal property"; instead of "structural relation" "internal relation.")

I introduce these expressions in order to indicate the source of the confusion between internal relations and relations proper [external relations], which is very widespread among philosophers.)

It is impossible, however, to assert by means of propositions that such internal properties and relations exist: rather, they make themselves manifest in the propositions that represent the relevant states of affairs and are concerned with the relevant objects.

§4.124 The existence of an internal property of a possible situation is not expressed by means of a proposition: rather it expresses itself in the proposition representing the situation, by means of an internal property of that proposition.

It would be just as nonsensical to assert that a proposition had a formal property as to deny it.

It appears that the conclusion we are to draw from these passages is that trying to say *with* a proposition what can only be shown *by* a proposition produces nonsense.

Readers of the *Tractatus* have rightly found this kind of conclusion baffling. In his introduction to the book, Russell expresses "some hesitation in accepting Mr. Wittgenstein's position. . . . What causes hesitation is the fact that, after all, Mr. Wittgenstein manages to say a good deal about what cannot be said."[8] Russell's concern can be put this way: In the remarks quoted above, Wittgenstein seems to argue for certain conclusions about what can and cannot be said with propositions. But his arguments imply that these very conclusions are themselves nonsensical. The upshot is that we appear to be left with the paradox that these conclusions are somehow true but inexpressible.

One way some interpreters have dealt with this problem has been to proceed as though many of the passages that Wittgenstein would condemn as nonsensical are perfectly intelligible philosophical claims about such topics as semantics and philosophical logic. Consequently, they can be straightforwardly evaluated and compared with the approaches and conclusions of other theories. Wittgenstein's claim that these sentences are nonsense is therefore read as a bizarre confusion or an inexplicable blindness on his part, or it is seen as some strange quirk on his part, indicative of his hostility toward philosophy and perhaps a result of his penchant for mysticism.[9]

This way of reading the *Tractatus* has the advantage that it avoids ascribing what looks like a paradoxical view to the author of the book. It also makes possible two further things, which are perhaps even more important to its advocates. It makes the book available as a source of useful insights into logic and language, and it opens up what seem to be the substantive claims of the book to ordinary philosophical criticism. Nevertheless, in one important respect at least, it seems a poor attempt at philosophical interpretation, if only because such total disregard for the author's intentions on such a crucial issue can hardly be a promising interpretative starting point.[10] Consequently, other commentators have attempted to deal with the question of the role of nonsense in the book by introducing a distinction into the very idea of nonsense itself.[11] Such a distinction can be seen as having its textual basis in remarks such as §4.122, quoted above. There we find Wittgenstein telling us "it is impossible, however, to assert by means of propositions that such internal properties and relations exist"—an assertion that only appears to convey to us that we may not speak of internal properties and relations by doing so. These commentators argue that nonsensical sentences such as §4.122 serve as guides to what one can say through the quite particular ways in which they themselves fail to say anything. In claiming that nonsense sentences like §4.122 have this special character, these interpreters have tried to take the edge off the apparent paradox that Wittgenstein wants to convey inexpressible truths via this nonsense. Concerning such "truths," Elizabeth Anscombe writes, "an important part is played in the *Tractatus* by the things which, though they cannot be 'said,' are yet 'shown' or 'displayed.' That is to say: it would be right to call them 'true' if, *per impossibile*, they could be said; in fact they cannot be called true, since they cannot be said, but 'can be shewn,' or 'are exhibited,' in the propositions saying the various things that can be said."[12] Anscombe goes on to suggest that we can perhaps see that a different kind of nonsense results from attempts to contradict certain would-be statements that, though nonsense, are somehow correct. These attempts result in nonsense too, but since they, so to speak, try to deny the deeper truth about things, they contain as she says "more error, or more darkness" than attempts to say what is "quite correct." To explain Wittgenstein's motivations for presenting his reader with nonsense in the first place, Anscombe suggests that "It would presumably be because . . . Wittgenstein regards the sentences of the *Tractatus* as helpful, in spite of their being strictly nonsensical according to the very doctrine that they propound; someone who had used them like steps 'to climb out beyond them' would be helped by them to 'see the world rightly.' "[13]

P. M. S. Hacker develops an approach to this problem that is similar to Anscombe's in many respects. He holds the view that the Wittgenstein of the *Tractatus* believed that there were inexpressible truths: "Wittgenstein did think, when he wrote the *Tractatus*, that there were ineffable metaphysical necessities."[14] Moreover, like Anscombe, Hacker argues that we can better deal with the problem of nonsense in the *Tractatus* by making a distinction in the way we talk about it:

> Philosophers try to say what can only be shown, and what they say, being nonsense, does not even show what they try to say. Nevertheless, even within the range of philosophical . . . nonsense we can distinguish, as we shall see, between what might (somewhat confusedly) be called illuminating nonsense, and misleading nonsense. Illuminating nonsense will guide the attentive reader to apprehend what is shown by other propositions which do not purport to be philosophical; moreover, it will intimate, to those who grasp what is meant, its own illegitimacy.[15]

"Misleading" nonsense, often a result of unreflectively practicing traditional philosophy, indicates a lack of insight on the part of the speaker into the nature of language. On the other hand, by intentionally "violating" or "flaunting" the laws of logical syntax, one person might employ illuminating nonsense to guide another to understand these laws and thus to "see the world aright."[16] Hacker writes: "The source of the error of past philosophy lies in its failure to understand the [unstatable] principles of the logical syntax of language which are obscured by grammatical forms."[17] Accordingly, Hacker concludes that we need not attribute any serious confusion to the author. "Wittgenstein was quite correct and consistent; the *Tractatus* does indeed consist largely of pseudopropositions. Of course, what Wittgenstein meant by these remarks . . . is, in his view, quite correct, only it cannot be said. Apparently what someone means or intends by a remark can be grasped even though the sentence uttered is strictly speaking nonsense."[18]

I have been discussing how some noted interpreters have dealt with the question of how we ought to regard the role of nonsense in the *Tractatus*. The discussion as I have framed it thus far has touched only on questions concerning the nature of logic and language. Now I want to turn to some of the passages toward the end of the book, which touch on the themes of ethics, aesthetics, and the mystical. What follows is an extremely condensed overview, intended only to convey the logic, as it were, of Wittgenstein's discussion there.

At §6.41, we read:

The sense of the world must lie outside the world. In the world everything is as it is, and everything happens as it does happen: *in* it no value exists—and if it did exist, it would have no value.

If there is any value that does have value, it must lie outside the whole sphere of what happens and is the case. For all that happens and is the case is accidental.

What makes it non-accidental cannot lie *within* the world, since if it did it would itself be accidental.

It must lie outside the world.

§6.42 and §6.421 continue in a similar vein:

And so it is impossible for there to be propositions of ethics.

Propositions can express nothing that is higher.

It is clear that ethics cannot be put into words.
Ethics is transcendental.
(Ethics and aesthetics are one and the same.)

Now I want to skip ahead to §6.521 and §6.522.

The solution of the problem of life is seen in the vanishing of the problem.

(Is not this the reason why those who have found after a long period of doubt that the sense of life became clear to them have then been unable to say what constituted that sense?)

There are, indeed, things that cannot be put into words. They *make themselves manifest*. They are what is mystical.[19]

We have already read that ethics, indeed *everything* of value, lies *outside* the world, apparently beyond the picturing possibilities of propositions. From these last lines, we seem to be led to believe, moreover, that our somehow coming to understand such *things* constitutes the "problem of life." This is suggested by the parenthetical passage, where we read of "those who have found . . . that the sense of life became clear to them." But what is clear to such persons, the sense of life, is also the sense of the world, since "The world and life are one."[20] Yet we have already read at §6.41, quoted above, that "The sense of the world must lie outside the world . . . *in* it no value exists." This would appear to entail that those to whom the sense of life becomes clear, those for whom the problem vanishes, are clear about some *thing* that lies *outside* the world, beyond what can be said. How is this possible? "There are, indeed, things that cannot be put into words. They *make themselves manifest*. They are what is mystical."

1.3

For commentators who seek to place these last remarks in some sort of historical context, there has been a tendency to see in them the influence of Schopenhauer.[21] In her book on the *Tractatus*, Anscombe writes, "If we look for Wittgenstein's philosophical ancestry, we should rather look to Schopenhauer; specifically, his 'solipsism,' his conception of 'the limit,' and his ideas on value will be better understood in the light of Schopenhauer than any other philosopher."[22] Hacker is even bolder in this regard, claiming that Schopenhauer "moulded [Wittgenstein's] conception of the metaphysical self and his notion of the mystical."[23] Hacker thus includes "a detailed comparison of some of Wittgenstein's doctrines on solipsism with those of Schopenhauer from whom they are derived" as an essential part of his interpretative strategy.[24]

Schopenhauer, of course, considered himself a disciple of Kant and professed to make only a few, albeit significant, corrections to the master's thought. Among them was the claim that Kant had erred in making Reason (*Vernunft*) a possible source of moral or practical knowledge.[25] Against this, Schopenhauer argues that Reason is a purely formal linguistic capacity that humans possess and that allows them to think abstractly.[26] As such, it is entirely barren as a source of knowledge. In Schopenhauer's eyes, Kant's attribution of anything to Reason beyond this formal ability both marked a deviation from his own better judgment and opened the floodgates for philosophers such as Hegel to ascribe to Reason what are, for Schopenhauer, incredible powers of suprasensible knowledge of reality.[27] Schopenhauer holds, against idealists like Hegel, that knowledge comes only from either empirical or synthetic a priori representations, both of which are rooted in and conditioned by the understanding. In short, for Schopenhauer, one can know the world only as representation, and there is no knowledge of things-in-themselves or the Absolute, which he thinks amount to the same thing. In this sense, he is closer to Kant than are the idealists whom he shunned.

From afar, however, Schopenhauer seems closer to the idealists than he would no doubt wish to appear. For his doctrine of the world as Will, a sort of mystical monism that he derives in large part from his interpretation of Hindu and Buddhist philosophy, does amount to the sneaking admission that we can glimpse behind the veil of appearances; he simply refuses to call this knowledge. We would do better to call such glimpses insights into the nature of things. Schopenhauer's writings are full of vivid descriptions of the occasions for such insights, such as when we are confronted with terrible forces of nature.

> The storm howls, the sea roars, the lightning flashes from black clouds, and thunder-claps drown the noise of storm and sea. Then in the unmoved beholder of this scene the twofold nature of his consciousness reaches the highest distinctness. Simultaneously, he feels himself as individual, as the feeble phenomenon of will, which the slightest touch of these forces can annihilate, helpless against powerful nature, dependent, abandoned to chance, a vanishing nothing in face of stupendous forces; and he also feels himself as the eternal, serene subject of knowing, who as the condition of every object is the supporter of the whole world, the fearful struggle of nature being only his mental picture or representation; he himself is free from, and foreign to, all willing and needs, in the quiet comprehension of the Ideas. This is the full impression of the sublime.[28]

Two avenues for attaining such insight are given particular attention by Schopenhauer: asceticism and art. The ascetic who renounces all willing sees through the illusion of the *principium individuationis* by which the world appears to be a manifold of different objects. Instead, he perceives that everything, including his own empirical personality, is merely a manifestation of one evil, lusting Will and that the only way to happiness and tranquility is the cessation of all desire.[29] Similarly, the artist, in losing himself in pure aesthetic contemplation, also loses a sense of a separate "I" and thus all sense of willing. In such moments, the artist is able to grasp timeless "Ideas," the Platonic forms that function as archetypes in Schopenhauer's metaphysics.[30]

Now from the mere tenor of the remarks that make up most of the last few pages of the *Tractatus*, a strategy such as the one Hacker suggests, which would attempt to interpret them as expressions of a modified version of Schopenhauer's metaphysics, is certainly tempting. Once one takes into account biographical sources and the *Notebooks*, from which much of the *Tractatus* is drawn, it could seem inevitable.[31] In truth, the *Notebooks* do occasionally read like meditations on *The World as Will and Representation*. Passages like the following are just a few of the many that would serve to justify such an approach.

What do I know about God and the purpose of life?
I know that the world exists.
That I am placed in it like my eye in its visual field.
That this meaning does not lie in it but outside it. (*Cf* 6.41)
That life is the world. (*Cf* 5.621)
That my will penetrates the world.
That my will is good or evil.

I can only make myself independent of the world—and so in a certain sense master it—by renouncing any influence on happenings.[32]

Only remember that the spirit of the snake, of the lion, is *your* spirit. For it is only from yourself that you are acquainted with spirit at all.[33]

Elsewhere, Wittgenstein simply seems to be paraphrasing, if not rehearsing, lines from Schopenhauer:[34] "As my idea is the world, in the same way my will is the world-will";[35] "The work of art is the object seen *sub specie aeternitatis*; and the good life is the world seen *sub specie aeternitatis*. This is the connexion between art and ethics."[36] And in the *Tractatus* itself, we find what sound like echoes of Schopenhauer's mystical monism: "To view the world sub specie aeterni is to view it as a whole—a limited whole. Feeling the world as a limited whole—it is this that is mystical."[37] One might even claim to find Schopenhauer's metaphysics making its way into the "Lecture on Ethics" that Wittgenstein delivered to the Heretics Society in Cambridge on November 17, 1929. There, Wittgenstein's description of his experience of "absolute or ethical value" might sound like an echo of Schopenhauer's description of the sublime.

Now in this situation I am, if I want to fix my mind on what I mean by absolute or ethical value. And there, in my case, it always happens that the idea of one particular experience presents itself to me which therefore is, in a sense, my experience *par excellence* and this is the reason why, in talking to you now, I will use this experience as my first and foremost example. . . . I believe the best way of describing it is to say that when I have it *I wonder at the existence of the world* . . . I will mention another experience straight away which I also know and which others of you might be acquainted with: it is, what one might call, the experience of feeling *absolutely safe*. I mean the state of mind in which one is inclined to say "I am safe, nothing can injure me whatever happens."[38]

Now the point here is not that all, or even most, of the "Schopenhauerian" remarks in the *Tractatus* or the *Notebooks* formally accord with all of the details of Schopenhauer's philosophy. Nor is it that any of the commentators who see his handiwork in them are so simpleminded as not to notice important differences. Anscombe, for example, points out that Wittgenstein's treatment of the will, at least in the *Tractatus*, looks fundamentally different from Schopenhauer's.[39] Regarded in their entirety, nevertheless, these remarks certainly could indicate something like the following interpretation: In the remarks on the will, solipsism, value, ethics, aesthetics, and the mystical, Wittgenstein employs nonsense in order to *intimate* to his reader the "quite correct" truth that the totality of statable facts comprises a limited world whole. In thus gesturing at the limit of this world whole, he is also conveying something about what lies beyond it, a noumenal domain of value ("what is higher") that is in some way graspable by us through mystical insight but about which we can *say* nothing, on pain of speaking nonsense. This sort of interpretation is not idiosyncratic. Janik and Toulmin are explicit about this: "The world—the totality of facts—relates to the will, in Wittgenstein's view, in very much the same manner as Schopenhauer's world as representation relates to the world as will, as husk to kernel, as *phenomenon* to *noumenon*."[40] One thus ends up with an interpretation of the *Tractatus* in which Wittgenstein is combining important parts of Schopenhauer's ethics and ontology with a more rigorous logical theory. It is worth pointing out that Schopenhauer, too, is at least dimly aware of the problematic nature of sentences concerning the ineffable. With this in mind, he occasionally warns his reader that these descriptions of sublime experiences are to be treated with caution: "Certainly . . . we fall here into mystical and figurative language, but it is the only language in which anything can be said on this entirely transcendent theme."[41] As Schopenhauer has not thought through his semantic theory to the same extent as Wittgenstein, however, he still conceives of such utterances as having an (albeit unusual) semantic content.[42] He thus fails to see these descriptions for what they really are: nonsensical utterances that *say* nothing and therefore must ultimately be thrown away but that can be used to *show* the sensitive reader something higher. Concerning such matters as ethics and aesthetics, therefore, Schopenhauer's reader is left in a semantic no-man's-land. Wittgenstein's more rigorous logical standards, on the other hand, will lead his reader to a knowing silence. Hacker summarizes this view when he writes of Wittgenstein's doctrines of the ineffable that

> They express a doctrine which I shall call Transcendental Solipsism. They involve a belief in the transcendental ideality of time (and presumably space), a rather perverse interpretation of the Kantian doctrine of the unity of apperception together with the acceptance of Schopenhauer's reification of the unity of

consciousness, and other related and undigested theories about ethics, the will, aesthetics and religion. The originality of the doctrines in Wittgenstein is negligible, their ancestry is of dubious legitimacy, and their validity more than a little questionable. Wittgenstein's originality in the matter lies in his attempt to dovetail these doctrines into the sophisticated theory of meaning with which most of the *Tractatus* is concerned. Unlike Kant and Schopenhauer, Wittgenstein thought that his transcendental idealist doctrines, though profoundly important, are literally inexpressible.[43]

If what Hacker says here is right, then it seems plausible to read Wittgenstein as attempting to complete Kant's project of limiting the scope of science and reason, thereby protecting what is "higher," in a way that Kant himself did not envision. Hacker concludes: "The Kantian idea echoes in Wittgenstein, but what in eighteenth-century Königsberg led to an *a priori* critical rationalist ethics, produced in the twentieth century a romantic ethics of the ineffable."[44] Janik and Toulmin concur: "In short, the primary concern of the author of the *Tractatus* is to protect the sphere of the conduct of life against the encroachments from the sphere of speculation."[45] And: "His world-view expresses the belief that the sphere of what can only be *shown* must be protected from those who try to *say* it."[46]

1.4

The ineffabilist approach just described broadly accords with the accounts favored by many well-known commentators besides Anscombe and Hacker.[47] Yet this way of reading the *Tractatus* has serious drawbacks and, for several years now, so-called resolute readers, most notably Cora Diamond and James Conant, have roundly attacked it.[48] If one can discern a general basis for their criticism, it is their view that readings like Anscombe's and Hacker's force an incoherent position onto Wittgenstein without any compelling textual or other interpretative justification for doing so. The incoherence lies in the idea that there are two *different kinds* of nonsensical utterances and that one of these kinds can be identified by *internal* features of the pseudopropositions that are used to make them. Hacker's reading, in particular, rests on the view that the nonsensical sentences of the *Tractatus* are intended to serve as guides to what one can say through the specific ways in which they themselves violate the principles of logical syntax.

Conant has termed the kind of view just described a "substantial" conception of nonsense. Although Hacker has vigorously denied it, Conant has nevertheless argued that Hacker's view in effect invites us to imagine against hope (that Wittgenstein thought) that there could be something like an identifiable nonsensical-sense that some nonsense makes.[49] Against this view, he and Diamond have argued for what Diamond has dubbed an "austere" view of nonsense in the *Tractatus*.[50] Rejecting the substantial view and adopting an austere attitude toward nonsense requires us to abandon the idea that there are different kinds of nonsense at work in the *Tractatus* and that these can be distinguished from one another by attention to internal features of certain nonsensical sentences in isolation from any context of use.[51] Diamond and Conant thus dispense with the idea that Wittgenstein believed that nonsense could be divided into a deep variety that gestures at sublime truths and at garden-variety nonsense. One significant consequence of this interpretation is that after we throw away Wittgenstein's nonsensical elucidations, the only sentences remaining are those that can be used to say something: *ordinary* sentences.[52] On the austere view, nonsense arises not from a violation of the principles of logical syntax but simply from someone's failure "to give a meaning to certain signs in his propositions."[53] While confusing combinations of signs (e.g., "Green is green") will not be permitted in a perspicuous notation, we can in fact give a meaning to any string of signs whatsoever. According to Diamond and Conant, there is no independently identifiable and inherently "important nonsense" that Wittgenstein employs to somehow convey or gesture at ineffable truths of logic, metaphysics, or anything else.

In developing her account, Diamond takes seriously Wittgenstein's suggestion to Ficker that the preface and conclusion are central for a proper understanding of the *Tractatus*, since, as he puts it, "they give the most direct expression" of its point. Recall that Wittgenstein begins the preface with the following remark: "Perhaps this book will be understood only by someone who has himself already had the thoughts that are expressed in it—or at least similar thoughts.— So it is not a textbook [*ist kein Lehrbuch*]." Commenting on this, Diamond writes, "to read the *Tractatus* with understanding, Wittgenstein tells us, is not to read it as a *Lehrbuch*. His intention is not that the book should teach us things that we did not know; it does not address itself to our ignorance."[54] This suggests, then, that the book imparts no new theories, doctrines, or truths of the kind ordinarily associated with philosophical treatises. Now, the remarks on value at the end of the book are not the only passages where Wittgenstein has been taken as trying to convey ineffable truths. It is possible to champion different ineffable topics: the necessary existence of simple objects, logical form, formal concepts, solipsism, and so on. Diamond, on the other hand, is happier to take Wittgenstein at his word, when Wittgenstein writes in the preface:

In order to be able to draw a limit to thought, we should have to find both sides of the limit thinkable (i.e. we should have to be able to think what cannot be thought).

It will therefore only be in language that the limit can be drawn, and what lies on the other side of the limit will simply be nonsense.[55]

There is no intimation here on Wittgenstein's part that in fact nonsense can be divided into a deep variety that gestures at sublime truths (logical or ethical/aesthetic) and garden-variety nonsense like "piggle wiggle tiggle": "His statement that what is on the other side of the limit is plain nonsense seems to be meant to rule out exactly the idea that some of our sentences count as nonsense but *do* manage to gesture towards those things that cannot be put into plain words."[56]

But this still leaves unexplained the most puzzling feature of the *Tractatus* that ineffabilist interpretations were supposed to account for: the conjunction of Wittgenstein's claim at §6.54 that his propositions serve their elucidatory purpose when they are recognized as nonsense with his claim in the letter to Ficker that his book has an ethical point. To get clear about these questions, I want to begin with a passage from a paper by Conant. As it has been a few years since the paper was written, I am not certain whether this passage still reflects precisely what Conant (not to speak of anyone else in this debate) thinks. Nevertheless, to my mind it stands as a concise and elegant description of Wittgenstein's conception of the *Tractatus*, one that I believe amenable to at least most resolute readings of the book. Conant writes,

> The guiding assumption of the *Tractatus* is that the philosopher typically suffers from an illusion of understanding, from the projection of an illusory sense onto a (pseudo-) proposition which has not yet been given a clear sense. The task, therefore, is not to disagree with what he thinks, but to undo his illusion that there is something which he is thinking—to show that what he imagines himself to be thinking fails to amount to a thought (that there isn't a "what" there for him to think). The method of the *Tractatus* relies upon the thought that under such circumstances the only procedure that will prove genuinely elucidatory is one that attempts to enter into the philosopher's illusion of understanding and explode it from within.[57]

Conant connects two difficult ideas in this passage. The first idea is that the traditional philosopher suffers from a kind of illusion. The second idea is that the only way for one to clear up this illusion ("the only procedure that will prove genuinely elucidatory") is to somehow find a way into that illusion oneself. On the view of the *Tractatus* that Conant is espousing in this passage, this activity of entering into the philosopher's illusion is called "elucidation" (*Erläuterung*). As to the first idea, Conant notes elsewhere that Wittgenstein is far from alone in the history of philosophy in holding that the proper response to traditional philosophical questions is to come to see them as chimeras.

> Taken by itself, there is nothing new in the thought that progress in philosophy will come not with the formulation of better answers to the old questions, but rather by accounting for the source of our attraction to the questions—by (to look no further than the opening words of the *Critique of Pure Reason*), for example, showing that "human reason has this peculiar fate that . . . it is burdened by questions which, as prescribed by the very nature of reason itself, it is not able to ignore, but which . . . it is also not able to answer." (A vii) The overarching task that guides the tradition formed by Lessing, Kant, Kierkegaard and Wittgenstein (among others) is to show that the disputes in philosophy we are tempted to take sides in are often illusory.[58]

Michael Kremer gives us a concise explication of the second idea, that of *Tractarian* elucidation, as Conant, Diamond, and others understand it:

> The propositions of the *Tractatus* do not begin by making sense, only to be gradually reduced to nonsense. They are nonsense all along. The only thing that is corroded is our view of ourselves as making sense of them. We start under the illusion that we understand certain strings of signs. Under this illusion we manipulate these strings "logically" so as to arrive at other strings, relying on apparent "structural" similarities to sensible argumentation. As we are led along by the seeming logic of the "argument" we come upon (illusory) "conclusions" that so puzzle us that we lose our grip on the idea that we were ever making sense at all, so also that we were following an "argument."[59]

In order to elaborate a bit on the relation between illusion and elucidation on a resolute reading of the *Tractatus*, I want to bring in something Diamond has written about the early Wittgenstein's conception of philosophical activity. She sees the *Tractatus* as responding to the philosopher's predicament through a self-conscious employment of imagination.

> To want to understand the person who talks nonsense is to want to enter imaginatively the taking of that nonsense for sense. . . . The *Tractatus*, in its understanding of itself as addressed to those who are in the grip of philosophical

nonsense, and in its understanding of the kind of demands it makes on its readers, supposes a kind of imaginative activity, an exercise of the capacity to enter
into the taking of nonsense for sense, of the capacity to share imaginatively the
inclination to think that one is thinking something in it. If I could not as it were
see your nonsense as sense, imaginatively let myself feel its attractiveness, I could
not understand you. And that is a very particular use of imagination.[60]

This description is meant to apply, of course, to Wittgenstein's own understanding
of his relation to the reader of the *Tractatus*. The sentences of that book are chosen and arranged, if Diamond is right, through Wittgenstein's own imaginative
activity, through his permitting his own imagination to wander and feel the
attraction of words that he imagines others may take for the expression of profound philosophical truths. It is therefore such a use of imagination that is central
to these sentences serving as philosophical elucidations, which the reader might
"overcome" so that she can "see the world aright."

Now recall from above that Diamond and Conant have claimed that there is a
confusion in the idea that one can internally distinguish one bit of nonsense from
another in order to separate off what we take to convey metaphysical truth from
that which we take for mere gibberish. Nevertheless, in the following Diamond
indicates a different way in which we might conceive of distinguishing between
different occurrences of nonsense:

> In a particular case of the utterance of a nonsense-sentence, its utterance may fail
> to reflect an understanding of oneself or of others; it may depend on this or that
> type of use of imagination. But there is no way of taking any nonsense-sentence
> and saying that, by the sentence it is, it is philosophical elucidation, not meta-
> physical nonsense. For a sentence that is nonsense to be an elucidatory sentence
> is entirely a matter of features external to it.[61]

The external features of a nonsensical utterance concern its context, which
include the intentions of the speaker and his imaginative relation to what is said.
Diamond discusses three ways in which imagination can mediate our relation
to metaphysical nonsense. One way is the tendency to assume that the mental
images one has when one utters or hears a sentence are intrinsically connected
with the logical and semantic features of that sentence. But the mental images I
may connect with a particular utterance often have little or nothing to do with the
way a sentence conveys information about the world, with the way another person can understand something by it through its being logically articulate. Rather,
such images form part of the causal chain of my mental history; they are a fact

about me. Combating this kind of psychologism about meaning is something that Wittgenstein made a lifelong task, and, as Diamond notes, it forms part of his inheritance from Frege.[62] Psychologism, then, is one of the ways that imagination is involved in the production of metaphysical nonsense. Diamond writes, "We are attracted by certain sentences, certain forms of words, and imagine that we mean something by them. We are satisfied that we mean something by them because they have the mental accompaniments of meaningful sentences."[63]

We imagine that these mental accompaniments were themselves somehow sufficient to guarantee that a sentence made sense. This leads to a kind of indolence in our relations to what we say; it inclines us away from careful attention, since the conjuring up of images that we take for an adequate guarantor of meaning something is a largely passive phenomenon. Closely related to this is the second case of false imagination that Diamond sees as one of Wittgenstein's targets in the *Tractatus*. This is the unreflective assumption that there can be philosophy in the traditional sense.

> The attractiveness of the forms of words expressive of philosophical confusion arises out of the imagining of a point of view for philosophical investigation. And it is precisely that illusory point of view that the *Tractatus* self-consciously imagines itself into in an attempt to lead one to see that there was only false imagination in the attractiveness of the words one had been inclined to come out with.[64]

The illusory point of view out of which the *Tractatus* tries to lead us is one from which we imagine that we can, so to speak, objectively consider the limits of thought and the nature of the world as a whole. Here we can perhaps see an important conceptual relation to the illusory perspective of transcendental realism that Kant saw as leading to the *Antinomies*. He diagnoses the underlying difficulty as stemming from the tacit premise that one can consider the world and all of its conditions as an object of knowledge. Kant's resolution of the *Antinomies* is based on his claim that, because of the subjective nature of the conditions of synthesis that make experience possible, there is no such objectifiable totality. Thus, Kant problematizes the very notion of a world whole that would provide the metaphysician with the perspective he (thinks he) requires.[65]

To see the possibility of a third way in which imagination may be related to nonsense, consider the opening sentences of the *Tractatus*: "The world is all that is the case. The world is the totality of facts, not of things." We have here sentences, indeed magisterial-sounding sentences, that silently invite us to imagine ourselves as enjoying a bird's-eye view on "the world and all of its conditions" and that what follows will be a discourse from just this view. On Diamond's and Conant's reading of the *Tractatus*, however, such sentences are expressions of an activity called elucidation, by which Wittgenstein tries to enter imaginatively into the viewpoint of the would-be practitioner of metaphysics, a person who is inclined to come out with sentences about the "world as a whole" and to imagine that he means something by them. Diamond writes,

> Here, then, is a description,—an external description—of the difference between the propositions of the *Tractatus* and the propositions of the metaphysician. The former are recognized by their author to be plain nonsense, the latter are not; the former are in the service of an imaginative understanding of persons, the latter are the result of a sort of disease of imagination, and the philosopher who comes out with them lacks that understanding of himself which the *Tractatus* aims to secure for us.[66]

1.5

In the course of explicating Diamond's and Conant's reading of the *Tractatus*, we have so far seen two different possible attitudes characteristic of a speaker of nonsense: that of the traditional philosopher or metaphysician, whose nonsense is said to reflect his false imagination that there is a perspective for philosophical investigation, and Wittgenstein's self-conscious nonsense, which is spoken in the service of philosophical elucidation. Diamond argues that "ethical sentences," as understood by Wittgenstein, constitute a third group. That is to say, the intentions behind such utterances are different both from the intentions behind the elucidations of the *Tractatus* and from the intentions behind traditional metaphysical utterances. The reader of the *Tractatus* is supposed to see that sentences that he initially took for real philosophical theses concerning the nature of the world, logic, mathematics, and ethics are in fact nonsense, and this realization is then supposed to break the hold that such word formations have on his imagination. There is a definite sense, then, in which the sentences of the *Tractatus* are supposed to affect the reader. Diamond, however, understands the intentions behind "ethical" utterances as distinct from those at work in the *Tractatus*: "The intention of the would-be engager in ethics is not like that, is not in that way therapeutic. So 'ethical sentences' are distinguishable from those of the *Tractatus* by the intention with which they are uttered or written. They are distinguishable from philosophical nonsense-sentences by their relation to the self-understanding towards which the *Tractatus* aims to lead us."[67]

There is actually an important common feature of the intentions characteristic of ethical nonsense sentences as understood by Wittgenstein and metaphysical nonsense: both kinds of nonsense reflect the attraction exerted on our imagination of there being a point of view on the world as a whole. The metaphysician tries to imagine himself into a standpoint over and against the world, from which he can propound theories not about this or that aspect of the world but rather about what I have been calling "the world and all of its conditions." Recall from the "Lecture on Ethics" Wittgenstein's own examples of the kind of ethical nonsense that he finds compelling:

> I believe the best way of describing it is to say that when I have it *I wonder at the existence of the world*. . . . I will mention another experience straight away which I also know and which others of you might be acquainted with: it is, what one might call, the experience of feeling *absolutely safe*. I mean the state of mind in which one is inclined to say "I am safe, nothing can injure me whatever happens."

So we see that the imaginative activities involved in these two kinds of utterance are not totally distinct. Nevertheless, they differ crucially in the way that the imagination of the speaker is connected with his intentions. The metaphysician has the sober intention of propounding theories that, whatever their truth value, he at least imagines make sense; the reflective speaker of ethical nonsense is not under this illusion, though his intentions are perhaps no less sober. But whereas, according to Diamond, "as Wittgenstein saw traditional philosophical activity, it would not survive recognition that the intentions in it were incompatible with making sense,"[68] for the self-conscious speaker of ethical nonsense, the imaginative appeal of sentences such as "The world of the happy man is a different one from that of the unhappy" would not necessarily suffer from this recognition. She concludes,

> If we understand ourselves . . . we shall not come out with ethical sentences under the illusion that we are talking sense. We may show this by framing our sentences; for example, someone might say "I am inclined to say 'The goodness of life does not depend on things going this way or that.'" Words like "This is what I am inclined to say," used to frame such sentences, may thus mark both that they are recognized by the utterer as nonsense, and that that recognition does not involve their losing their attractiveness, their capacity to make us feel that they express the sense we want to make.[69]

This last remark suggests how we can distinguish Wittgenstein's views clearly from those of the logical positivists, who of course rejected traditional philosophical ethics on the grounds that ethical statements were unverifiable and thus nonsensical pseudostatements. This is an important point, since on the surface Wittgenstein and the positivists might seem to be close here. Indeed, it can hardly be surprising if Wittgenstein has often been mistaken for a kind of proto-positivist on ethics, especially as some well-known positivists took their views to be inspired in part by him. Maybe the best-known and influential case of this was A. J. Ayer's widely read *Language, Truth, and Logic*, a book that, particularly in the English-speaking world, functioned as a sort of summary introduction to the doctrines of logical positivism. The preface to the 1936 first edition begins with the claim that "the views which are put forward in this treatise derive from the doctrines of Bertrand Russell and Wittgenstein, which are themselves the logical outcome of the empiricism of Berkeley and David Hume."[70]

Looking at Ayer's discussion, we see that, on the one hand, he wanted to do away with any kind of discourse that failed to conform to a verificationist criterion of meaning. This not only included eliminating all traditional ontological theorizing but also the attempt to treat ethics as a genuine sphere of knowledge.

> It is our business to give an account of "judgements of value" which is both satisfactory in itself and consistent with our general empiricist principles. We shall set ourselves to show that in so far as statements of value are significant, they are ordinary "scientific" statements; and that in so far as they are not scientific, they are not in the literal sense significant, but are simply expressions of emotion which can be neither true nor false.[71]

First, note that from the vantage point of a resolute reading, according to which Wittgenstein does not intend to put forth anything like a semantic theory of meaning in the *Tractatus*, Ayer's explicit reliance on "general empiricist principles" should already make one suspicious about the degree to which his views can be properly regarded as deriving from Wittgenstein's book. Second, and more immediately relevant, is the way in which Ayer understood his own metaethical enterprise as one of treating utterances that purported to say something ethical as utterances that indicated something about the psychology of the speaker, for example, about his or her preferences, feelings, or dispositions.

> In every case in which one would commonly be said to be making an ethical judgement, the function of the relevant ethical word is purely "emotive." It is used to express feeling about certain objects, but not to make any assertion about them.... In fact we may define the meaning of the various ethical words in

terms both of the different feelings they are ordinarily taken to express, and also the different responses which they are calculated to provoke.[72]

These "ethical" feelings and responses may in turn be investigated systematically—not by the philosopher but rather by the psychologist and sociologist.

> We find that ethical philosophy consists simply in saying that ethical concepts are pseudo-concepts and therefore unanalysable. The further task of describing the different feelings that the different ethical terms are used to express, and the different reactions that they customarily provoke, is a task for the psychologist. There cannot be such a thing as ethical science, if by ethical science one means the elaboration of a "true" system of morals. . . . All that one may legitimately enquire in this connection is, What are the moral habits of a given person or group of people, and what causes them to have precisely those habits and feelings? And this enquiry falls wholly within the scope of the existing social sciences. . . . It appears, then, that ethics, as a branch of knowledge, is nothing more than a department of psychology and sociology.[73]

This passage makes clear that Ayer sees no difficulty in using the traditional term "ethics" to describe this wholly naturalized new field of study. Diamond remarks in this regard that the positivist project of metaethics "reflects the idea that sentences which are in some way 'ethical' can be recognized and discussed philosophically in sentences that make sense and that do not wholly ignore whatever is ethical in those sentences."[74] According to Diamond, it is precisely this having it both ways that Wittgenstein thinks represents a confusion in one's attitude toward ethics. If we are clear here, we will see that we are instead presented with a choice: "Grasp the sentences in question as ethical by imaginatively treating nonsense as sense or stick to talking and thinking sense yourself and lose touch with anything ethical in the sentences."[75] Diamond's way of putting it is to say that the positivists were confused about what language they wanted to be in. Their attempt at making sense of ethical utterances by grounding our understanding of them in empirical psychology was, for Wittgenstein, to miss what was at the very heart of ethics as he saw it. This can be seen again from what he says in the following passage from the "Lecture on Ethics," where he argues against the idea that there can be a correct logical analysis of ethical utterances:

> I see now that these nonsensical expressions were not nonsensical because I had not yet found the correct expressions, but that their nonsensicality was their

very essence. For all I wanted to do with them was just *to go beyond* the world and that is to say beyond significant language. My whole tendency and I believe the tendency of all men who ever tried to write or talk Ethics or Religion was to run against the boundaries of language.[76]

Just before this remark, Wittgenstein asserts that he would reject any analysis that succeeded in making sense of an ethical utterance *on the very grounds of its significance*.[77] If this is the case, then quite apart from whatever Wittgenstein's view comes to, it certainly seems wrong to lump him in with the logical positivists on the subject of ethics (and aesthetics), even if we do reject the ineffabilist reading of the *Tractatus*. Diamond thus draws the following lesson: "What I am warning against is any idea that we should take Wittgenstein's remarks about ethics to constitute philosophical analysis of a kind of discourse, rather than as remarks aimed at bringing about a kind of self-understanding through the reader's imaginative activity."[78]

It is worth connecting what I have just been saying about the difference between Wittgenstein's and Ayer's respective understandings of ethics with a strand of thought that Diamond finds in Kant. Much of my discussion above turns on the importance of the sense/nonsense distinction. Diamond sees a relevant connection here with another pair of complementary concepts from Kant: transcendental and empirical. We have seen that one of the ways the positivists differed from Wittgenstein on ethics concerned the idea that one can give an analysis of ethical utterances by treating them as though they could be made sense of in terms of laws of empirical psychology. We have also seen how for Wittgenstein this leaves out something that he saw as essential to ethics. Kant, too, would have rejected any attempt to make ethics a matter of descriptive psychology. According to Kant, ethics can never be grounded in the empirical world, because the empirical world is governed by the law of causality, and that makes the freedom necessary for morality impossible. Diamond puts the analogy between the two this way:

In reading Wittgenstein or Kant, we can take the word "transcendental" as a kind of warning. For Kant, the connection between ethics and the transcendental subject is such that ethics is destroyed, there is no ethics, if you try to move ethical thought into the realm of what we can know, the empirical world. For Wittgenstein, the connection between ethics and the transcendental is not, as it was for Kant, a matter of tying ethics to something other than what we can know, other than the empirical world. But for him as for Kant, ethics is destroyed, there is no ethics, if we try as it were to push ethics into the empirical world.[79]

Diamond is suggesting here that we see Kant and Wittgenstein as sharing the attitude that it is misguided to look in the realm of the facts for what is ethical. One might go further and connect what Diamond says here about Kant and the empirical world with the concept of justification. For it is implicit in what she says about Kant that for him ethics cannot have as its grounds or justification any fact in the world. It was central to Kant's understanding of ethics that justification for action not be sought in any facts of the world but rather in Reason. Of course, he believed that facts *are* properly connected with justification in areas of life quite distinct from ethics, such as the natural sciences. For Kant, however, empirical facts can never serve as the basis for justification in ethics. Diamond's point is that the transcendental/empirical dichotomy in Kant can, to a certain degree, shed light on Wittgenstein's own outlook.[80] If this is true, then the concept of justification, which is intimately related to this distinction in Kant's thought, may well be important for a deeper understanding of the *Tractatus*. This is a point that I will explore further in the next chapter.

On an ineffabilist reading of the *Tractatus*, one is able to move fairly directly to an interpretation of Wittgenstein's claim that his book has an ethical aim. The rejection of ineffabilist interpretations required that I take an extended detour before I could return to this question. Now that an alternative and, I think, better interpretation of the book is at hand, I want to show in the next chapter how it allows us to understand this dimension of the *Tractatus* in altogether different terms.[81]

2

THE ETHICAL PURPOSE
OF THE *TRACTATUS*

2.1

The previous chapter served mainly to set the stage for my remaining discussion. As we saw, on a resolute reading, the ethical aim of the *Tractatus* is intimately connected to Wittgenstein's understanding and practice of philosophy as an activity whose goal is clarity rather than the establishment of philosophical truth or the refutation of philosophical theories. Indeed, the idea that Wittgenstein had as little desire to advance any sort of philosophical doctrine in the *Tractatus* as he did in his more mature philosophy is a point that resolute readers are particularly keen to emphasize as an important part of the continuity of his thought. On this point, Diamond remarks,

> Whether one is reading Wittgenstein's *Tractatus* or his later writings, one must be struck by his insistence that he is not putting forward philosophical doctrines or theses; or by his suggestion that it cannot be done, that it is only through some confusion one is in about what one is doing that one could take oneself to be putting forward philosophical doctrines or theses at all. I think that there is almost nothing in Wittgenstein which is of value and which can be grasped if it is pulled away from that view of philosophy. But that view of philosophy is itself something that has to be seen first in the *Tractatus* if it is to be understood in its later forms.[1]

One very important consequence of resolute readings is that after we have followed Wittgenstein's injunction at §6.54 to throw away the ladder of elucidatory nonsense that makes up the main body of the *Tractatus*, we should see that the only sentences with which we are left are *ordinary* sentences.[2] That is to say, we should see that the only sentences remaining with which we might *try* to say something are sentences that actually *do* say something, that is, the propositions of natural science, that is, sentences all of whose constituent signs have been given a meaning.[3] And, as Wittgenstein tells us, these sentences will have "nothing to do with philosophy" and so nothing to do with traditional ethics.[4]

At this stage, however, I think that one is still entitled to wonder about the *substance* of Wittgenstein's claim in the letter to Ficker. So far, the understanding we have seems largely negative, consisting mainly in a clearing away of misunderstandings about what kind of book the *Tractatus* is *not*. If Wittgenstein rejects *both* traditional philosophical ethics *and* the idea that there can be inherently "important nonsense" that manages somehow to "convey" or "gesture at" ineffable truths of ethics (in addition to gesturing at ineffable truths of logic or metaphysics), then how can we read the *Tractatus* as having an *ethical point*? Michael Kremer has made what I take to be roughly the same point. He argues that resolute interpreters have "to explain *why* Wittgenstein wrote a book consisting almost entirely of nonsense. *What* did he think he could accomplish through doing this?"[5] He adds, "Diamond suggests that the *Tractatus*'s aim will be achieved when the self-understanding of those attracted to philosophy leads to their losing that attraction. Yet this leaves one wondering what the source of this attraction *is*, and why bringing about the end of such an attraction is the aim of a book with an *ethical* purpose."[6] These kinds of questions are not pressing for interpreters such as Hacker; they have a ready answer: Wittgenstein wrote a book of nonsense in order to convey to his reader a number of ineffable truths about logic, metaphysics, and ethics. As we have seen, however, this is precisely the kind of answer that is not available to Diamond and like-minded interpreters of the *Tractatus*. I believe that Diamond does do more than merely point out that Wittgenstein hoped that the book would make philosophical nonsense unattractive to us. She also says that he thought that ethics would not lose its attractiveness to us merely through our recognition that it, too, was nonsense. Nevertheless, I agree with Kremer that she doesn't develop this point in much detail, and I think that Kremer is right in suggesting that this leaves us without an adequate sense of what Wittgenstein's ethical aim in writing the book might have been.[7]

This is the main question that I address in this chapter. I begin by taking a brief look at a difference between an ordinary way of thinking about conveying an intention and a difficulty for doing so in the context of reading the *Tractatus*. Most of the chapter is then taken up with articulating a way of understanding the ethical purpose of the *Tractatus* through comparison and contrast with certain themes from Heidegger's *Being and Time*. To this end, I first give a brief overview of Heidegger's phenomenological account of anxiety, the "they," and authenticity. I then turn to Wittgenstein's remarks on causality and mechanics in the *Tractatus*, showing how reading those remarks in light of what he says in the "Lecture on Ethics" and elsewhere makes evident a way in which the book is engaged in a form of cultural critique that is central to its ethical point. Next, I bring out some striking and substantive parallels and points of connection between Heideggerian authenticity and the relation to language that the *Tractatus* aims to bring about. This leads to an examination of a paper in which Michael Kremer has argued that the ethical point of the book can be fruitfully seen in relation to Saint Paul's and Saint Augustine's writings on justification and to an examination of an interpretation worked out by James Conant, who has argued that the book shares important philosophical goals and methods with some of Kierkegaard's pseudonymous works. I argue that problems with Conant's interpretation of Kierkegaard make his comparison of the latter's thought with Wittgenstein's problematic and that these problems are likely sources of trouble for Kremer as well. Finally, I argue that the ethical point of the *Tractatus* is to reawaken us to a sense of wonder, a sense of wonder that is perhaps best thought of in religious terms, although not necessarily along confessional lines.

2.2

There is a straightforward, perhaps commonsense way in which an intention, a desire, for instance, can be expressed in an ordinary sentence.[8] I might, for example, express my desire for ice cream by saying "I would really like some ice cream now." In this case, one can go from the sentence expressing the desire back to the nature of the desire itself. The logical articulateness of the sentence, along with its context of use, let us see what the desire is and what implications or possible outcomes it has. But imagine having an impulse like the one Wittgenstein describes in the "Lecture on Ethics," the very essence of which consists in the desire *not* to make sense. If there really is no such thing as articulating a bit of nonsense, no articulating the inarticulate, and if Wittgenstein's impulse when it comes to ethics is to come out with nonsense, then it follows that there is no such thing as straightforwardly articulating such nonsense so as to get an understanding of his intention, no such thing as analyzing the sentence and working back to the intention. Does it follow that the would-be speaker of ethical nonsense cannot be understood and is in a hopelessly isolated predicament? For his part, Wittgenstein left no doubt about the importance that this "urge to run up against the limits of language" had for him.[9] He concluded the lecture with this remark: "Ethics so far as it springs from the desire to say something about the ultimate meaning of life, the absolute good, the absolute valuable, can be no science. What it says does not add to our knowledge in any sense. But it is a document of a tendency in the human mind which I personally cannot help respecting deeply and I would not for my life ridicule it."[10] One would have to be exceptionally clear about the nature of this tendency or urge not to get confused about it. One would, for instance, constantly have to refrain from the temptation to make it seem like any ordinary desire, whose content could be given in an ordinary sentence.[11] That would mark confusion in oneself about what one really wanted to do when one felt the need to give expression to it. I believe that it was Wittgenstein's view that all (or most) people had within them the germ of such an impulse but that they had fallen into something like the confusion just mentioned.

In the everyday kind of cases just sketched above, understanding someone consists in our standing in relation to logical features of his utterance, such that we can be guided by these features directly to the intention behind the utterance, directly to the speaker himself, as it were. In the previous chapter, however, we read how the form that philosophical elucidation takes in the *Tractatus* could be seen as depending on particular uses of imagination, especially on how its sentences are constructed and arranged so as to make us feel the attraction of words suggesting a point of view for the philosophical investigation of the world as a whole. Our coming to see how a book consisting entirely of nonsense could be written with an ethical point is clearly different from the more ordinary kind of cases of understanding a speaker's intention. Necessarily, it is indirect.

I want to suggest also that if the ethical point of the *Tractatus* that Wittgenstein mentions in the letter to Ficker, what I take to be the intention that lies behind the writing of the book, cannot be articulated in terms of an ordinary sentence, then the only way that Wittgenstein can get us to understand his intention—and the only way that we might understand something similar in ourselves—is if something like this intention might already be in us, ready to be reawakened, as it were. Conveying this kind of intention, then, could not involve a mere assertion that the reader might grasp directly in order to see if he found the same in himself. Instead, we should see Wittgenstein's procedure as more of an *uncovering and a disentangling* of an intention in his reader, one with which all sorts of other ordinary intentions have been confused. We might only be able to approach this intention, however, through a kind of *via negativa*, by seeing in ourselves something left over, some impulse to keep going, when all the intentions connected to whatever can be said have been accounted for. With these thoughts in hand, I want to turn now to some central ideas in the early work of another twentieth-century philosopher.

2.3

Heidegger's project in *Being and Time* is to uncover and articulate the fundamental structures of human existence.[12] This attempt to arrive at the "meaning of Being of Dasein" (Heidegger's term for human being) was his way into the more ambitious (and ultimately abandoned) project of fundamental ontology, where the goal was to arrive at the "meaning of Being" in general.[13] An important conceptual-phenomenological distinction that Heidegger makes is that between what he calls "existential" (*existenzial*) and "existentiell" (*existenziell*). The first term, "existential," denotes a fundamental, ontological structure of human existence, while the second, "existentiell," refers to a particular instantiation of that structure, such as Dasein's interpretation of itself in a particular situation. "Existential" and "existentiell" thus form a complementary pair of terms.[14] A crucial ontological and methodological point for Heidegger to make concerns the connection between the *existential* structure of anxiety (*Angst*) and the *existentiell* possibility of authenticity (*Eigentlichkeit*). Heidegger calls anxiety a "ground mood" (*Grundstimmung*) and distinguishes it from the specific emotion of fear. Fear is always fear of some particular entity in the world.[15] On the other hand, "That in the face of which one has anxiety is Being-in-the-world as such."[16] He writes, in addition, that "Anxiety individualizes Dasein for its ownmost Being-in-the-world. . . . Therefore, with that which it is anxious about, anxiety discloses Dasein . . . as something individualized."[17]

Heidegger thinks that phenomenological reflection reveals that Dasein is a being who always brings to its activities a prereflective set of practices and ways of comporting itself that allow things to show up to it as intelligible. Heidegger calls this set of background practices an "Understanding-of-Being" (*Seinsverständnis*).[18] Anxiety, according to Heidegger, individuates Dasein by wrenching it out of its "fallenness" (*Verfallenheit*), its seamless absorption in the everyday world as this gets disclosed to it through the average, banal interpretations of these background practices by what Heidegger terms the "they" (*Das Man*). Indeed, Heidegger emphasizes that most of the time, Dasein understands not only the everyday world but even its own existence in terms of the "they-self":

> Dasein is for the sake of the "they" in an everyday manner, and the "they" itself articulates the referential context of significance. When entities are encountered, Dasein's world frees them for a totality of involvements with which the "they" is familiar, and within the limits which have been established by the "they's" averageness. . . . Proximally, it is not "I," in the sense of my own Self, that "am," but rather the Others, whose way is that of the "they." In terms of the

"they," and as the "they," I am given to "myself." Proximally Dasein is "they," and for the most part it remains so.[19]

Nevertheless, it is important not to misconstrue the "they" as some kind of evil spirit hanging over Dasein.[20] Heidegger wants to demonstrate, rather, that the "they" is an existential structure of Dasein, one that is necessary if there is to be a publicly intelligible world at all. He writes, "*The 'they' is an existentiale; and as a primordial phenomenon, it belongs to Dasein's positive constitution.*"[21]

To elaborate a bit further, Heidegger claims that attention to the way it is most of the time shows that, contrary to the philosophical tradition's bias toward theoretical reflection, Dasein is primarily an agent in a world of concrete involvements that are intelligible to it by virtue of its shared skills and background understanding. In order for these skills to function as such, however, they must, as it were, "recede into the background." For example, when I am skillfully driving a car with a manual transmission in busy city traffic, I don't need to be thinking about what I am doing. The clutch pedal, the stick shift, brakes, and steering wheel, if they are all working properly, become mere extensions of my body as I use them to navigate through town.[22] In these and similar cases, there is often no need for deliberate thought, or what Heidegger calls "thematic awareness." I may *in fact* be thinking about something, but this need not have any relevant connection with the task that I am engaged in at the moment. Indeed, in the kind of case that I have described, quite often to the extent that I am deliberating about my actions, I am not engaging the situation skilfully.[23] One needs, in some sense, to "forget" the skills in order for them to permit one to cope adequately with the world.

In fallenness, however, Dasein reveals a tendency, as Heidegger puts it, "not only to forget the forgotten, but to forget the forgetting itself."[24] Charles Guignon comments, "to say that we are prone to forgetfulness is to say that we have a tendency to become so preoccupied with the way things show up for us in our world that we lose sight of the background conditions . . . that first make it possible to encounter anything at all."[25] With such "second-order" forgetting, Dasein loses sight of the "first-order" forgetting, wherein the practices and skills recede to the background. When Dasein "forgets the forgotten," however, it becomes not merely absorbed but "fascinated." Heidegger calls such fallen fascination "inauthenticity": " 'Inauthenticity' . . . amounts . . . to a quite distinctive kind of Being-in-the-world—the kind which is completely fascinated by the 'world' and by the Dasein-with of others in the 'they.' "[26] For our purposes here, the most important characteristic of the entities that Dasein encounters in its dealings with the world is that they have a fixed nature: a hammer *just is* a tool for carrying out various tasks, a dentist *just is* a professional who treats one's teeth, and so on.[27]

And, indeed, inauthentic Dasein interprets itself as essentially the bearer of some constellation of social roles that seem to confer on it an essential nature.[28] Inauthenticity, however, is not merely a matter of Dasein's embodying social interpretations and practices, because Heidegger sees these as a requirement for Dasein to have a world at all. Rather, in inauthenticity, one's relationship to such roles and practices is obscured in that one does not understand them for what they are.

Anxiety confronts Dasein with the understanding that none of these ways of being can give it any specific personal content, since they are anonymous, public, "anyone" ways of the "they-self" for comporting oneself.[29]

> [In anxiety], the totality of involvements . . . discovered within-the-world, is, as such, of no consequence; it collapses into itself; the world has the character of completely lacking significance.[30]
>
> In anxiety what is environmentally ready-to-hand sinks away, and so, in general, do entities within-the-world. The "world" can offer nothing more, and neither can the Dasein-with of Others.[31]

Thus, somewhat paradoxically perhaps, Heidegger claims that Dasein is *individuated* in anxiety precisely by being wrenched out of its everyday world, thereby seeing that it has *no fixed identity* and *can have none*. Dasein sees clearly that all of the practices of the "they-self" are publicly interpreted anonymous practices and that all of the everyday objects and equipment by which it is surrounded are anyone's freeways, anyone's streetcars, anyone's telephone, and so on. It is precisely the understanding of these "anyone" practices *as such* that makes it manifest to Dasein *that* it is in a publicly interpreted world: "The utter insignificance which makes itself known . . . does not signify that the world is absent, but tells us that entities within-the-world are of so little importance in themselves that on the basis of this *insignificance* of what is within-the-world, the world in its worldhood is all that still obtrudes itself."[32]

When faced with anxiety, Dasein has two *existentiell* possibilities: authenticity or inauthenticity. Authentic Dasein holds on to the insight that it has gained through anxiety concerning the general, leveled nature of the average background practices. Inauthentic Dasein, on the other hand, flees back into the "tranquilized" comfort of the "they."[33] Anxiety, Heidegger thus writes, "brings Dasein back from its falling, and makes manifest to it that authenticity and inauthenticity are possibilities of its Being."[34] When authentic Dasein holds on to anxiety, its new relation to the "they" need no longer be one of simply falling for the banal, rigid interpretations of its practices. Rather, in an authentic relation to the "they," Dasein can gain a new possibility, which Heidegger terms "resoluteness"

(*Ent-schlossenheit*).[35] Resolute Dasein maintains a kind of constant openness to new possibilities, and Heidegger's description of resoluteness militates against a reading in which it is interpreted as anything like an intentional choice made by a deliberating subject. "One would completely misunderstand the phenomenon of resoluteness if one should want to suppose that this consists simply in taking up possibilities which have been proposed and recommended, and seizing hold of them."[36] Rather, resoluteness should be understood more on the order of an openness to being called by anxiety: " 'Resoluteness' signifies letting oneself be summoned out of one's lostness in the 'they.' "[37]

In resolute openness, Dasein no longer interprets itself as having an essence, given once and for all by the current roles and projects that it has taken over from the "they." More to our present point, since resolute Dasein no longer takes on the banal interpretations of the "they" as simply obvious and necessary but instead *as* practices, Heidegger claims that these same ordinary background practices allow things to show up for resolute Dasein in a more variegated and nuanced fashion. Specifically, resolute Dasein's openness affords it the possibility of responding to what Heidegger calls the "Situation": "The existential attributes of any possible resolute Dasein include the items constitutive for an existential phenomenon which we call a 'Situation' and which we have hitherto passed over."[38] In being open to the Situation, Dasein no longer encounters whatever or whoever constitutes its current involvement in a general, one-size-fits-all, banal way. Instead, resolute Dasein is called forth "into a clear and honest appreciation of where it is placed, of what it is that calls for decision, and away, therefore, from the They's facile interpretations which serve only to 'close off' the nature of its Situation."[39] To this extent, then, resolute Dasein is distinguished from the "they," since "the 'they' knows only the 'general situation.' "[40] It is crucial to appreciate, however, that resolute Dasein's projects are in principle no less shared and public than before. Rather, its openness to the Situation is ultimately dependent on its more sensitive relation to the average, everyday practices already available to it. Heidegger is clear that, although in resolute authenticity Dasein can realize its "ownmost potentiality for being," it in no way becomes, so to speak, more of a Dasein or in any way otherworldly. "Resoluteness, as authentic Being-one's-Self, does not detach Dasein from its world, nor does it isolate it so that it becomes a free-floating 'I.' . . . Resoluteness brings the Self right into its current concernful Being-alongside what is ready-to-hand, and pushes it into solicitous Being with Others."[41] Moreover, because Dasein always finds itself in a concrete situation in the world, there is no need for Dasein to, as it were, "re-enter the world by *making* a resolution" or "to be called back to the world." Instead, Dasein can once again take up its projects, but in a way that manifests its essential nullity, that is, without the illusion that these involvements and projects alone can give it an essential identity.[42]

Since that part of Heidegger's account of authenticity that I have summarized above does not yet indicate a way in which authentic Dasein's life might be any different from inauthentic Dasein's life in terms of content, we can understand it as concerning the *form* of Dasein's involvements in the world. What has been emphasized is the view that the "they" cannot provide Dasein with a telos of its own through which it might attain a unique differentiating content. Moreover, this aspect of Heidegger's description of authenticity does not distinguish between particular cultures in which Dasein may find itself but rather is meant to bring out a structural possibility of Dasein, regardless of its specific historical context. This involves Dasein's maintaining constancy in its life in terms of resolute openness toward the world and the ways of the "they." In saying, however, that a feature of authenticity for early Heidegger involves overcoming the tendency to live as though the leveled practices of the "they" could provide any personal meaning to one's life, one comes quite close to saying that the particular facts of the world to which resolute Dasein relates are not what is most important to this struggle. Authentic and inauthentic Dasein inhabit the same world, but their way of inhabiting that world differs. Heidegger writes, "The 'world' which is ready-to-hand does not become another one 'in its content,' nor does the circle of Others get exchanged for a new one; but both one's Being towards the ready-to-hand understandingly and concernfully, and one's solicitous Being with Others, are now given a definite character in terms of their ownmost potentiality-for-Being-their-Selves."[43] Staying open to anxiety thus lets Dasein take up its projects again authentically, not in the lostness of the "they," and win for itself a kind of life not possible for inauthentic Dasein. Heidegger writes, "Along with the sober anxiety which brings us face to face with our individualized potentiality-for-Being, there goes an unshakable joy in this possibility."[44] With this background in place, I now turn to bringing out some related themes in the *Tractatus*.

2.4

The mere idea of the *Tractatus* as engaged in a kind of cultural critique should not come as too radical of a suggestion. Indeed, as I will go on to argue, this critique is essential for understanding the book's ethical point.[45] There have, after all, been various proposals for reading *Philosophical Investigations* this way, an understanding that to some extent Wittgenstein himself encourages by, for instance, his choosing for the book's motto a line taken from a play by an Austrian cultural critic and by his expression in the preface of his doubts about its reception in the "darkness of this time."[46] The idea gains in plausibility from the fact that Wittgenstein's sense of the philosophical significance of cultural matters and his sense of the state of Western culture were fairly constant from the time he wrote the *Tractatus* until the end of his life.[47] Of particular significance for him in this regard was what he saw as the distorting effect that causal-scientific modes of thought exerted on our understanding both in philosophy and in the broader intellectual and spiritual life of the West.[48] The two following passages are fairly representative of numerous remarks on this subject that one finds scattered throughout the *Nachlass*: "That is the fatal thing about the scientific way of thinking (which today possesses the whole world), that it wants to respond to every disquietude with an explanation"[49] and "The insidious thing about the causal point of view is that it leads us to say: 'Of course, it had to happen like that.' Whereas we ought to think: it may have happened like that—and also in many other ways."[50] Although Wittgenstein recorded these comments in 1933 and 1940 respectively, I will show how the attitude that they exhibit toward a particular way of thinking motivates the remarks concerning the law of causality and mechanics in the *Tractatus* and how this attitude is crucial for a proper understanding of what the book sets out to accomplish.[51]

In raising the possibility that the *Tractatus* engages in a form of cultural critique, I do not mean to suggest that it seeks to alter its readers' aesthetic taste (although it may have that consequence). Instead, I mean to point to the possibility that the book attempts to engage the self-understanding of a reader who is likely to come to it with a certain cast of mind that includes unexamined commitments from a particular cultural context. On my understanding of the overall method of the *Tractatus*, it stands to reason that this particular mode of engaging the reader would have to be part and parcel of the overall therapeutic aim of the book. Given both the continuity of Wittgenstein's cultural outlook and that outlook's continued significance for his work in philosophy, gaining a better understanding of what it is that obstructs the *Tractatus* from achieving its ethical and cultural aims should be an important step in assessing whether those aims might be more successfully integrated and pursued in a work like *Philosophical Investigations*.[52]

2.5

On May 6, 1930, Wittgenstein recorded this recollection in one of his manuscript books: "When I had the thought 16 years ago that the law of causality might in itself be without content, and that there is a way of looking at the world that it does not envisage, I had the feeling of the dawn of a new epoch."[53] The recollection apparently refers to the spring of 1914, a period when Wittgenstein was living in Skjolden, Norway. Unfortunately, there is no mention of this insight in the small amount of written material that has survived from this time. He mentions the law of causality in a letter to Russell written in January 1914, but the point Wittgenstein makes there seems to be a quite different one from what he is talking about in the remark above.[54] The notes dictated to G. E. Moore in April 1914 make no mention of the law of causality at all.[55] But in the notebooks from which most of the text of the *Tractatus* would eventually be taken, we do find the following remarks, recorded on March 29, 1915, that seem to express at least an important part of the insight about the law of causality to which Wittgenstein is referring above. They read,

> The law of causality is not a law, but the form of *a* law.
>
> "Law of Causality" is a class name. And just as in mechanics—let us say— there are minimum laws—e.g., that of least action—so in physics there is a law of causality, a law of the causality form.
>
> Just as men also had an inkling of the fact that there must be *a* "law of least action," before precisely knowing how it ran.
>
> (Here, as so often happens, the *a priori* turns out to be something purely logical.)[56]

Apart from some minor changes, these remarks would eventually come to be §6.32, §6.321, and §6.3211, respectively, of the *Tractatus*. In addition to what these passages say concerning the law of causality, the §6.3s also tell us that Newtonian mechanics belongs to the class of causal laws specified by the law of causality, which we just saw Wittgenstein describe as a class name.[57] Moreover, the relation between mechanics and the description of the world that it yields is compared to the description one would obtain by laying a square mesh over a surface and then reading off whether any given square seen through the mesh is black or white. The individual scientific propositions one would obtain by imposing a unified form of description such as Newtonian mechanics on the world are then supposed to be understood by analogy with the color propositions obtained in the manner just described. In any case, whichever "mesh" of laws we choose to apply to the world for the purpose of describing it, just as the mesh is "*purely* geometrical; all its properties can be given *a priori*," so, too, because they provide an a priori form that our descriptions of the world take, the laws of mechanics are "purely logical," that is, without content.[58]

In the recollection quoted above, Wittgenstein makes a connection between his insight about the law of causality and "a way of looking at the world that it does not envisage." At *Tractatus* §6.45, we find such a way described:

> To view the world *sub specie æterni* is to view it as a whole—a limited whole.
>
> Feeling the world as a limited whole—it is this that is mystical.[59]

We don't need to assume that there must be some kind of logicodeductive relation, either between individual remarks of the *Tractatus* or between its various groupings of remarks, in order to suppose that there is philosophical significance in the placement of these words at the end of the §6.4s' treatment of ethics and in the fact that these remarks are placed immediately after the treatment of causality and mechanics in the §6.3s. But any uncertainty about the fact or significance of this relation is removed by Wittgenstein himself in the "Lecture on Ethics." There, we saw him describe his own "experience *par excellence*" of what he means by "absolute or ethical value" as an experience of wonder at the existence of the world.[60] Somewhat further on, now nearing the end of the lecture, he elaborates on this experience in a way that connects directly with my discussion:

> Let me first consider, again, our first experience of wondering at the existence of the world and let me describe it in a slightly different way; we all know what in ordinary life would be called a miracle. It obviously is simply an event the like of which we have never yet seen. Now suppose such an event happened. Take the case that one of you suddenly grew a lion's head and began to roar. Certainly that would be as extraordinary a thing as I can imagine. Now whenever we should have recovered from our surprise, what I would suggest would be to fetch a doctor and have the case scientifically investigated and if it were not for hurting him I would have him vivisected. And where would the miracle have got to? For it is clear that when we look at it in this way everything miraculous has disappeared; unless what we mean by this term is merely that a fact has not yet been explained by science which again means that we have hitherto failed to group this fact with others in a scientific system. This shows that it is absurd to say "Science has proved that there are no miracles." *The truth is that the scientific way of looking at a fact is not the way to look at it as a miracle.* For imagine whatever fact you may, it is not in itself miraculous in the absolute sense of that term. For we see now that we have been using the word "miracle" in a relative and an absolute sense. And I will now describe the experience of wondering at the existence of the world by saying: it is the experience of seeing the world as a miracle.[61]

The language Wittgenstein uses here to express his wonder has clear resonances with the language we find at *Tractatus* §6.45, where, as we just saw, he writes of the eternal view and mystical feeling of the world as a "limited whole" (*ein begrenztes Ganzes*). To help bring out the importance of the relation between what Wittgenstein says at §6.45 and what he says in the passage from the lecture, it will be useful to emphasize a difference between the meaning of the German expression that he uses to describe the world at *Tractatus* §1.1 and §1.12, "*eine Gesamtheit*" ("totality"), and the expression he uses elsewhere, "*ein Ganzes*" ("whole"). This contrast perhaps comes out less clearly in English than it does in German, where the sense of the former term tends to be that of a collection or heap of individuals (or individual facts, as the case may be), while the latter expression tends to have the holistic sense of being an organic unity. To speak of the world in the terms proper to being a totality is to speak of it in terms of discrete, contingently related facts and entities, while to talk of feeling the world as a limited whole is to talk of a feeling where one imagines the world as an organic unity in which everything has its place, where everything is as it should be, must be, necessarily. Whereas with a totality it makes perfectly good sense to speak of discrete events and entities as standing in comprehensible causal relations to one another, to view the world as a limited whole is to imagine there being no genuinely discrete events or entities in the first place and so no causal explanations of their relations.[62] Imagined from such a perspective, *whatever* happens in the world (and not merely what is exotic or temporarily inexplicable) must be regarded as both happening of necessity *and* as being miraculous. This (to some perhaps perverse) combination of the concepts of the necessary and the miraculous has clear overtones of a religious perspective from which it is natural to speak of regarding whatever happens in the world as being brought about by the will of almighty God, an image that Wittgenstein invokes later in the lecture when he says "But this allegory also describes the experience [of wonder] which I have just referred to. For [this] is, I believe, exactly what people were referring to when they said that God had created the world."[63] However we interpret Wittgenstein's understanding of expressions of wonder, his claim in the lecture that "we cannot express what we want to express and that all we *say* about the absolute miraculous remains nonsense" makes evident that he thought of the place they might have in our life as clearly distinct from the role played by ordinary scientific assertions.[64]

2.6

My discussion so far makes it clear that the "ethical point" of the *Tractatus* is closely connected to its attempt to achieve clarity about the difference between what Wittgenstein describes in the ethics lecture as a way of regarding the world as a miracle and a way of understanding natural phenomena in causal-scientific terms. But, above, we also read Wittgenstein recall how his insight into the nature of the law of causality brought with it the feeling of the dawn of a new epoch, and in line with this I want to argue for the idea that there is an essential cultural dimension to this enterprise as well. I begin by looking at *Tractatus* §6.371–§6.372, which I think provide some strong, textual support for the idea that a particular sort of cultural critique has a significant role to play in the book.

> The whole modern conception of the world (*die ganze moderne Weltanschauung*) is founded on the illusion that the so-called laws of nature are the explanations of natural phenomena.
>
> Thus people today stop at the laws of nature, treating them as something inviolable, just as God and Fate were treated in past ages.
>
> And in fact both are right and both wrong: though the view of the ancients is clearer in so far as they have a clear and acknowledged terminus, while the modern system tries to make it look as if *everything* were explained.[65]

It may be tempting to interpret these passages as *denying* that the laws of nature really *are* the explanations of natural phenomena. But the remarks can also be taken as posing a challenge to the reader to try to make sense of the expression "explanation" as it occurs here.[66]

On the one hand, it is far from obvious what is wrong with regarding the laws of nature as explanations, because of course there are very harmless ordinary contexts in which they *can* function as explanations of natural phenomena. If someone were to ask me why a ball falls in the way it does, there is nothing wrong if I answer, "Because of the law of gravity." This answer won't necessarily mean the end of the discussion, but that it *could* (perhaps after a bit more filling out) shows that there are contexts where invoking a law of nature is accepted as providing an explanation. Naturally, it may be that my invoking a law of nature as an explanation is not accepted, even with some elaboration. It is conceivable that the person who asks me the question might respond by saying "No, that's not right. I don't believe your explanation!" Whether I find this response strange or irritating, and however I choose to go on from there (perhaps I offer different kinds of support for my explanation), there is no doubt that this person's denial of the truth of the law of gravity is not somehow self-contradictory. Furthermore, the fact that it is possible for her to reject the law of gravity as part of my explanation shows how it is functioning here as a full-blown proposition with a sense.[67] In a different context, however, the law of gravity might play a very different role. If I were teaching a high-school physics class and a student were to ask me to explain why a ball of a certain mass that is shot straight up into the air with a certain initial velocity takes a certain amount of time to return to the earth's surface, I may derive the answer from the law of gravitation (or a simplified version of it), and this answer might be all that is required of my explanation. There may be no need to *assert* the law of gravity before proceeding with my derivation, and one way of understanding this is to see that in this case the law of gravity is not so much functioning as a substantive part of my explanation as it has *already been accepted* as providing the *form* of the propositions that will constitute my explanation.

I take the upshot of the instability of "explanation" in §6.371–§6.372 to be to bring out how we moderns want to have it both ways. We want the laws of nature to function as true assertions with explanatory force, as the law of gravity does in the first context, *and* we want them to have the kind of logical necessity they have when they function as the law of gravity does in the second context.[68] Passages §6.371–§6.372 can thus be read as part of Wittgenstein's attempt to deconstruct what he sees as a characteristically modern illusion that we can have it both ways, an illusion belonging to the same family as superstitious belief in the causal nexus.[69] The "clarity" of the ancients, then, seems to have consisted in this: that while they perhaps believed God's power could explain the facts, it is really we moderns who try "to make it look as if *everything* were explained" by treating the laws of nature as though they could magically explain both the facts and "the logic of the facts."[70]

We find further evidence for thinking that a kind of cultural project is integral to the *Tractatus* in a long remark recorded on November 11, 1930, where Wittgenstein criticizes the nineteenth-century social theorist Ernst Renan.

> In Renan's "Peuple d'Israël" I read: "Birth, sickness, death, madness, catalepsy, sleep, dreams, all made an immense impression and, even nowadays, only a few have the gift of seeing clearly that these phenomena have causes within our constitution."
>
> On the contrary there is absolutely no reason to wonder at these things, because they are such everyday occurrences. If primitive men can't help but wonder at them, how much more so dogs and monkeys. Or is it being assumed that men, as it were, suddenly woke up and, noticing for the first time these things that had always been there, were understandably amazed?—Well, as a matter of fact we might assume something like this; though not that they become aware of these things for the first time but that they do suddenly start to wonder at them. But this again has nothing to do with their being primitive. Unless it is called primitive not to wonder at things, in which case the people of today are

THE ETHICAL PURPOSE OF THE *TRACTATUS* 57

really the primitive ones, and Renan himself too if he supposes that scientific explanation could remove (*heben*) wonderment.

As though lightning were more commonplace or less astounding today than 2,000 years ago.

Humans have to awaken to wonder—and so perhaps do peoples. Science is a way of sending him to sleep again.

In other words it's just false to say: Of course, these primitive peoples couldn't help wondering at everything. Though perhaps it is true that these peoples *did* wonder at all the things around them.—To suppose they couldn't help wondering at them is a primitive superstition. (It is like supposing that they *had* to be afraid of all the forces of nature, whereas we of course have no need to be afraid. On the other hand we may learn from experience that certain primitive tribes are very strongly inclined to fear natural phenomena.—But we cannot exclude the possibility that *highly* civilized peoples will become liable to this very same fear once again; neither their civilization nor scientific knowledge can protect them against this. All the same it's true enough that the *spirit* in which science is carried on nowadays is not compatible with fear of this kind.)[71]

I read Wittgenstein to be claiming here that it is nothing more than a modern prejudice to assume, as Renan does, that the wonderment with which the Israelites beheld the phenomena of birth, death, dreams, and so on was necessarily a common feature of their humanity and ours, some kind of primitive version of our scientific curiosity, so that we can simply take for granted that this wonderment is, as it were, smoothly continuous in its evolution with the goals of modern scientific explanation. Rather, their wonderment may have belonged to an altogether different way of inhabiting and seeing the world.[72]

I have quoted this long passage in full because I think it brings out two extremely important points. First, there is its clear implication that there is nothing in the content of modern science itself that is incompatible with wonder but that something about the cultural climate in which science takes place blocks a reawakening to wonder. Second, given the striking parallels between the wording of this passage and the wording of much of the ethics lecture, as well as the equally striking parallels between the "primitive peoples" and "people of today" spoken of here and the "ancients" and the "modern system" spoken of at *Tractatus* §6.371–§6.372, there are compelling reasons not only for thinking that clarity concerning the nature of causal-scientific explanation was essential to the ethical aim Wittgenstein claimed for the *Tractatus* in his letter to Ficker, an aim that it now appears reasonable to understand as intimately connected to reawakening us to the possibility of wonder, but also that the book was written with the awareness that this endeavor only makes sense if understood in a particular historical and cultural context.[73] Specifically, this means clearing away certain cultural prejudices that Wittgenstein thought were embedded in confusions about the nature of scientific explanation. Now we read at *Tractatus* §6.53:

> The correct method in philosophy would really be the following: to say nothing except what can be said, i.e. propositions of natural science—i.e. something that has nothing to do with philosophy— and then, whenever someone else wanted to say something metaphysical, to demonstrate to him that he had failed to give a meaning to certain signs in his propositions.[74]

While the claim here is that only the propositions of natural science say something, it is clear from what Wittgenstein says at the end of his "Lecture on Ethics" that he did not believe it followed from this that we need to confine ourselves to those expressions. On the contrary, it is only when we (moderns) become clear about what we want to do when we use sentences that say something that we will also have clarity about the very peculiar impulse to give expression to wonder. This is why in the lecture Wittgenstein also claims that he would reject any analysis that succeeded in making sense of an ethical utterance *on the very grounds of its significance*.[75] For, by his lights, to imagine such an analysis betrays a failure (and a failure that he thought passed for common sense in the modern West) to recognize the distinct natures of these two intentions. The book thus tries to lead its reader to understand that while the propositions of natural science may exhaust the propositions of meaningful language, and while it is the essence of meaningful language that making an ordinary assertion cannot give expression to wonder at the world, this understanding need not lead us to rationalize away the impulse to express wonder.

But what might help to prevent expressions of an intention to speak ethical nonsense from being confused with ordinary "anyone" sentences expressing ordinary intentions? How can these expressions be marked off from "all the claptrap about ethics—whether intuitive knowledge exists, whether values exist, whether the good is definable"?[76] On the one hand, the first part of a passage from Waismann's notes suggests that one could avoid confusion here simply by keeping quiet: "Is talking essential to religion? I can well imagine a religion in which there are no doctrinal propositions, in which there is thus no talking."[77] On the other hand, the second part of the passage, while reaffirming this possibility, also makes clear the importance of attention to context in those cases where we choose not to remain silent: "Obviously the essence of religion cannot have anything to do with the fact that there is talking, or rather: when people talk, then this itself is part of a religious act and not a theory. Thus it also does not matter at all if the words used are true or false or nonsense."[78] As Diamond has argued, there is no way of categorizing nonsense into various kinds; all that can give a particular nonsensical sentence its "ethical significance" is its particular external circumstances, including the intentions of the speaker and various ways in which she might signal that her utterance is not intended to be taken as a straight-out declaration of fact. Attention to the way an utterance is framed by other words, for example, may lessen our temptation to take it seamlessly out of context and pass it on as an ordinary assertion. Take "I am inclined to say 'I am safe, nothing can injure me whatever happens.'" Reported directly, "Wittgenstein said 'I am safe, nothing can injure me whatever happens'" is simply nonsense: it has the form "Wittgenstein said 'p,'" where "p" makes no sense. It is true, however, that the sentence "Wittgenstein said 'I am inclined to say, "The goodness of life does not depend on things going this way or that"'" is *not* nonsense. But the hope is that the "I am inclined to say" part of this sentence will flag the (at least somewhat alert) listener's attention in such a way that he'll be less tempted to take this utterance for a report where Wittgenstein asserts "I am safe, nothing can injure me whatever happens." That is to say, the listener will be warned off of passing this utterance on seamlessly as something Wittgenstein *said*, as something that he the listener agrees with or disagrees with; he won't ask whether it's really true, won't ask "Who does Wittgenstein think he is anyway? How could he possibly know *that*?" He might even respond to this "I am inclined to say" by asking, for instance, "Where was Wittgenstein when he said this, what was his mood like? What else was going on? What is this inclination?" Inquiring into the circumstances of the utterance in this way might bring him to treat it differently from an ordinary utterance, and of course treating it differently might just mean coming to think that Wittgenstein is sounding off again incomprehensibly. That would, at any rate, be a far more perceptive response than taking the utterance as obviously and unproblematically accessible to oneself and others, as just one more assertion on which everyone is free to offer his or her opinion.

2.7

I now want to articulate a point of deep philosophical resonance that I find between, on the one hand, an understanding of Dasein's fundamental structure, which Heidegger's phenomenology is supposed to impart to his reader, and, on the other hand, an insight into our relation to language, to which Wittgenstein aims to lead his reader by way of his employment of elucidatory nonsense. The resonance consists in this: Heidegger wants to show how anxiety makes authenticity possible for Dasein by revealing to it that the average, everyday understanding and self-interpretations in which it is immersed cannot in themselves satisfy its apparent need for a stable unique identity and a differentiated world of its own.[79] Anxiety lets Dasein see instead that the ordinary background practices of the "they" are actually anonymous, "anyone" ways of understanding itself and its world. Analogously, Wittgenstein wants his reader to see that once the *Tractatus*'s ladder of elucidatory nonsense has been thrown away, all that remain are the ordinary, anonymous, "anyone" sentences of natural science. But this clarification of language is at the same time a clarification of the impulse to run up against its limits and so opens for a clarified, authentic experience of wonder with the realization that these "anyone" sentences cannot give this impulse any support or justification.[80] Quite the contrary. As we saw, Wittgenstein makes clear in the "Lecture on Ethics" that these sentences, as publicly intelligible descriptions of states of affairs in the world and when regarded from the perspective of wonder, must be rejected on the grounds of their own significance. These are important and difficult connections that I will try to make clearer.

Heidegger interprets anxiety as an existential ground mood that makes manifest to Dasein that the world as it is articulated and interpreted in terms of the average understanding of the "they" is incapable of providing it with anything like a set of meaningful distinctions having essential reference to it as a unique person. By bringing this to light, anxiety individuates Dasein, lifting it out of its everyday lostness in the "they" and making it possible for it to take up its projects in resolute authenticity, where so far this has been distinguished from inauthenticity not so much by the facts that constitute its world but by the character of authentic Dasein's relation to those facts. Now a central thrust of resolute interpretations of the *Tractatus* involves reading the book as abandoning the search for any special moral and aesthetic facts, either in the "empirical" world or in any "noumenal" domain. On these readings, Wittgenstein thought that the search for such special facts showed a kind of confusion about language that was symptomatic of a deeper confusion about what was essential to what he wanted to call "ethics." I think that part of reading the *Tractatus* this way involves the idea that it is essential to the book's "ethical point" that the reader come to see that the meaning of any (ordinary) sentence does not depend on who utters it or on her attitude or intention in doing so. Nor does the meaning of a sentence depend on there being any facts that one might be tempted to say have a "special relation" to some people but not others. If this is true, then the facts encountered by someone who is clear about the nature of the proposition, the person who sees that any sentence that makes sense is unsuitable for expressing "absolute value" or "anything that is higher," are the same facts as those encountered by someone who is not. This is because there simply *are no* special facts to which the *Tractatus* tries to draw our attention.

Thus, the ethical aim of the *Tractatus* that Wittgenstein hoped his employment of elucidatory nonsense would achieve should be understood as a change in the reader's self-understanding through a change in her relationship to language. Viewing this change in self-understanding through the prism of Heidegger's description of authenticity leads me to suggest further that we understand this change in self-understanding as specifically involving the isolation and clarification of the nature of the reader's impulse to "run up against the limits of language," her desire for something more than the ordinary, "anyone" sentences of natural science could give her. I think it is also true to say that this clarity would necessarily have an individualizing effect on such a person. For if the "anyone" sentences of ordinary language are seen in this way, then naturally discovering that one had an impulse to somehow go beyond them cannot help but in some sense set one apart from them.[81] With this in mind, it is worth returning again to what Wittgenstein described in the "Lecture on Ethics" as his own "experience par excellence" of an urge to run up against the limits of ordinary language. He said, "I believe the best way of describing it is to say that when I have it I wonder at the existence of the world."[82] A bit later, he describes this experience again: "And I will now describe the experience of wondering at the existence of the world by saying: it is the experience of seeing the world as a miracle." He then immediately adds a further description: "Now I am tempted to say that the right expression in language for the miracle of the existence of the world, though it is not any proposition *in* language, is the existence of language itself."[83] There are two points that I would like to make against the backdrop of this quotation. The first concerns a connection between authenticity and the ethical aim of the *Tractatus* that I have already mentioned, where I suggested that a person's clarity about the impulse to go beyond the "anyone" sentences of ordinary language would have an individualizing effect on that person. I suggest here that we regard the words Wittgenstein uses to describe his experience as an example of the very sort of individual psychological distance to the sentences of ordinary language that I was talking about. We see this distance manifest in his temptation to say that the right expression for the miracle of the world is no proposition in language but the existence of language, the totality of language itself. It is important that I emphasize what I am *not* attributing to Wittgenstein here. I am not attributing to him the claim that such experiences involve a synoptic view of the totality of language that would enable him to arrive at and somehow communicate sublime truths about logic, language, and the world. That would be to smuggle in the very view of Wittgenstein that I take Diamond and others to have rightly rejected. That is why I have couched my discussion in psychological and not epistemological terms, and it is probably also why immediately after the remark quoted above, Wittgenstein adds, "for all I have said by shifting the expression of the miraculous from an expression by means of language to the expression by the existence of language, all I have said is again that we cannot express what we want to express and that all we say about the absolute miraculous remains nonsense."[84] The second point concerns what I will call a "reciprocal clarity" that I believe Wittgenstein thinks lies at the root of such experiences. The reciprocity concerns both clarity about the nature of ordinary sentences and clarity about one's impulse to transcend them. Clarity about either entails clarity about the other.[85] In *Being and Time*, Heidegger is trying to uncover anxiety as something that calls us to clarity about our relationship to the anyone practices of the "they." Living in this clarity is what he calls authenticity. My claim here is that Wittgenstein's attempt in the *Tractatus* to clarify language and the impulse to go beyond its limits and Heidegger's attempt in *Being and Time* to uncover anxiety as a source of understanding into Dasein's fundamental structure ought to be seen as serving what are in central respects the same philosophical end.[86]

2.8

At this point, I want to address what might be a nagging concern even for those who are generally sympathetic to my attempt to draw certain lines of philosophical contact between the early Wittgenstein and the early Heidegger. As I have been trying to articulate it so far, this contact concerns the nature of Wittgenstein's attempt to clarify what we heard him call in the "Lecture on Ethics" a "tendency of the human mind" to express wonder (a tendency whose clarification I have argued we see as essential to the ethical aim of the *Tractatus*) and Heidegger's attempt to reveal anxiety as a phenomenon that clarifies our relationship to the anyone practices of the "they-self." Now, quite apart from the oddity that some may find in my bringing into contact two books with such different forms and methods as the *Tractatus* and *Being and Time*, the nagging concern has to do with the fact that the point of contact I try to bring out between wonder and anxiety would seem to point to very different phenomena. For, it might be thought, given the positive feelings we commonly associate with "wonder" and the negative feelings we commonly associate with "anxiety," these two expressions would seem to point to two quite distinct and in some respects even opposing phenomena. Indeed, the second description that Wittgenstein gives in the "Lecture on

Ethics" of what he calls an "experience of absolute or ethical value" is what he calls the "experience of feeling absolutely safe." Heidegger, on the other hand, tells us repeatedly that Dasein does not heed the clarifying call of anxiety but instead flees back into the inauthentic, tranquilized ways of "the they." What I want to do now in addressing this concern is to show that there is in fact no genuine problem here with the way in which I have brought Wittgenstein and Heidegger into contact. In fact, addressing this concern actually strengthens the plausibility of their philosophical contact as I have laid it out so far.[87]

First, we should recall this description that Heidegger gives of a life led in resolute authenticity: "Along with the sober anxiety which brings us face to face with our individualized potentiality-for-Being, there goes an unshakable joy in this possibility." Heidegger provides a slightly reformulated but substantially similar description in his inaugural lecture "What Is Metaphysics?" given in Freiburg in July 1929. There he says: "the anxiety of those who are daring cannot be opposed to joy or even to the comfortable enjoyment of tranquilized bustle. It stands—outside all such opposition—in secret alliance with the cheerfulness and gentleness of creative longing."[88] If anxiety goes with unshakable joy and is in secret alliance with the cheerfulness and gentleness of creative longing, it is evidently far from an unambiguously "negative" phenomenon.[89] More telling is that in *Being and Time* Heidegger actually implies a close link between anxiety and wonder. The link goes through the contrast Heidegger points out between wonder and curiosity. He writes, "In not-staying, curiosity makes sure of the constant possibility of *distraction*. Curiosity has nothing to do with the contemplation that wonders at being, *thaumazein*, it has no interest in wondering to the point of not understanding. Rather, it makes sure of knowing, but just in order to have known."[90] Curiosity, moreover, is described by Heidegger as a mode of inauthenticity:

> Curiosity . . . does not make present what is objectively present in order to *understand* it, staying with it, but it seeks to see *only* in order to see and have seen. . . . Greed for the new indeed penetrates to something not yet seen, but in such a way that making present attempts to withdraw from awaiting. Curiosity is altogether inauthentically futural, in such a way that it does not await a *possibility* but in its greed only desires possibility as something real.[91]

If wonder is incompatible with inauthenticity, which is characterized by Dasein's fleeing anxiety through distraction, it must have some connection to authenticity, which requires that Dasein remain open to anxiety. Indeed, Heidegger makes this connection explicit in "What Is Metaphysics?" where he claims that *anxiety makes wonder possible* by revealing the nothing (*Das Nichts*) in the ground of

Dasein and that it is only on the ground of wonder that we pose "the basic question of metaphysics which the nothing itself impels: 'Why are there beings at all, and why not rather nothing?' "[92] In Heidegger's case at least, the concern that the expressions "wonder" and "anxiety" must denote incompatible phenomena, because of various associations we might have with them, is groundless; quite the opposite turns out to be the case.

If we turn now to Wittgenstein, we see that not everything he says in the "Lecture on Ethics" about these matters invites us to have purely "positive" associations with the "tendency of the human mind" to speak ethical nonsense. In addition to characterizing what he calls his experience of ethical value as "wonder at the existence of the world" and as the experience of "feeling absolutely safe," he also describes this experience in a third way, as feeling guilty, which he glosses as the feeling that "God disapproves of our conduct."[93] Furthermore, the passage I have quoted above where he criticizes Renan suggests that Wittgenstein sees a close connection between the feeling of wonder and a particular sort of deepseated fear of natural phenomena.[94] Significantly, the passage makes it clear that he does not think that what he describes as an inclination to fear natural phenomena often found among "primitive peoples" has any necessary connection to scientific ignorance, since he also says that peoples from scientific cultures might also, once again, become liable to this same kind of fear (and wonder) if their science were carried on in a different spirit.

Elaborating the connection Wittgenstein sees between a certain kind of fear and wonder will strengthen the connections I am trying to make between an aspect of Heideggerian authenticity and Tractarian ethics. In section 2.2, I described how the ethical aim of the *Tractatus* required a kind of indirect uncovering or disentangling of an intention in the reader to speak ethical nonsense. This requirement pertained to the peculiar nature of the intention itself. Now, it may not seem as though getting clear about such an impulse would be something we would naturally want to flee or avoid, especially if one describes the experience behind the inclination as "wonder at the existence of the world." But, from the perspective on human life from which the *Tractatus* is written, it looks as though we (especially we moderns) often do, in fact, resist staying open to wonder and the impulse to express it without interposing a philosophical justification. On December 30, 1929, a few weeks after the "Lecture on Ethics," Waismann recorded Wittgenstein as remarking, "The inclination, the running up against something, *indicates something*: St. Augustine knew that already when he said: 'What, you swine, you want not to talk nonsense! Go ahead and talk nonsense, it does not matter!' "[95] Wittgenstein seems to echo this thought many years later when he writes "Don't for heaven's sake, be afraid of talking nonsense! But you must pay attention to your nonsense."[96] The connection I now want to elaborate concerns Wittgenstein's understanding and appropriation (both in the *Tractatus* and in the "Lecture on Ethics") of descriptions of a certain class of experiences, descriptions that are found in some of those works that had the most profound influence on his philosophical imagination.

Perhaps most relevant among these works for my discussion here is William James's *Varieties of Religious Experience*, a book that Wittgenstein read with enthusiasm as a young man and that he continued to recommend to friends and students later in life. In a 1912 letter to Russell, Wittgenstein writes:

> Whenever I have time I now read James' "Varieties of Religious Experience." This book does me *a lot* of good. I don't mean to say that I will be a saint soon, but I am not sure that it does not improve me a little in a way in which I would like to improve *very much*: namely I think that it helps me to get rid of the *Sorge* (in the sense in which Goethe used the word in the 2nd part of *Faust*.)[97]

James's book is famously full of detailed descriptions of conversion experiences. I quote at length here James's introduction to one of these descriptions, followed by the description of the experience itself:

> Let us turn now to the feelings which immediately fill the hour of the conversion experience. The first one to be noted is just this sense of higher control. It is not always, but it is very often present. . . . The need of such a higher controlling agency is well expressed in the short reference which the eminent French Protestant Adolphe Monod makes to the crisis of his own conversion. It was at Naples in his early manhood, in the summer of 1827.
>
> My sadness, he says, was without limit, and having got entire possession of me, it filled my life from the most indifferent external acts to the most secret thoughts, and corrupted at their source my feelings, my judgement, and my happiness. It was then that I saw that to expect to put a stop to this disorder by my reason and my will, which were themselves diseased, would be to act like a blind man who should pretend to correct one of his eyes by the aid of the other equally blind one. I had then no resource save in some influence from without. I remembered the promise of the Holy Ghost; and what the positive declarations of the Gospel had never succeeded in bringing home to me, I learned at last from necessity, and believed, for the first time in my life, in this promise, in the only sense in which it answered the needs of my soul, in that, namely, of a real external supernatural action, capable of giving me thoughts, and taking them away from me, and exerted on me by a God as truly master of my heart as

he is of the rest of nature. Renouncing then all merit, all strength, abandoning all my personal resources, and acknowledging no other title to his mercy than my own utter misery, I went home and threw myself on my knees, and prayed as I never yet prayed in my life. From this day onwards a new interior life began for me: not that my melancholy had disappeared, but it had lost its sting. Hope had entered into my heart, and once entered on the path, the God of Jesus Christ, to whom I then had learned to give myself up, little by little did the rest.[98]

Compare this description to a passage from Schopenhauer already cited in chapter 1, the kind of passage with which Wittgenstein will certainly have been familiar:

The storm howls, the sea roars, the lightning flashes from black clouds, and thunder-claps drown the noise of storm and sea. Then in the unmoved beholder of this scene the twofold nature of his consciousness reaches the highest distinctness. Simultaneously, he feels himself as individual, as the feeble phenomenon of will, which the slightest touch of these forces can annihilate, helpless against powerful nature, dependent, abandoned to chance, a vanishing nothing in face of stupendous forces; and he also feels himself as the eternal, serene subject of knowing, who as the condition of every object is the supporter of the whole world, the fearful struggle of nature being only his mental picture or representation; he himself is free from, and foreign to, all willing and needs, in the quiet comprehension of the Ideas. This is the full impression of the sublime.

Before or during the time when he wrote the *Tractatus*, Wittgenstein would have encountered descriptions of mystical or conversion experiences in many writers besides James and Schopenhauer.[99] Like James, what interested Wittgenstein was not the "cognitive significance" of these experiences or their descriptions. What struck both men as significant above all was the persistent recurrence of such descriptions in the annals of human thought.[100]

Here I want to draw attention to a particularly striking feature that these descriptions share with each other as well as with Heidegger's description of anxiety. This concerns a way in which such descriptions seem to indicate a subverting of the integrity or everyday givenness of our normal sense of ourselves as subjects. By this I mean to point to a way of imagining these descriptions as expressing a kind of psychological distance from, and in some sense an impulse to reject, the "anyone" sentences ordinarily used to describe one's subjective experience.[101] But if for the moment we understand this rejection in relation to what Wittgenstein says in the "Lecture on Ethics," where he claims that he would refuse any analysis of utterances like "I wonder at the existence of the world" or "I feel absolutely safe" on the grounds of their very significance, then we should be wary of taking these descriptions of mystical experiences or conversion experiences or anxiety as intending to provide ordinary first-person reports: such ordinary reports can be written in a *Begriffsschrift* and can be studied by the science of psychology.[102] And if this is so, then the "tendency of the human mind" to speak of a "higher controlling agency," of a "real external supernatural action, capable of giving me thoughts, and taking them away from me," of a "supporter of the whole world," or of a mood where neither the world nor other people can offer anything more, a mood in which the world has the character of completely lacking significance, all these can be understood as the human mind's own tendency to undermine its ordinary sense of itself as a self-sufficient sphere of the inner. This is not to imagine the isolation of a Cartesian ego, a mind cut off from the outer world but otherwise intelligible to itself with all of its contents intact. This is to imagine the stripping away of the very content that gives the self its presumed identity in the first place, a threat to its very structure.

It may help to make my discussion clearer to connect it to a stretch of remarks that I have yet to address. The remarks I mean are *Tractatus* §5.6–§5.641, where the themes taken up include the a priori, the limits of logic and language, solipsism, and the subject as limit of the world. Rather than reading these remarks as, for example, either flatfooted statements of, or nonsensical gestures at, an ineffable Schopenhauerian or Weiningerian metaphysics, I suggest instead that their function in the text be understood in terms of what we saw Diamond claim for "ethical nonsense." In other words, we should regard many of the sentencelike structures one finds among these remarks such as "The world and life are one" (§5.621) and "I am my world (The microcosm)" (§5.63) as sentence-signs that Wittgenstein felt would not necessarily lose their attractiveness to us even after we recognized them as nonsensical.[103] If this is right, then that these sentences are nonsense may not exclude the possibility that I will understandingly allow them to exercise a pull on my imagination and so use them to express my feeling. But at the same time, my authentic use of these and similar expressions requires that I am clear about what I am doing in using them, that in a certain sense I acknowledge my relatedness to them, that I recognize *that I am using them*, and so that I am not, so to speak, seamlessly one with them when I use them. This is what I take to be the upshot of a remark by Wittgenstein recorded by Waismann about one year after the "Lecture on Ethics": "At the end of my lecture on ethics I spoke in the first person. I think that this is something very essential. Here there is nothing to be stated any more; all I can do is to step forth as an individual and speak in the first person. For *me* a theory is without value. A theory gives me nothing."[104] Thus the self can bring itself into philosophy through the authentic use of sentences like

"The world is my world." The "nonpsychological way" in which philosophy can talk about the self,[105] the way in which a speaker can show himself as the "metaphysical subject and limit of the world," is to show his understanding and responsibility for making utterances like these, utterances that say nothing (§5.641). If these are things that I find myself drawn to say even if I see they are nonsense, then in acknowledging the draw and accepting responsibility for speaking thus, I acknowledge an impulse in myself to thwart my everyday sense of myself. But at the same time, I acknowledge a degree of responsibility for my meaningful uses of language, because the world is partly mine to uncover as intelligible in the ways in which I make signs into symbols.[106] Real wonder wrenches me from the comfort of the "modern worldview" and reveals the disturbing insight that I am not wholly satisfied with that comfort. It distances me from the everyday sentences of the "they" and reveals that whether I intend to speak nonsense or sense, I am the one who is speaking.[107] But in either case, the acknowledgment would outstrip any ordinary justification, which is to say any justification at all, that I can give of myself.[108] And so the *Tractatus* must be written in the expectation that achieving its ethical aim of awakening the reader to wonder will meet with resistance and evasion.[109] This is because acknowledging wonder goes against the grain of what Wittgenstein saw as the modern worldview's self-understanding that anything one wants to say should be justified with reference to the so-called laws of nature; it crashes with an especially powerful modern aversion to acknowledging the importance of any impulse to speak that does not seek refuge in the comfort of the "anyone" propositions of natural science.[110]

2.9

I have been discussing how we might better understand the ethical aim of the *Tractatus* by examining it in relation to part of Heidegger's account of authenticity. Bringing the *Tractatus* into contact with Heidegger's thought in this way also points to a way of resolving a possible difficulty for resolute readings. In the closing remarks of the preface to the *Tractatus*, Wittgenstein writes, "The *truth* of the thoughts that are here set forth seems to me unassailable and definitive. I therefore believe myself to have found, on all essential points, the final solution of the problems."[111] This passage looks like it poses a serious difficulty for resolute readings, because Wittgenstein speaks of the "truth of the thoughts that are here set forth," whereas for instance on Diamond's and Conant's reading, §6.54 tells us to throw away the main body of the book as plain nonsense. Interpretations of the book where Wittgenstein is read as trying to get his reader to grasp certain ineffable truths of logic and metaphysics might seem to be better suited to account for what Wittgenstein says about truth in the preface. While we are far from compelled to adopt such a reading, it might seem as though no other alternative is available. In fact, it is possible (and preferable) to make sense of what Wittgenstein says about truth in the preface to the *Tractatus* from within an overall resolute approach to the book. And I will suggest that Heidegger's account of truth in *Being and Time* may be of help in laying out just such an alternative reading.

There is, of course, a sound internal textual basis for resisting the temptation to understand the "truth" that Wittgenstein speaks of in the preface as concerning particular truths that the book tries to convey to its reader. For at the very beginning of the preface, Wittgenstein says that the *Tractatus* is *not* a textbook (*ist kein Lehrbuch*). It is not a book that purports to teach us any doctrines. Instead, I suggest that we not hear Wittgenstein as speaking from within the web of concepts and argumentative terms that make up the traditional philosophical lexicon when he speaks of truth in the quoted passage from the preface. A good description of what I mean here by "traditional" is given by Heidegger himself, who writes in *Being and Time* of theses that "characterize the way in which the essence of truth has been traditionally defined: (1) that the 'locus' of truth is assertion (judgment); (2) that the essence of truth lies in the 'agreement' of the judgment with its object."[112] In a later passage, Heidegger describes what he thinks is the more fundamental sense of truth that comes to light as a result of his ontological investigation of Dasein.

> Resoluteness is a distinctive mode of Dasein's disclosedness. In an earlier passage, however, we have Interpreted disclosedness existentially as the *primordial truth*. Such truth is primarily not a quality of "judgment" nor of any definite way of behaving, but something essentially constitutive for Being-in-the-world as such. Truth must be conceived as a fundamental *existentiale*. In our ontological clarification of the proposition that "Dasein is in the truth" we have called attention to the primordial disclosedness of this entity as the *truth of existence*; and for the delimitation of its character we have referred to the analysis of Dasein's authenticity.[113]

This is a very dense passage, and I do not pretend to give anything like a full explication of it here. But I take Heidegger to be saying in effect that through an examination of Dasein's authenticity, the "primordial" truth is revealed, that is, that a world becomes intelligible through Dasein's Understanding-of-Being, the largely implicit background understanding that already orients its various sense-making activities, including the philosophical inquiry into the grounds of truth. Earlier in *Being and Time*, Heidegger remarks that the expression "Being-in-the-world" stands for a unitary phenomenon.[114] By this he means that the world that gets disclosed through Dasein cannot be understood in conceptual isolation from Dasein *and* that Dasein cannot be understood in conceptual isolation from the world: this is what makes it even possible for Dasein to make particular true (and false) judgments about the world. This points to an important way in which Heidegger means to undermine traditional debates between metaphysical realism and metaphysical idealism.

Wittgenstein, too, wants his reader to regard such debates as resting on a false dichotomy, and the person who attains the authentic relation to language to which the book seeks to bring her understands that the world is only intelligible or "disclosed" through ordinary sentences and that these same ordinary sentences make no sense in conceptual isolation from the world.[115] So Wittgenstein is not referring to a traditional conception of truth in the preface, something like correspondence between a proposition (or even a quasi-proposition that cannot really be uttered) and its object; rather, the *Tractatus* is meant to reveal the emptiness of attempts to arrive at anything like a philosophical theory of truth. We should instead let our sense of what he means by truth in the preface be mediated by what he says in the penultimate proposition of the book (§6.54), where he writes that the reader who has understood him will "see the world aright."[116] But then it seems that the question of truth here must come back to the question of the ethical point of a book consisting of a ladder of elucidatory nonsense. I have already claimed that central to the ethical aim of the *Tractatus* is an attempt to isolate and clarify the reader's impulse to express her sense of wonder through a change in her relationship to language. I take myself to be saying the same thing in claiming here that central to the ethical aim of the book is an attempt by Wittgenstein to guide his reader to being "in the truth" in the sense discussed here.[117] Against the inclination to respond with skepticism to the idea that a book so taken up with language might have an ethical point (I have heard it said, with a tone of bored contempt, "So it's just about language; you are saying that all this about the ethical point of the book is just about language"), I am saying that what Wittgenstein took to be the definitive unassailable truth of the thoughts set forth in the *Tractatus*'s effort to overcome the kind of confusion that underlies debates between realists and idealists is of a piece with an effort to bring out a sense of wonder and reverence at the fit between word and world (call this the "miracle of science") and so of a piece with an attempt to foster an appreciation for how deeply language is interwoven with what is special about human life. Earlier, I quoted a passage from the "Lecture on Ethics" where Wittgenstein says, "Now I am tempted to say that the right expression in language for the miracle of the existence of the world, though it is not any proposition *in* language, is the existence of language itself."[118] The ethical aim of the *Tractatus*, the exploding of the philosopher's illusion when he throws away the ladder of the book's elucidatory nonsense, would be achieved if its reader appropriated the significance of three words: we can talk.[119]

I have been arguing at length for the idea that it can help our understanding of the *Tractatus* if we think about some of its most central and most puzzling features in relation to certain themes found in *Being and Time*. For all the undeniable differences between them, especially when it came to philosophical methodology, the early thought of both Wittgenstein and Heidegger is shaped by a certain common vision of philosophy wherein one of its primary tasks is to bring to light a pervasive problem of clarity. The problem concerns the need for an acknowledgment of those general forms of intelligibility that open us up to a common world, on the one hand, and our individual and collective need to wrest something away from these general forms, on the other, even if (perhaps especially, in the early Wittgenstein's case) doing intellectual justice to these general forms seems to allow for not much more than an insistence on the significance of the need itself. The felt intensity of this problem even made it natural or inevitable for both men to adapt the descriptions of central parts of their projects to the language of religious crisis and conversion. In the early Wittgenstein, this needs to be seen in the way his understanding of logic and (what he calls) ethics interpenetrate each other. In particular, I have argued that Wittgenstein's way of working out this problem, so to speak, mimics the logic of Heidegger's attempt to uncover anxiety as a phenomenon that individualizes Dasein from the anyone ways of the "they." Wittgenstein's understanding of logic and the nature of philosophical confusion, taken together with his religious-psychological reading of the descriptions of mystical and conversion experiences to be found in Schopenhauer, Tolstoy, James, Augustine, and others, come together in the *Tractatus* as an attempt to undermine the idea that the anyone sentences of natural science can provide any foundation or justification to the "tendency in the human mind" to express wonder. After having brought these two thinkers together philosophically in this way, however, I now want to examine briefly the possible meaning of a different kind of connection.

2.10

In his notes for December 30, 1929, Friedrich Waismann records the following:

> To be sure, I can imagine what Heidegger means by being and anxiety. Man feels the urge (*Trieb*) to run up against the limits of language. Think for example

of the wonder (*das Erstaunen*) that anything at all exists. This wonder cannot be expressed in the form of a question, and there is also no answer whatsoever. Anything we might say is a priori bound to be mere nonsense. Nevertheless we do run up against the limits of language. Kierkegaard too saw that there is this running up against something and he referred to it in a fairly similar way (as running up against paradox). This running up against the limits of language is *ethics*.[120]

Given the low esteem in which Heidegger was held by members of the Vienna Circle, the statement seems remarkable in itself for the apparent openness that Wittgenstein shows toward Heidegger's words. More remarkable still, however, is that he goes on to connect what "Heidegger means" to his own understanding of ethics. Naturally, the salient question here becomes *how* Wittgenstein might have understood that connection with ethics and, in particular, how he might have imagined what Heidegger meant by being and anxiety. Now, the mere existence of an affinity between Wittgenstein's thinking about ethics at this time (a period during which I would still broadly classify his thinking about ethics as Tractarian) and Heidegger's thought from the late 1920s, an affinity that I've tried to articulate as mediated by the themes of wonder and anxiety, does not depend on what Wittgenstein actually imagined in this case. Still, that this brief remark can be read as touching on the very points I have been elaborating suggests that the affinity may not have been altogether unrecognized by Wittgenstein himself.

In looking at this issue, we first have to try to decide *which text* from Heidegger Wittgenstein is referring to in the passage.[121] It's not of course unnatural to assume that the text would have been *Being and Time*. McGuinness, for example, seems to give a tacit endorsement to this idea by providing a footnote reference to *Being and Time* that includes an excerpt from the book's discussion of anxiety that could have been the basis for Wittgenstein's remark.[122] Wittgenstein's reference to Kierkegaard appears to lend further plausibility to the idea that he was familiar with *Being and Time*, since in a footnote Heidegger cites Kierkegaard as an important source for the concept of anxiety: "The man who has gone farthest in analyzing the phenomenon of anxiety—and again in the theological context of a 'psychological' exposition of the problem of original sin—is Søren Kierkegaard."[123] Nevertheless, and apart from my simply finding it hard to believe that Wittgenstein read extensively in *Being and Time* (my incredulity being no argument, I realize), I think a much likelier source of any familiarity that Wittgenstein had with Heidegger's thought would have come through his contact with members of the Vienna Circle itself, where he could have heard discussions of or read comments on Heidegger's work.

One obvious source to consider in this vein is Rudolf Carnap's paper "The Elimination of Metaphysics Through Logical Analysis of Language," a paper in which Carnap singles out certain sentences from Heidegger's lecture "What Is Metaphysics?" for treatment as prime examples of metaphysical nonsense.[124] The following is the largest block of text from the lecture to appear in Carnap's paper:

> What should be examined are beings only, and besides that—nothing; beings alone, and further—nothing; solely beings, and beyond that—nothing. What about this nothing?—— Is the nothing given only because the "not," i.e., negation, is given? Or is it the other way around? Are negation and the "not" given only because the nothing is given?—— We assert that the nothing is more original than the "not" and negation.—— Where shall we seek the nothing? Where will we find the nothing?—— [W]e do know the nothing . . . —— Anxiety reveals the nothing.—— [T]hat in the face of which and for which we were anxious was "really"—nothing. Indeed: the nothing itself—as such—was there.—— How is it with the nothing?—— The nothing itself nihilates.[125]

We know from his so-called *Diktat für Schlick* that Wittgenstein read at least some of "The Elimination of Metaphysics," since this dictation contains comments on Carnap's method in the paper, in particular his treatment of "The nothing itself nihilates."[126] Given, however, that the paper was published in the second issue of *Erkenntnis* for 1931, there is a question as to whether Wittgenstein *could* have read Carnap's paper already by the time of his conversation with Schlick and Waismann on December 30, 1929. But it is quite possible that the paper had been written well before then. In an addendum to the end of his paper, Carnap refers to a radio lecture given by Oskar Kraus on May 1, 1930, where Heidegger's *Nichts-Philosophie* is denounced. If Carnap heard the radio broadcast already then, and if this is a late addition to the proofs, then it seems quite possible that the paper had been written well before May 1930 and so possible that Wittgenstein had already seen a manuscript as early as December 1929. On the other hand, in the same note Carnap also refers to the printed version of Kraus's lecture, which dates from 1931, and so it may well be that this is where he first learned of Kraus's talk.

At any rate, I think that what Wittgenstein says in conversation with Schlick and Waismann comes so strikingly close to words and themes from Heidegger's lecture—the one speaks of an urge to wonder that anything at all exists, the other of our being impelled to wonder why there are beings at all and why not rather nothing[127]—that it's hard to believe he had read or heard nothing more of the lecture than those impoverished blocks of text printed in Carnap's paper.[128] Given his contact with Carnap and other members of the Vienna Circle, it seems plausible that Wittgenstein could have had access either to the text of "What Is Metaphysics?" or at least to a reliable set of lecture notes. And this prospect raises some final questions that I think must remain open but that nevertheless are worth raising in their own right. First, assuming that Wittgenstein is indeed commenting on Heidegger's lecture in his conversation with Schlick and Waismann and that he had indeed read or heard substantial portions of the lecture before the conversation, are his comments best understood as taking Heidegger to be *making a point about wonder*, for example, making a point about wonder as it could be connected to anxiety (as Wittgenstein might have imagined that connection from the lecture alone and without having read *Being and Time* in any detail)? His grouping together of Heidegger with Kierkegaard and Augustine, where it seems clear enough that the latter two are being referred to here as *making points* about the speaking of ethical nonsense and not merely *as speakers* of ethical nonsense, makes it natural to understand Wittgenstein as taking Heidegger's words in this way as well.[129] Wittgenstein's own practice, both in the preface and conclusion of the *Tractatus*, in conversation, and in the "Lecture on Ethics" make it unreasonable to exclude this possibility. Or, should Wittgenstein's comments be understood more on the order of a sympathetic response to an actual example of ethical nonsense that he imagines Heidegger coming out with in the lecture? Perhaps in the context of this conversation Wittgenstein (or Waismann) simply was not concerned with distinguishing between these two different ways of imagining what Heidegger meant. But, of course, this is not the only place where one finds a striking resonance between Heidegger's lecture and Wittgenstein's words. Wittgenstein is, in fact, echoing themes here that he had already touched on in the lecture he gave to the Heretics Society in Cambridge only one month before this conversation with Schlick and Waismann took place in Vienna. And this means that we have to take seriously the possibility that Wittgenstein actually appropriated some of Heidegger's rhetoric for the "Lecture on Ethics."

I have argued at length for the idea that it deepens our understanding of the ethical point of the *Tractatus* if we bring to light the striking conceptual and structural similarities its philosophical perspective on human life and language shares with a significant part of the early Heidegger's account of authenticity. If I am correct there, then what is surely strangest about Wittgenstein's encounter with Heidegger in 1929 is that he responds to Heidegger's words from a philosophical perspective that in crucial respects is structurally similar to much of Heidegger's own description of authenticity in *Being and Time* without his having any detailed knowledge of *Being and Time* itself.[130]

2.11

Much of this chapter has been taken up with exploring how the ethical point of the *Tractatus* can be usefully understood in relation to Heidegger's account of authenticity from *Being and Time*. That required some care, because the description of authenticity that was relevant for my discussion in section 2.3 and then in sections 2.7–2.10 was entirely concerned with Dasein's relation to the banal, everyday interpretations of the Understanding-of-Being that Dasein takes over from the "they." This explains my repeated use of phrases such as "part of," "aspect of," and "feature of" when referring to Heidegger's account of authenticity. But Heidegger's discussion includes more than a mere description of Dasein's formal constancy when it is "in the truth" about the anonymous practices of the "they." He also indicates an important additional possibility for resolute Dasein. Heidegger writes, "The resoluteness in which Dasein comes back to itself, discloses current factical possibilities of authentic existing, and discloses them *in terms of the heritage* which that resoluteness, as thrown, takes over."[131] In what follows, I want to explore how this points to an important *difference* between the *Tractatus* and *Being and Time*.

Hubert Dreyfus understands what Heidegger says here in terms of what Dreyfus calls "marginal practices." As Dreyfus explains them, marginal practices may have been part of the everydayness of Dasein's culture in the past, but they have been displaced by the anonymous practices of the "they" that have become dominant in that culture since. For example, Dreyfus suggests that resolute Dasein can be open to possibilities such as engaging in a version of Christian caring modeled on early Christian practice. He comments, "Such alternative possibilities, precisely because they do not make good, average, everyday sense but rather seem old-fashioned, trivial, or meaningless, would neither be undermined by anxiety nor levelled by the public. They would therefore attract authentic individuals."[132] Heidegger thus thinks that resolute Dasein's life is characterized not only by its authentic relation to the dominant everyday practices of the "they" but also in terms of the nonbanal marginal practices from its heritage to which Dasein is now open and that make possible for it a kind of *differentiating content*. In the same vein, David Cooper writes that when Dasein avails itself of its heritage, it "is not left without guidance as to the possibilities on which to resolve, for the 'authentically historical' person who 'takes over' his heritage will draw these possibilities precisely *from* that heritage. For what the heritage offers are 'the possibilities of the Dasein that has-been-there.'"[133] In sum, authentic Dasein will be able to attain both a certain constancy in its life, in terms of its resolute openness toward the "they," and will also gain the possibility of differentiating itself, since by taking up possibilities from its heritage it acquires specific content.

Heidegger does not claim that Dasein must be aware that it is taking up marginal practices in order to do so. It seems that authentic Dasein may just be naturally sensitive to the neglected alternatives that its historical culture has to offer; it can pick up on them and is, as it were, attuned to them as possibilities. With this possibility in mind he states, "there is hidden a *handing down* to [Dasein] of the possibilities that have come down to it, but not necessarily *as* having thus come down."[134] Heidegger maintains, however, that such appropriation from the heritage can also be explicit and conscious: "The existentiell ability-to-be-upon which it projects itself can be gleaned *explicitly* from the way in which Dasein has been traditionally understood. The resoluteness which comes back to itself and hands itself down, then becomes the *repetition* of a possibility of existence that has come down to us."[135] Finally, Dasein may repeat a possibility of existence on the model of someone from the culture who has gone before and who is a particularly noteworthy embodiment of the marginal practice that authentic Dasein wishes to take up. Heidegger calls this "the possibility that Dasein may choose its hero."[136]

In sections 2.7 through 2.10, I argued that it is useful to think about the ethical point of the *Tractatus* in relation to the part of Heidegger's description of authenticity in *Being and Time* that concerns the form of Dasein's engagement with the world. My discussion in this section, on the other hand, brings to light an important difference between Heideggerian authenticity and the ethical point of the *Tractatus*. James Conant has attempted to articulate what the ethical aim of a book consisting simply of nonsense might be by bringing Wittgenstein's method in the *Tractatus* into contact with some of Kierkegaard's pseudonymous writings, in particular with the *Concluding Unscientific Postscript*.[137] Michael Kremer, also writing from a resolute perspective, has suggested a way of understanding the ethical aim of the *Tractatus* in terms of St. Paul's and St. Augustine's writings on justification. What I want to show next is how this difference between Heidegger and Wittgenstein that I have been sketching can be understood as a secular version of a difference between the *Tractatus* and the writings of St. Paul, St. Augustine, and Kierkegaard that, in my view, makes problematic some of the connections between their thought and Wittgenstein's that Conant and Kremer have tried to establish.[138]

2.12

Michael Kremer has argued that an appreciation of the discussions of justification and faith in the writings of St. Paul and St. Augustine can bring us closer to understanding the meaning of Wittgenstein's claim that the *Tractatus* has an ethical aim. Kremer cites St. Paul's argument in the letter to the Romans that obedience to the Mosaic Law cannot provide justification before God but only condemnation. Justification is not through works under the law but through faith.[139] Kremer aptly points out that Paul is not advocating in the letter that we merely subjugate ourselves before God in faith rather than doing so through obedience to the law, for that might suggest that what we need for faith is a particularly strong act of willpower.

> This superficial reading, suggesting that faith is something we can do, a work we can perform in accordance with a new commandment—"accept Jesus Christ as your personal savior, and you will be redeemed"—misses the point entirely. The repentance Paul calls for is not something we can do by obeying some or other command; it is an inner conversion that has to be brought about in us by God's grace. The law condemns us not just because we are unable to obey it, but because our need to justify ourselves through obedience to it is itself a sign that we are sinful. . . . Justification before God, a setting things right in which harmony and peace are restored, is accomplished not through "faith" in the sense of "voluntary assent" but rather through God's grace, which transforms our lives by bringing faith into them. [140]

Kremer finds similar themes in Augustine, for example in his criticisms of the attempts by pagan philosophers to formulate ethical theories and systems that could serve as justifications for action. As Kremer points out, for Augustine such philosophers are guilty of the sin of pride: "They represent the false hope that human beings can on their own power discover how the universe must be ruled and put this into effect."[141] Kremer connects these considerations with the *Tractatus* by making what I think is the very interesting suggestion that one of Wittgenstein's fundamental goals in that book was to expose as illusory all attempts for ultimate justification in logic, metaphysics, and, of course, ethics.

In fact, Kremer sees the very notion of *ineffable truth*, which interpreters including Hacker claim Wittgenstein was trying to express in the *Tractatus*, as one that in fact Wittgenstein wants to expose as empty an attempt at justification. In the search for ultimate foundations for a theory, whether in metaphysics or ethics does not matter, we often find that whatever propositions we arrive at to serve as our foundation have further conditions that they rely on for their truth or intelligibility. In this case, we are faced with the threat of an infinite regress:

> To stop the looming regress we seem to need something sufficiently like a proposition to serve as a justification, an answer to a question, yet sufficiently different

from a proposition to need no further justification, to raise no further questions in turn. The doctrine that there are "things" that can be shown—and so can be "meant," "grasped," and communicated, and can also be "quite correct"—but which cannot be said—and so cannot be put into question—seems to fit the bill. The thought is that by appeal to such ineffable "things" we can solve our problems of justification once and for all.[142]

Kremer argues, persuasively I think, that, far from being what Wittgenstein is try-ing to get his reader to grasp, the hope that ineffable truths that might ground a philosophical theory is instead a sort of last-ditch effort in the search for justifi-cation, in particular for ethical justification: "The *Tractatus* aims to relieve us of this need for ultimate justification by revealing that all such justificatory talk is in the end meaningless nonsense."[143] The connection with Paul and Augustine that Kremer draws from this revelation is that in it we see that we are finite creatures who are unable to provide ourselves with the foundations of knowledge and right action. Kremer concludes, "we will find what we sought only by abandoning the search for justification altogether, and with it the prideful hope that we can give meaning and value to our lives. In this way we will be awakened to the value and meaning that was there all along."[144]

This last remark by Kremer indicates an important connection between his interpretation of the ethical point of the *Tractatus* and that advocated by James Conant. Besides being one of the original proponents and subsequently most important advocates of resolute readings of the *Tractatus*, Conant has argued for a reading of the book according to which we see it as sharing important goals with much of Kierkegaard's work, in particular with the works published under the pseudonym Johannes Climacus.[145] Conant focuses most of his attention on the *Concluding Unscientific Postscript*, and, in addition to reading the *Postscript* and the *Tractatus* as having similar goals, he also claims that the two books have quite similar methods as well: "Wittgenstein's *Tractatus Logico-Philosophicus* can be seen to have both the same aim (one of providing a mirror in which the reader can recognize his own confusions) and the same method (one of having the reader climb up a ladder which in the end he is to throw away) as the [*Concluding Unscientific Postscript*]."[146] Each of these books, Conant says, employs an "indirect method," and he explains both books having this method as a function of their substantially similar aims.

In a well-known passage from the *Postscript*, Kierkegaard's pseudonym Clima-cus describes how two different modes of relating to an object, subjectivity and objectivity, are correlated with distinct spheres of existence:

In the ethico-religious sphere the accent is not on the "what," but on the "how." But this is not to be understood as referring to demeanor, expression or the like; rather it refers to the relationship sustained by the existing individual, in his own existence, to the content of his utterance. Objectively the interest is focused merely on the thought-content, subjectively on the inwardness. At its maximum this inward "how" is the passion of the infinite, and the passion of the infinite is the truth. But the passion of the infinite is precisely subjectivity, and thus subjectivity becomes truth.[147]

This passage and others like it in his work have prompted both defenders and attackers to view Kierkegaard as an extreme irrationalist, in particular when it concerns the claim that he appears to be making here that in an infinitely passionate relationship to the paradox of the god-man, subjectivity becomes truth. Conant wishes to resist this interpretation. He asks,

> Is it not the widespread consensus of the scholarly community that Kierkegaard is the apologist par excellence for the possibility of some category of higher nonsense? Everything will hinge here on what, in the end, one takes Climacus' endless dialectical manipulations of the category of "the absolute paradox" to be in service of.[148]

Conant's description of the philosophers for whom he believes Kierkegaard is writing, as well as of those interpreters of the latter's work who read him as pleading for a category of "higher nonsense," should sound like Kremer's description of those who hope that the ineffable truths they claim to find in the *Tractatus* can serve as justifications for ethics and logic:

> Since no ordinary form of belief seems to suffice to effect the transformation of oneself into a Christian, one assumes it must require some extraordinary form of belief: a form of belief that requires something extraordinary of the intellect—that one strive to believe against the grain of one's understanding, that one attempt to hold fast to the absurd.[149]

Exploding the illusion that there is any kind of "extraordinary belief" to hold on to is what, on Conant's view, Climacus's manipulations of the category of the absolute paradox is supposed to effect. Indeed, this is one of the most important methodological features he sees the *Tractatus* and *Postscript* as sharing: "These works exhibit certain nonsensical (yet apparently innocent) propositions and build on them until the point at which their full nonsensicality will (hopefully) become transparently visible."[150]

This similarity between Conant's interpretation of the *Tractatus*, which relies on his understanding of Kierkegaard, and Kremer's reading of the book that we discussed above, becomes even clearer when we look at what Conant has to say about the purpose of Kierkegaard's employment of nonsense. Echoing Wittgenstein in the *Tractatus*, Conant writes, "[Kierkegaard's] aim is to show [the philosopher] that where he takes there to be a problem there isn't one. The solution to what he takes to be the problem of life is to be found in the vanishing of the problem."[151] He adds, "the problem is not one of teaching the reader something he does not know but rather one of showing him that, with respect to the activity of becoming a Christian, there is nothing further he needs to *know*."[152] Conant believes that interpreters of Kierkegaard who ascribe to him a doctrine of "higher nonsense" fail to see that he is not arguing that becoming a Christian involves attaining any special knowledge that could serve as a foundation for faith. Instead, he is trying to get the philosopher to see that the belief that such special knowledge is vital for becoming a Christian is the result of taking a distorted view of the ordinary or everyday, a view in which their real significance as the starting place for becoming a Christian is concealed. And so typically, the philosopher interested in understanding Christianity only engages the ordinary in his life in terms of a philosophical theory and a confused view of genuine religiousness: "His eagerness to be able to represent his knowledge to himself as an intellectual achievement forces the philosopher to come to know 'the simple' (i.e. what we otherwise all already know) by means of a reflective detour."[153] According to Conant, Kierkegaard thinks that normally the philosopher who seeks to understand Christianity as an abstruse doctrine flees the everyday, what we otherwise all already know, because he can't see how *this* could provide him with the kind of justification he thinks he needs in order to become a Christian. But on Conant's understanding of Kierkegaard, the real problem is not one of epistemic justification at all: "The philosopher interprets the task of becoming a Christian to require the cultivation and application of his understanding, postponing the claim that the Christian teaching makes upon his life, deferring the insight that what is required is the engagement of his will—the achievement of resolution."[154] On Conant's view, then, the philosopher flees "the simple" in his life, because he cannot envisage how it, with all of its contingencies and uncertainties, could serve as the kind of foundation he imagines he needs for making the commitments essential to becoming a Christian. Conant's point, however, is that the foundation the philosopher seeks is simply irrelevant to this task and that what is needed is, as he says, the achievement of resolution. Conant connects this account of Kierkegaard with the *Tractatus* in an effort to get us to see that for Wittgenstein, once our attraction to philosophical theories has been exposed as an attempt to evade the requirements that life makes on us to act, then perhaps we will be in a position to commit ourselves to acting with resolution. His understanding of the ethical aim of the *Tractatus* is thus one with his understanding of Kierkegaard's goals in works such as the *Postscript*: "It is, I believe, against the background of such a vision of us in flight from our lives (and hence ourselves) that one should first attempt to understand what Wittgenstein and Kierkegaard each might have meant by the claim that what he had written was a work of ethics."[155] While there are differences (perhaps of interpretation, at least of emphasis) between Conant's and Kremer's accounts, they share two key ideas concerning the ethical point of the *Tractatus* with which I am in fundamental agreement. The first idea is that Wittgenstein's employment of elucidatory nonsense is intended to achieve a change in the reader's self-understanding through a change in her relationship to language. The second idea is that this change in self-understanding that Wittgenstein wanted to effect in his reader is not primarily of a cognitive nature, not, that is, the sort of change we tend to associate with accepting the truth of a theory. It would be characterized primarily by how we do or do not act, not by what we do or do not know. Nevertheless, I argue in the next section that Kremer and Conant each overlook a fundamental disanalogy between the aims of St. Paul's, St. Augustine's, and Kierkegaard's thought on the one hand and the aims of the *Tractatus* on the other.

2.13

While it should be obvious that Conant's work is central to my own understanding of the *Tractatus*, I have serious differences with his reading of Kierkegaard and deep reservations about the way in which he brings this reading into contact with the early Wittgenstein. Put succinctly, the main difference between Conant's understanding of Kierkegaard and my own concerns what realization Kierkegaard wants to bring about in his reader. For Conant, this is the discovery by the philosopher that he has avoided making the commitments that a Christian life requires of him and has instead taken the "reflective detour" of speculative philosophy. While a critique of speculative philosophy is certainly part of the story, I take Kierkegaard to be trying to bring his reader to see that the true predicament of the self is despair, that the self lacks the resources to *make* any genuinely meaningful commitment, and so that what the self needs is some object outside of itself that would *confer* meaning and value on its life and at the same time *solicit* a commitment from it.[156]

Because on my understanding of Kierkegaard he is close to Paul and Augustine on this matter, it may help to return to my discussion in the last section, where we can see a possibly parallel issue crop up with Kremer's claim that Wittgenstein shares something like Paul and Augustine's view on justification. There we saw Kremer make clear that according to these two saints, all attempts at self-justification are futile and even sinful. We saw further that justification can only be had through faith and that faith is not a relation that can be entered into by an act of will but must itself be bestowed upon one through God's grace. This lets me bring out an important ambiguity in the claim by Kremer that I took to suggest an affinity with Conant. Recall that after arguing that Wittgenstein's ethical aim in the *Tractatus* is to show the futility of the search for justification in metaphysics and ethics, Kremer writes, "we will find what we sought only by abandoning the search for justification altogether, and with it the prideful hope that we can give meaning and value to our lives. In this way we will be awakened to the value and meaning that was there all along." There is a way of taking this claim, which is entirely unproblematic, as a statement of Paul's and Augustine's points of view, so long as we distinguish "the value and meaning that was there all along" from Conant's understanding of "what we otherwise all already know." To see this, we should first realize that it follows from what Kremer says about Paul's and Augustine's criticisms of others, that they do not abandon the idea that the self *needs* justification but only the idea that it can provide itself with justification through its own efforts. "The value and meaning that was there all along," then, could be taken to indicate something like the value and meaning that God gives to each human as one of His special creations, and so what in each case He has already given to one before one commits the sin of pride by trying to provide oneself with justification. It could even be plausibly taken to mean something like "the *possibility* that was there all along of getting value and meaning through faith."

On the other possible interpretation that I have in mind, Kremer might intend the phrase "the value and meaning that was there all along" to mean the "ordinary" or "everyday" in Conant's sense, one in which these terms carry with them no definite religious associations and, as Conant points out, imply that what is required of the individual is courage and resolution. If that is the case, however, then Kremer would come close to contradicting what he says about grace, for there it was clear that the faith required for transforming a person, which I am assuming for Paul and Augustine, at least, is intimately connected to any meaning and value I might discover having been in my life all along, is something that must come from God.[157] No act of will can bring a person into a relation of faith with God. Assuming that he would not want to lose hold of his correct insights concerning Paul and Augustine by ascribing to them the same sort of view that

Conant ascribes to Kierkegaard, we now can see a serious disanalogy that Kremer has overlooked between the two saints and Wittgenstein. As I said earlier, neither Paul nor Augustine does away with the *need* for justification. They believe, rather, that there is no possibility (and thus also no need) for *self*-justification, and both point to the real source of justification, namely God. But there is nothing analogous in the *Tractatus* to this last part of Paul's and Augustine's thinking. Put simply, in the *Tractatus* there is no concrete "god-term" outside of the self that is pointed to in the book that might *provide* the self with the very justification, that, on Kremer's reading, it purports to show is beyond our reach.

This touches on what I take to be a related problem with Kremer's description of the kind of transformation he believes the *Tractatus* to be capable of bringing about. Kremer sees the book not only as leading the reader to an abandonment of the search for justification in ethics and metaphysics but also as potentially fostering specific virtues in the reader, especially Christian humility. In this vein he writes,

> It would be a mistake to conclude that in showing us how to abandon the search for self-justification, and so the search for ethical principles by which to rule our lives, Wittgenstein means to free us to "do as we please" and so give license to unbridled self-gratification, or to a kind of ethical anarchy. For St. Paul, faith frees us from the law not by freeing us to sin, but rather freeing us to do what the law commands. For St. Augustine, humility transforms our basic attitude towards our condition as creatures, and so makes it possible for us to act out of true concern for others. Similarly, Wittgenstein aims at a conversion which will free us not only from the need for justification but from the conflicted and impossible desires which this need both engenders and signifies. As our motivations and desires are transformed, so will our lives and actions. There are many things that those who have learned the lesson of the *Tractatus* will not, in fact, do, simply because they lack any desire to do them.[158]

He adds a bit further on, "I take the *Tractatus* to be aimed at inculcating such virtues as humility, and the love of one's neighbor, which I, with Augustine, would see as a virtual corollary of humility."[159] In effect, this claim faces the same objection that I have made above concerning the important differences on justification between Wittgenstein, on the one hand, and Paul and Augustine, on the other. Once the requirement and possibility for self-justification have been shown to be incoherent, it is unclear to me what would prevent someone from wanting to emulate a figure such as Napoleon instead of a figure like Jesus. The implications of what Kremer says about dropping the requirement for self-justification, for example, seem to me very consistent with much of what can be found in Nietzsche, and there we do not find much worth put on specifically *Christian* forms of humility.

Kremer does not merely claim that there are actions from which the person who understands the author of the *Tractatus* will refrain. He goes even further, in seeming to suggest that through understanding the intention of the author of the *Tractatus* in writing a book of nonsense, the reader can see him as an example of someone who embodies both humility and other virtues: "In recognizing [Wittgenstein's propositions] to be nonsense, we understand Wittgenstein, and come to see how to live"[160] and "Wittgenstein aims to provide us with such an example in writing the *Tractatus*—an example that we can follow in coming to a new way of life, if we understand him."[161] But these ideas are deeply problematic, particularly in light of what Kremer says himself: "True humility, like St. Paul's faith, is not something that one brings about, but rather a gift of God's grace that recognizes itself as such; the truly humble person is the one whose gratitude to God encompasses and includes her own humility."[162]

Because wonder and humility are close in certain respects, it may seem strange for me to be criticizing Kremer on this point, having put so much weight on the role that the former concept plays in the overall aim of the *Tractatus*. I don't want to deny that the *Tractatus* may (try to) set a kind of spiritual or intellectual example. But I believe that Wittgenstein himself would stress that much more is needed to show us how to live, including how to live according to specifically Christian virtues, than his book. With no God, no savior, nor even any prophets or saints in his text who might *humble* us or give us specific concrete examples of how to embody humility and other virtues, it is difficult for me to see how the mere recognition that the search for ultimate justification in philosophy is an illusion can bring about the kind of transformation Kremer claims for the book.[163]

We see, then, that what should be regarded as a fundamental religious dimension in the writing of these other figures makes too close a comparison with the work of the early Wittgenstein problematic, because this integral part of their thought finds no correspondence in the conception of the *Tractatus*. My way of putting this difference just now was to say that in the *Tractatus* there is no concrete "god-term," no God or savior outside of the self that is pointed to who might provide the self with justification or confer meaning and value on its life. To see the difference from Heidegger that I discussed in section 2.11 as a secular version of this difference from Paul, Augustine, and Kierkegaard, we need to move up a level of abstraction. One might say that the difference between Paul, Augustine, Kierkegaard, and Heidegger, on the one hand, and the early Wittgenstein, on the other, is that the reader of the *Tractatus* who understands Wittgenstein, one who is left at the end of the book with only ordinary sentences, is not directed to any

definite concrete *thing* outside of himself, whether that be a savior, marginal practice, or hero, that entering into a relation with could give unique value and meaning to his life.[164] This also indicates that if Wittgenstein intended the *Tractatus*
to bring about the same kind of transformation in his reader as Paul, Augustine,
Kierkegaard, and Heidegger hoped to bring about in theirs, then quite apart from
the success or failure of their attempts, there seem to be good grounds not only for
thinking Wittgenstein's book to be unsuitable for this task but also for seeing it as
misguided in its conception.[165] I will argue in the next section, however, that we
do not need to view the ethical purpose of the book that way.

2.14

If one of Wittgenstein's goals in writing the *Tractatus* had been to show his reader
how to live, then given that I have claimed that the reader who is able to "throw
away the ladder" at the end of the book will see that he is only left with ordinary
"anyone" sentences, one would be justified in concluding that the *Tractatus* fails in
one of its essential tasks so badly as to impugn Wittgenstein's right to claim that
it had an ethical aim. However, there is a very good reason for not thinking this,
which we can begin to see by returning to the preface.

Consider, first, the initial sentence of the second paragraph of the preface:
"The book deals with the problems of philosophy, and shows, I believe, that the
reason why these problems are posed is that the logic of our language is misunderstood." Wittgenstein tells us here that his book deals with the *problems of philosophy*. This in itself does not entail that the book is not also concerned with what
could be called "the problems of life," but Wittgenstein does not at any rate say
anything to this effect. In fact, I believe that what he goes on to say about the
connection between the problems of philosophy and "the logic of our language"
makes it even more plausible that his book is aimed primarily at a narrow swath of
philosophers rather than to thoughtful members of a broader public who might
pick up a work of philosophy that did explicitly address itself to the meaning and
problems of life.

Next, I want to turn to the last paragraph of the preface, where we read the
following: "The *truth* of the thoughts that are here set forth seems to me unassailable and definitive. I therefore believe myself to have found, on all essential points,
the final solution of the problems. And if I am not mistaken in this belief, then
the . . . thing in which the value of the work consists is that it shows how little is
achieved when these problems are solved." I have already proposed in section 2.9 a
way in which we might understand the "truth" that Wittgenstein speaks of in this

passage. That concerns the character of the relationship to language to which the book tries to lead its reader. Wittgenstein goes on to say that based on this "unassailable" truth, he has found the "final solution" to the problems of philosophy. Notice, however, that in the final sentence of the preface Wittgenstein writes *how little* is achieved when the problems of philosophy are solved. This doesn't sound like the sort of thing an author would say if one of his main purposes in writing a book were to show a reader how to live a meaningful life. Thus, Kremer's suggestion to the contrary is *precisely* the kind of thing that I am arguing the *Tractatus* understands itself as unsuited to accomplish. More to the point, if Wittgenstein thought that entering into the "unassailable," "definitive" "truth" that solves the problems of philosophy would lead one to see how to live or to discover the meaning (or lack of meaning) in one's life, it seems extremely odd to me to describe such a momentous occasion by declaring *how little* is thereby achieved.

So the *Tractatus* does not fail in its attempt to lead its reader to a realization about the meaning and value in his life, or in trying to show him how to live, since these were never part of its "ethical aim" in the first place. I think that Wittgenstein's own "ethical" ambitions for the book were, while very ambitious in one sense, more modest than what Kremer or Conant have argued. Wittgenstein felt that traditional philosophy rested on illusions, perhaps even on illusions that the philosopher entered into as an evasion of life, what we heard Conant call earlier a "reflective detour." If, after reading the *Tractatus*, one was left with the insight that there are only ordinary sentences, then this would of course mean that, as Diamond has put it, the idea that there can be philosophy in the traditional sense would be shown up as an illusion. That would certainly constitute a "final solution" to these problems (or perhaps more appropriately, a "final dissolution"). While I do not believe that Wittgenstein thought that reorienting his philosophical reader's relation to language in this way would automatically lead him in any particular life direction, such as becoming a Christian, I do believe that he hoped that imparting this insight into the nature of language would remove at least one important obstacle that blocks this sort of transformation from taking place in the life of the philosopher, that obstacle being the illusion that a work consisting of philosophical sentences can show him how to live. And this *preparatory* act is certainly integral to what Wittgenstein saw fit to call the "ethical aim" of his book. Recall, furthermore, that earlier I used the word "individualized" to characterize the situation of the reader of the *Tractatus* who understands that none of the ordinary sentences with which he is left after he has thrown away the book's nonsensical ladder can do justice to his tendency to come out with ethical nonsense, since this very tendency would tend to create a kind of psychological distance between himself and those very sentences. Whether Wittgenstein assumed that as a result of being individualized in this way the philosopher would take his search for meaning in a quite different direction, and what Wittgenstein thought that direction would or should be, is not something about which he believed his book had anything to say. Given his understanding of the nature of philosophical activity at the time he completed the *Tractatus*, the removal of the obstacle of speculative philosophy is all, I believe, he thought philosophy itself could achieve.

3

A RESOLUTE FAILURE

3.1

The previous chapter involved an extensive cross-examination of certain themes in the thought of the early Wittgenstein and the early Heidegger so as to get a better understanding of what the ethical purpose of the *Tractatus* is and is not. In and of itself, there is nothing novel in comparing the thought of these two philosophers, at least since the last twenty years or so. Such comparisons tend to line up these two thinkers in different temporal directions than I have done in the previous chapter, however. It is more usual, that is, to compare the thought of the Heidegger of *Being and Time* with the Wittgenstein of *Philosophical Investigations*.[1] For example, Richard Rorty finds this way of comparing the two apt, based on his understanding of the development of Wittgenstein's thought as running from an early Schopenhauerian mysticism in the *Tractatus* to what he finds to be the naturalistic pragmatism of the *Investigations*. On the other side, Rorty finds the development of Heidegger's thought as running in something like the opposite direction, moving from a fruitful pragmatism in *Being and Time* to an opaque reification of language in his later thought.[2] There is, of course, nothing wrong in comparing the work of the early Heidegger and the later Wittgenstein; clearly the significance of practices in each makes such a comparison natural and attractive. But from the perspective of a resolute approach to the *Tractatus*, there must be something fundamentally wrong with one of the vectors making up Rorty's comparison, based as it is on a standard reading of the book as a work that tries to gesture at ineffable truths.[3]

Nevertheless, these considerations alone do not dispose of an issue that I indicated at various points in chapter 2. My discussion of the ethical aim of the

Tractatus was necessarily shaped (and constrained) by what I take to be Wittgenstein's own philosophical commitments concerning language at the time of writing that book. Specifically, this meant that if my discussion purported to be true to his self-understanding, it would have to take into account the predicament of an author who wishes to convey an intention where it is not possible to convey that intention in meaningful language. In chapter 1, I discussed Diamond's suggestion that the *Tractatus*'s employment of elucidatory nonsense requires a particular engagement of the reader's imagination.[4] But Wittgenstein's reliance on a certain kind of imaginative activity points to a clear difference with Heidegger's method in *Being and Time*. Whereas Wittgenstein attempts to clarify the nature of language and at the same time uncover our impulse to run up against its limits through his use of elucidatory nonsense, Heidegger's philosophical practice is informed by the idea that the results of his existential phenomenology, the uncovering of Dasein's *existentiale*, its fundamental structure (and the first stage of his project of fundamental ontology) can be given in, if not exactly ordinary, at any rate perfectly respectable sentences. And this may seem to point to a serious enough disanalogy in the conceptions behind the two books to vitiate my idea that it is useful to consider the ethical aim of the *Tractatus* in terms of Heidegger's account of authenticity in *Being and Time*. It will further our understanding of the *Tractatus* to see how in a crucial respect this evidently real methodological distinction does not make an important enough philosophical difference.

As we have seen, the ethical aim of the *Tractatus* is intimately connected to Wittgenstein's understanding and practice of philosophy as an activity whose goal is clarity rather than the establishment or the refutation of philosophical theories. Indeed, the idea that Wittgenstein had as little desire to advance any sort of philosophical doctrine in the *Tractatus* as he did in his more mature philosophy is a point that resolute readers are particularly keen to emphasize as an important part of the continuity of his thought. In what follows, I want to show how an underlying metaphysics of language, akin in spirit to the early Heidegger's quasi-foundationalist view of the structure of intelligibility, runs through the fabric of the *Tractatus* and ultimately vitiates the ethical point that Wittgenstein claimed for the book. Given, moreover, the important *differences* between the *Tractatus* and Wittgenstein's later work, gaining a better understanding of what it is that obstructs the *Tractatus* from achieving its ethical aim will be an important step in appreciating whatever "ethical point" a work like *Philosophical Investigations* may have.

3.2

The success of the *Tractatus* in achieving its ethical aim is dependent on at least two related general ideas, ideas that I elaborated in chapter 2 in terms of authenticity and wonder. The first idea is that Wittgenstein's employment of elucidatory nonsense is intended to achieve a change in the reader's self-understanding through a change in her relationship to language. The second idea is that this change in self-understanding is not primarily of a cognitive nature, not, that is, the sort of change we tend to associate with accepting the truth of a theory. I assume here that these two ideas, or ideas very close to them, will be part of any attempt to articulate the ethical point of the *Tractatus* on a resolute reading. In the remainder of this chapter, I will argue why I think that the *Tractatus* is ultimately unsuccessful in making its ethical point or in achieving its ethical aim. I hope to carry out this criticism in some of the same terms that Wittgenstein himself used when he came to mistrust his earlier work. I should make clear that in speaking of Wittgenstein's later criticisms of his earlier work, I do not mean to suggest that his later writing marks a clean break with his earlier philosophy. In particular, many of the early remarks in *Philosophical Investigations* can be interpreted as aiming at a straightforward refutation of philosophical theories that Wittgenstein held in the *Tractatus*.[5] Though certainly tempting, I believe such an interpretation can be misleading. On the other hand, while there is a high degree of continuity in Wittgenstein's philosophy, it remains true that there are very significant differences as well and, indeed, ones that are relevant for understanding why the *Tractatus* fails in its attempt to effect the change in its reader's relationship to language that I have claimed is necessary for its achieving its ethical aim. Wittgenstein is critical of his earlier philosophy, at times in ways that are fairly unambiguous, and it is one of these criticisms in particular that I wish to stress here.

The main shortcoming of the *Tractatus* that I wish to examine in this context, a shortcoming that makes it especially easy to misconstrue the book's non-metaphysical aspirations and strategy, concerns an important limitation of its method. In an earlier paper, Conant claimed that Wittgenstein came to believe that the book's employment of a ladder of elucidatory nonsense made it ineffective because such a strategy will almost inevitably lead the reader to believe that philosophical theses are being put forward.

> When Wittgenstein himself criticizes the *Tractatus*' mode of philosophical presentation it is not simply . . . on the grounds that its doctrine is flawed, but on the grounds that its *method* is flawed: it is inherently dogmatic—the work cultivates the impression that things are being dogmatically asserted. This way of putting

the criticism is meant to suggest, I take it, that the procedure employed is not well suited to the task of remaining neutral in a dialectical conflict.... The *Tractatus* does, of course attempt to address this problem. It attempts to insist about its own sentences that they are not meaningful propositions but only elucidations. But Wittgenstein's later criticism of his work seems to be that this declaration will almost always come too late.[6]

Conant contrasts the earlier method with that of the *Investigations* by emphasizing Wittgenstein's practice in this later work of keeping in closer contact with his reader through the frequent exchanges with his interlocutor. He notes in this regard, "Wittgenstein's later method is to round on his interlocutor at every point, to press at every juncture the question whether the words he is attracted to in his philosophizing can be entered as a claim."[7] This procedure spares the reader the mental contortion of having had the impression all along of following a long and complex chain of arguments intended to establish certain truths, only to have the author try to remove this impression all at once in the space of a few remarks.

Conant was certainly correct to point out this problematic aspect of Wittgenstein's method in the *Tractatus*. But as I believe he would agree, to leave matters there is to go too easy on Wittgenstein. It seems to imply that the most important defect in the *Tractatus* is that in composing it Wittgenstein did not take a psychological limitation of his readers into account. It's almost as if to say that the book could have accomplished its tasks if only most of us had longer attention spans—as though we were the kind of people who were only capable of understanding short jokes, since with lengthier ones the long wait for the punch line made us think we were hearing a narrative instead. At any rate, the *Tractatus* is more deeply flawed than that, and Wittgenstein made more than a tactical error in writing it as he did. One way of putting my point is to say that the *Tractatus* fails in its ethical aim because it remains too intellectualist in nature. If, as Wittgenstein writes in the second paragraph of the preface, "The book deals with the problems of philosophy, and shows, I believe, that the reason why these problems are posed is that the logic of our language is misunderstood,"[8] then it will also be true that the shape that philosophical elucidation takes in the book should conform to the shape of that misunderstanding and so, too, to the shape of the phenomenon that has been misunderstood. The book can succeed only if its attempt to clarify and right our relationship to language can, to paraphrase the *Investigations*, get its reader to *look* at the phenomenon of language in use and not *think* about how it must be.[9] But given Wittgenstein's own distorted view of language at this time, this is precisely what it is unable to do.

Let us look at two remarks that any interpretation of the *Tractatus* must account for. There is first this passage from the preface:

> The *truth* of the thoughts that are here communicated seems to me unassailable and definitive. I therefore believe myself to have found, on all essential points, the final solution of the problems.[10]

Next, there is the second-to-last remark of the book, §6.54, where we read:

> My propositions serve as elucidations in the following way: anyone who understands me eventually recognizes them as nonsensical, when he has used them— as steps—to climb up beyond them. (He must, so to speak, throw away the ladder after he has climbed up it.)
>
> He must overcome these propositions, and then he will see the world aright.

On a resolute reading of the *Tractatus*, we understand the author when we see at the end of the book that we have been taken in by his nonsense and that we have imaginatively taken his propositions for philosophical theses about the nature of logic and the structure of the world as a whole.[11] On recognizing that we have been so taken in, we are to realize further that what we took for propositions (or pseudopropositions expressing ineffable truths) were in reality *einfach Unsinn*; all that we are left with are ordinary sentences. Recall from my discussion in the last chapter, however, that this recognition was supposed to lead us to abandon our search for philosophical foundations when we become clear about the futile nature of such attempts. At the same time, our recognition of the real significance of this search for foundations, what it says about us and why it had to fail, was also supposed to have a profound, transformative effect on how we understand ourselves.

What I am most interested in looking at here is the nature of this transition from metaphysical confusion to this "ethical" clarity. On coming to the end of the *Tractatus*, an astute reader will not have forgotten Wittgenstein's promise in the preface to have provided a final, definitive solution to the problems dealt with in the book, problems that he has told us concern our misunderstanding of the logic of our language. The reader will likely connect these words with Wittgenstein's injunction at the end to overcome his propositions so as to see the world aright. What, after all, could be more tantalizing to a philosopher than the prospect of seeing the world aright once and for all? But, just here, I have serious doubts about whether Wittgenstein has really given his reader the resources required to "throw the ladder away." For right there, in holding out the hope that one could free oneself once and for all from metaphysical confusion through gaining clarity into *the* nature of language, there seems to me to be the germ of the commitment to the view that this clarity consists in being clear about one thing, say, in having a definitive insight into the nature of what sort of thing a sentence essentially is and how a sentence really means what it means. And I want to suggest that this false hope itself rests on a confusion on the part of the author of the *Tractatus* and that it finally must undermine what he took to be his own ethical aim in writing the book.

Consider, in this regard, the pride of place that Wittgenstein gives to the work of Frege and Russell in the composition of the *Tractatus*. Even if we read Wittgenstein as employing aspects of this work as part of an imaginative activity intended to bring his reader to see its shortcomings, it is nonetheless true that the language of the new logics developed by Frege and Russell, along with the biases built into their conception, became crucial for that activity. So crucial, in fact, that Wittgenstein's preoccupation in the *Tractatus* with the kinds of problems he sees arising out of Frege's and Russell's projects suggests that he thought that their work indicated essentially *the* right place to engage metaphysical confusion. Conant summarizes this point well when he contrasts the early and later Wittgenstein:

> Thus our predicament (as captives to an illusion) can be rendered visible through the construction of a single large mirror in which the entire etiology of our confusion is depicted. Wittgenstein . . . comes to distrust this strategy of authorship. But he also recants its underlying conception of the etiology of our confusion. For the later Wittgenstein, the etiology of philosophical confusion is as complicated—and as difficult to survey—as are our lives and our language. So the procedure of uncovering our individual confusions must remain a piecemeal one—one of constructing lots of little mirrors in which the reader can come to recognize himself in each of his moments of being tempted to insist emptily.[12]

Once Wittgenstein abandons the idea of there being one method for the removal of all philosophical confusion, he no longer conceives of his treatments of different philosophical problems as merely touching on different regions of an otherwise unified logical space. Instead, he sees himself as clarifying many different kinds of problems with many different kinds of examples of clarification. This change is pervasive in *Philosophical Investigations*, and we hear it signaled at various points. At §23, after listing a number of different language games that often go unnoticed in philosophical accounts of language, Wittgenstein notes "it is interesting to compare the multiplicity of the tools in language and of the ways they are used, the multiplicity of kinds of word and sentence, with what logicians have said about the structure of language. (Including the author of the *Tractatus-Logico Philosophicus*)." Later, at §133 we read:

> The real discovery is the one that makes me capable of stopping doing philosophy when I want to.—The one that gives philosophy peace, so that it is no longer tormented by questions which bring *itself* in question.—Instead, we now demonstrate a method, by examples; and the series of examples can be broken off.—Problems are solved (difficulties eliminated), not a *single* problem.
>
> There is not *a* philosophical method, though there are indeed methods, like different therapies.[13]

Wittgenstein's claim in the preface of the *Tractatus* "to have found, on all essential points, the final solution of the problems" more than suggests that he understands his book as providing an example of *the* method for overcoming philosophical confusion.[14] I understand the import of these and other remarks from the *Investigations*, on the other hand, to be that such an enormous assumption, built into the very structure of the *Tractatus*, is itself a product of a kind of false imagination. I mean that Wittgenstein came to realize that his own method in the *Tractatus* presupposes a view of language and philosophical confusion that is far too narrow and that this view in turn is what drives the method of the book. Throughout his later writings, on the other hand, we find him constantly striving to undermine this tendency in the attention he gives to the multiplicity of language games and in the emphasis he puts on different philosophical methods for resolving different types of confusion that are liable to arise.

We can get a better sense for why Wittgenstein would later describe his procedure in the *Tractatus* as "dogmatic" if we look more closely at the way a particular conception of philosophical clarification is internal to how elucidations are supposed to work in the book.[15] That conception of philosophical clarification is manifest in the importance that Wittgenstein invests in the idea of something like a *Begriffsschrift* and the way in which this both serves and shapes the elucidations in the *Tractatus*.[16] Frege understood a correct *Begriffsschrift* as a notation that makes the logical articulation of sentences clear in the very manner in which those sentences are written.[17] In remarking here how the idea of something like a *Begriffsschrift*'s serving as a tool for philosophical clarification exercised a powerful hold on Wittgenstein's imagination, I do not mean to overlook the very significant differences played by such an idea in his own and in Frege's thought. Just to take one example, Frege's logicist ambitions in mathematics are entirely foreign to Wittgenstein's aims. More generally, the role that something like a *Begriffsschrift* is meant to play in the *Tractatus* need not be seen as reflecting Wittgenstein's intention to advance any particular theory of logic or language. Rather, its role is entirely subordinated to the elucidatory goals Wittgenstein sets for the book. Elucidations making use of a sign language that excludes errors[18] are supposed to exhibit a method for clarifying propositions that, by making clear the logic of our language, allows philosophical problems to vanish.[19] This is because in following Wittgenstein's "attempts" to clarify philosophical propositions, the reader is supposed to come to see that, because they cannot be written down in a *Begriffsschrift*, philosophical propositions have no logical articulation and so are not propositions at all.[20] In coming to understand the logic of our language, moreover, the reader is to see that each point along the path of this trajectory has consisted of plain, elucidatory nonsense. Her having mistaken any stage along this path for sense was merely the result of philosophical confusion, which now evaporates, leaving no residue from the path taken.[21]

But in trying to draw the reader along a single trajectory toward clarity about the logic of our language, the method of elucidation employed in the *Tractatus* forces us into imagining that philosophical confusion about that logic can only arise along one conceptual dimension, a dimension already projected by what is susceptible to the kind of analysis embodied in the notion of a *Begriffsschrift*. But this seems to involve the tacit claim that some quite specific thing, something like the *essential* nature of language and thought, is *there* for us to grasp or not to grasp. Pushing this thought further reveals that Wittgenstein's reliance on the idea of *Begriffsschrift* brings with it a commitment to ideas such as, for example, that all propositions are logically articulated in the same way (this is why a *Begriffsschrift* supposedly has the power it has), that all inferential relations between propositions are truth-functional and that therefore there must be a single system containing all genuine propositions, that is, the propositions of natural science, where the unified logical space of assertions, causal laws, and hypotheses that constitute the system called mechanics enjoys a privileged position.[22]

These features of Tractarian elucidation have prompted an apt remark by Oskari Kuusela, namely, that "in the *Tractatus* metaphysics dresses in the gown of methodology. It takes refuge in the philosophical method which Wittgenstein supposedly establishes."[23] In the same vein, Diamond comments, "The search for the essence of language is, in theory, *überwunden*, overcome. But it is really still with us, in an ultimately unsatisfactory, unsatisfying, conception of what it is to clarify what we say."[24] Thus there is a certain implicit, metaphysical conception of language and thought that drives the method of the book, and this method for dissolving philosophical confusion in turn reflects such a conception. When we throw away the ladder at the end of the *Tractatus*, it would seem that to see the world aright we are required not only to realize that we have been taken in by the author's nonsense but that we must also see *exactly why* it is the essence of a sentence that it cannot do what we imagined it might, by seeing *essentially what kind* of a thing a sentence is, instead of seeing that there are various ways that we make sense with sentences.[25] The concept of the *use* of a sentence or of an expression certainly has a significant role to play in the *Tractatus*. This is clear from some (I believe somewhat neglected) passages in the *Tractatus* where Wittgenstein tries to bring out the importance of looking at linguistic use for our understanding of language.[26] But saying that linguistic use is important is not the same as actually looking at it, and for the most part the book does not really try to make contact with the complexities of our concrete everyday experience with language. I might put it by saying that the early Wittgenstein did not fully appreciate the *logical* significance of life with language. In the end, requiring the reader to grasp *the kind* of thing a sentence is contains an implicit commitment to metaphysical assumptions about the nature of language, which, in spirit at least, the *Tractatus* sets out to expose as illusory. Call these the *Tractatus*'s unacknowledged *existentiale*.

Now it may well be true, as resolute readers argue, that Wittgenstein did not intend to put forward any philosophical doctrines in the *Tractatus* and that it is therefore deceptive at the very least to attribute a "picture theory of the proposition" to him, as is often done. Nevertheless, I think that a good argument can be made for the claim that the method of the *Tractatus* envisions only something like the *picturing function* of propositions.[27] We read at *Tractatus* §6.53:

> The correct method in philosophy would really be the following: to say nothing except what can be said, i.e. propositions of natural science—i.e. something that has nothing to do with philosophy—and then, whenever someone else wanted to say something metaphysical, to demonstrate to him that he had failed to give a meaning to certain signs in his propositions.

The implication here seems to be that the essential function of propositions is to state facts, to be true or false, and that this is done by a certain narrow class of propositions—but not a word about what this comes to in our life with language, nothing about *how* meanings are given to the signs in a proposition. In particular, nothing about how we are taught to project a symbol in a sign. And so naturally too, then, nothing about virtues like courage and openness being helpful for learning how to speak the language (game) of wonder, something the book therefore converts from honest difficulty to total incomprehensibility. And I am tempted to say that Wittgenstein is mute on this point because, in envisioning only one kind of use of language, he himself is not yet in full contact with the richness of the phenomenon at hand. Wittgenstein wrote in the late 1940s, "The basic evil of

Russell's logic, as also of mine in the *Tractatus*, is that what a proposition is is illustrated by a few commonplace examples, and then pre-supposed as understood in full generality."[28] The suddenness with which the *Tractatus* ends, the finality of its proclamations, demand that something essential and necessary should have been grasped by the reader if he has understood the author.[29] And it is only fair to say that these senses of "essential" and "necessary" are ones that the later Wittgenstein saw as all too traditional.

I said above that the reason why I believe the *Tractatus* cannot succeed in its ethical aim is that it is too intellectualist. This is manifest in the way the book tries to lead us to a grasp of how it is the very essence of language that thwarts our attempts to make sense when we try to say something in ethics. Its attempt to set our intellects at peace relies on its giving us a synoptic view of what a sentence is. But because the idea of such a view is *itself* an illusion, this peace will never come, and so we can never understand the author's ethical intention in writing the book. We are left instead to ponder how the view of the sentence with which we are supposedly left really is capable of achieving *everything* contained in what we call language. Indeed, the *Tractatus* can be seen as an example of the very "craving for generality" and "contemptuous attitude towards the particular case" in philosophy that Wittgenstein would later bemoan.[30] A remark by Wittgenstein written twenty-five years after the publication of the *Tractatus* is pertinent here. It comes amid a discussion of different uses we might make of assertions, in particular the role that assertions play in our language game of talking about fate as opposed to when we make an ordinary assertion of fact. Arguably written with *Tractatus* §6.53 in mind, Wittgenstein is criticizing his earlier work on the very grounds I have been describing.

> The use of the word "fate." Our attitude to the future and the past. To what extent do we hold ourselves responsible for the future? How much do we speculate about the future? How do we think about past and future? If something unwelcome happens:—do we ask "Who's to blame?", do we say "Someone must be to blame for it"?,—or do we say "It was God's will," "It was fate"?
>
> In the way in which asking a question, insisting on an answer, or not asking it, expresses a different attitude, a different way of living, *so* too, in this sense, an utterance like "It is God's will" or "We are not masters of our fate." What this sentence does, or at least something similar, a commandment too could do. Including one that you give to yourself. And conversely a commandment, e.g. "Do not grumble!" can be uttered like the affirmation of a truth.
>
> Why now am I so anxious to keep apart these ways of using "declarative sentences"? Is it really necessary? Did people in former times really not properly

understand what they wanted with a sentence? Is it pedantry?—It is simply an attempt to see that every usage gets its due. Perhaps then a reaction against the over-estimation of science. The use of the word "science" for "everything that can be said without nonsense" already betrays this over-estimation. For this amounts in reality to dividing utterances into two classes: good and bad; and the danger is already there. It is similar to dividing all animals, plants and rocks into the useful and the harmful.

But of course the words "see that they get their due" and "over- estimation" express my point of view. I could have said instead: "I want to help this and this to regain respect."; only I don't see it like that.[31]

Passages such as this one reflect Wittgenstein's long-standing and deep hostility to what he perceived to be the undue influence of causal scientific modes of thought on modern culture in general and philosophy in particular. But such a remark can also provide us with an interesting perspective from which to view the ethical point of the *Tractatus* in light of Wittgenstein's later thought and work. Assuming the correctness of my claim that the *Tractatus* is meant, among other things, to render a cultural critique of the "the entire modern worldview," there is no small irony that Wittgenstein himself succumbed to one of modernity's greatest traps, an essentializing and thus flattening out of our various forms of intelligibility, encouraged by our overestimation of science.[32] So long as we remain in search of something like a *final* vision, an intellectualist illusion of disengaged rationality and a main theme in Wittgenstein's later work, we will not be able to "overcome" the *Tractatus*'s propositions. To use his own metaphor, we shall be unable to throw away the ladder because we will still be standing on it, thinking.

The *Tractatus* hinders us from having precisely the relationship to language that it seeks to secure for us. If the ethical aim of the book consists in trying to lead the reader to a kind of self-understanding gained through a proper relationship to language, then this is only attainable if its method is true to the phenomenon of language. And this means that it must connect up with the many different ways that language functions in our lives. Wittgenstein's attempt to overcome the attraction that philosophy exerts on us fails exactly on this point because its method, the best intentions to the contrary notwithstanding, will in the end divert our attention in the wrong direction, looking for the nature of the sentence ("This is how things stand"): the ethical aim of the book must remain unfulfilled.

CONCLUSION TO PART I

I want to close with a brief discussion of how these issues concern the way we see the *Tractatus* in relation to Wittgenstein's later work. First, I want to look at the context of the remark from May 6, 1930 (which I quote on 51–52), where Wittgenstein recalls his momentous feeling at being struck by the thought that there was a way of looking at the world not captured by the law of causality. That remark follows three related observations on the idea of "completed systems." Wittgenstein first writes,

> Reading Spengler, *Decline* etc. and finding, despite much that is irresponsible in specifics, *many* genuinely significant thoughts. Much, perhaps most of it, touches on what I myself have often thought. The possibility of several self-contained systems that, as soon as one has them, look as though one were a continuation of the other.
>
> And all of this also connects with the thought that we really don't know (or consider) how much can be taken from or given to humans.[1]

It is clear from the way that Wittgenstein notes the intersection between Spengler's thought and his own that he does not believe the question indicated in the last sentence concerns the very notion of a completed system but rather the idea that we have a single pregiven criterion for deciding what will count as a completed system in every case.[2] Two further elaborations make clearer the nature of the problem. The first elaboration, in part a reflection on Hanno Buddenbrooks's mental derangement, concerns problems with the idea of a pregiven, context-free criterion for there being a complete set of mental faculties (and so presumably with the complementary ideas of there being something like a complete set of concepts or a complete language). Wittgenstein suggests that even if a person were to lack a particular cognitive ability that we ordinarily take for granted, this in itself *need not* force us to describe the remaining faculties as somehow forming an inherently incomplete set. The second elaboration concerns what Wittgenstein calls Spengler's "hugely important" thought that string instruments assumed their completed form sometime between 1500 and 1600. Then there follows the recollection on the law of causality that I discuss in chapter 2.[3]

There are two points that I want to make about this train of thought. First, I want to suggest a way of understanding this sequence of passages where the connection between them is understood to be more than one of merely psychological association, where the recollection about the law of causality can be seen as having a conceptual relation to what precedes it. That is, I think we can read this sequence of remarks as indicating an important line of *continuity* between Wittgenstein's thought during the time he was working on the notebooks for the *Tractatus* and his thought in the early 1930s. In the Tractarian period we have, on the one hand, a system of truth-functional propositions of natural science, and, on the other hand, rules such as the law of causality, according to which we must construct such a system. At the time Wittgenstein recorded these remarks, he was inclined to speak of rules of a calculus or rules of syntax and the systems of propositions that result from our operating according to those rules.[4] A few years later, he would speak of grammatical remarks that give the forms of the language games we play and contrast these with the actual moves in those games.

My second point concerns how these remarks demonstrate a crucial respect in which Wittgenstein's thought had moved *away* from the *Tractatus*. His referring with approval to Spengler's idea of several self-contained systems of significant thought brings out just how far he had abandoned one of the central metaphysical commitments underlying the elucidations of the *Tractatus*, namely the idea of a single, unified logical space of assertions, causal laws, and hypotheses that constitute the system called mechanics.[5] Perhaps more important still is how it becomes evident that the cultural and ethical significance that the possibility of wonder had for Wittgenstein was not dependent on that earlier, problematic idea. This is clear from the fact that the long passage criticizing Renan in which Wittgenstein writes of our need to reawaken to wonder (see 56–57) was recorded six months after the series of remarks on Spengler and the possible multiplicity of systems of thought mentioned above.

I want to end here by briefly exploring an issue that touches on a related but nevertheless importantly different aspect of Wittgenstein's post-Tractarian interest in conceptual and linguistic multiplicity. At *Tractatus* §6.341 and §6.342 we are asked to compare Newtonian mechanics to a mesh consisting of a particular geometrical shape. We are to imagine the form imposed on our description of the world in mechanics as analogous to the form of description we would obtain by laying this geometrical mesh over the world. I have been arguing that the method of the *Tractatus* might have been informed by a far richer understanding of what is involved when we give expression to our wonder. Whatever purity and depth of philosophical understanding Wittgenstein may have thought the quest to recover true wonder demanded of himself and his reader, there are compelling reasons why we should have been given something more than an arid via negativa leading back to our attraction to certain word forms, a path that our following turned out anyway to depend on the problematic idea of our grasping the essence of language as that gets revealed through Tractarian elucidation. In later terminology, the wonder and the attraction themselves might have been articulated in terms of their connections to various specific language games. Putting this point in Tractarian terms, we could say that Wittgenstein should have provided us with the means for imagining a place in our lives for a "miracle mesh." But there is a risk in thinking about the matter in these terms, and it concerns the fact that the idea of a mesh as it is employed in the two remarks in the *Tractatus* is essentially connected to the possibility of *describing* the world.

In her book *Realism and Imagination in Ethics*, Sabina Lovibond explores some of the same aspects and implications of Wittgenstein's work that I have examined here. At one point she writes:

> Concepts of unconditional value—whether in morals or politics or aesthetics— are available for our (non-ironic) use only in so far as we can "find ourselves" in the specific repertoire of social practices which happen, historically, to "lie at the bottom" of evaluative discourse within the community to which we belong. They can be said to be available to us only in so far as an expressive relation can be said to exist between those practices and ourselves. Thus it is only where such a relation exists that we shall have access to the concepts of non-instrumental value which we need . . . if we are to find a meaning in life.[6]

Comments such as this one are made in the context of Lovibond's discussion of the significance of Wittgenstein's later writings for ethics. She finds in those writings an expressivist view of language as well as the basis for a kind of nonmetaphysical moral realism. Lovibond's view is that Wittgenstein in his later work has what she calls a "metaphysically neutral" view of indicative sentences.[7] For Lovibond, this involves a couple of related points. First, it involves a rejection of what she takes to be the *Tractarian* view of the proposition, what she calls a "normative view."[8] By this I take her to mean a view that involves the idea of there being something like an external metaphysical requirement on what can be called a proposition.[9] In particular, this involves for her the notion that Wittgenstein thought that what makes a sentential sign a genuine proposition is its being *about* some part of reality and that he thought that there must be an absolute, independent criterion for deciding whether that is the case for some sentential signs but not for others. The second point concerns what Lovibond takes to follow from the rejection of the normative view in Wittgenstein's later work, namely, that if something *looks* like an indicative sentence that says something about some part of reality, then quite apart from any philosophical picture we may want to impose on the matter, it *is* an indicative sentence that says something about some part of reality. There is, on this "metaphysically neutral" view, no philosophical criterion by which we can distinguish between those indicative sentences that *really are* about something ("reality") and those that are not. The key factor, instead, is whether an indicative sentence has a role to play in our lives, that is, as Lovibond says, whether we have an expressive relation to the shared practices where the discourses of which the sentence is a part have their home. Lovibond thus goes on to claim that Wittgenstein's later work makes a kind of nonmetaphysical moral realism possible, since on the view just adumbrated, sentences containing "concepts of unconditional value" have as good a claim to being *about* something as do sentences containing concepts from natural science, provided, of course, that these evaluative sentences and their constituent concepts have uses in our language and way of life.

While approving of Lovibond's emphasis on the expressivist strain in Wittgenstein's later work, Cora Diamond has nevertheless criticized the way Lovibond purports to find there the elements of a (nonmetaphysical) moral realism. Diamond writes,

> There is an assumption Lovibond is making, the assumption that there are just two alternatives: if we do not make a metaphysically-based distinction between sentences which genuinely describe reality (and are made true or false by the facts) and sentences which do not do so, then we shall accept an account in which all indicative sentences are treated equally as descriptions of reality, as "about" the things they grammatically appear to be about.[10]

Attention to Wittgenstein's later writings on mathematics shows that for him there are not just the two alternatives recognized by Lovibond. By making clear that those are not the only possibilities he provides a point of view from which we can question what Lovibond takes to be the implications of his views for ethics. Indicative sentences may have *various* functions: indicativeness itself indicates neither the kind of use a sentence has, nor whether it has any use.[11]

Diamond tries to bring out ways in which there can be uses of language that are not indicative sentences, do not involve the employment of any specifically moral vocabulary, yet that nonetheless can be seen by their use to belong to part of our moral discourse. If this is the case, however, then what is important to take from the later Wittgenstein's writings for our thinking about evaluative discourse is a recognition of the need to look carefully at our *uses* of evaluative language. If we do this, Diamond thinks we will be far less likely to find in Wittgenstein's later work a basis for moral realism, as we will no longer see in that work the germ of a defense for the idea that our ordinary moral discourse is logically in order because indicative sentences containing specifically moral terms can lay just as much claim as any other class of sentences to picking out features of reality and thus are about something as much as is any other class of sentences. We won't put weight on the "aboutness" in the way that Diamond thinks Lovibond still does.[12]

When seen against the backdrop of my discussion here, the long remark by Wittgenstein from 1947 on different types of assertions (quoted above on pages 97–98) can be read not only as criticizing the kind of view he had once held but also as anticipating Diamond's criticisms of Lovibond. The problem he points to there is *not* the exclusive attribution of meaning to assertions (though, of course, he also came to regard that idea as wrongheaded). The problem is rather the failure to recognize distinctions of use *within* the category of assertions itself.

PART
II

4

THE CONCEPT OF PROGRESS IN
WITTGENSTEIN'S THOUGHT

4.1

As a motto for the *Philosophical Investigations*, Wittgenstein chose to quote a line from Johann Nepomuk Nestroy's play *Der Schützling* (*The Protégé*): "Anyway, the thing about progress is that it always seems greater than it really is" ("*Überhaupt hat der Fortschritt das an sich, dass er viel grösser ausschaut, als er wirklich ist*").[1] The structure and content of this chapter reflect how I see the motto of the *Investigations* orienting the reader toward the remainder of that text, specifically prefiguring how the concept of progress is relevant for our grasping some of its central philosophical objectives. I see the motto as at once referring us to Wittgenstein's authorship and at the same time referring to the cultural context in which his work has been carried out. What I hope to accomplish is to give an account of how I see the *Philosophical Investigations* engaging in a critique of a certain understanding of progress in a cultural sense of that term, against the background of the way in which I understand the book to amount to a kind of philosophical progress in Wittgenstein's thinking.[2]

My discussion can be made a bit clearer by calling attention to an ambiguity in the chapter's title. "The Concept of Progress in Wittgenstein's Thought" can be understood to refer to certain features of the development of Wittgenstein's thought. But it could also be taken to refer to what Wittgenstein thought about the concept of progress, where "concept of progress" is connected to certain value judgments one makes when comparing, for example, different features of earlier and later historical periods. A central aim of this chapter is to show how it broadens our perspective on the nature and significance of Wittgenstein's later philosophy when we see that these two ways of thinking about the role of progress in his thought are actually woven together in his work. A further challenge follows from the way I try to reach this aim, since the chapter draws on and brings together what to some may seem to be not only individually controversial but also incompatible approaches to understanding Wittgenstein's thought as that is expressed in his texts.[3]

Section 4.2 briefly discusses some textual and literary-critical questions that bear on the nature of the motto as well as on the use I make of material that not only falls outside of *Philosophical Investigations* but outside of anything we might call Wittgenstein's "strictly philosophical" texts. In section 4.3, I elaborate on some assumptions I make regarding the relation between the *Tractatus* and the *Investigations*. Against the background of these assumptions, I show in sections 4.4 and 4.5 how the remarks on rule-following can be taken as an example of how the *Philosophical Investigations* attempts to lead the reader to a perspective on language that then prepares the way for a distinctive kind of cultural critique.

4.2

David Stern's "Nestroy, Augustine, and the Opening of the *Philosophical Investigations*" contains an informative discussion of the very regrettable publication history and subsequent neglect by commentators of the motto for the *Investigations*.[4] As Stern notes, the motto has yet to be translated for any of the bilingual German-English editions of the book and is omitted altogether from English-only translations.[5] Moreover, even though the motto itself appeared in earlier German editions, until Joachim Schulte's critical genetic edition from 2001 included the word "motto" in front of the line from Nestroy (as it appears in Wittgenstein's manuscript), readers were left to make an educated guess as to what the function of this line might be.[6] With such a history, it is not too surprising that the motto rarely figures significantly, if at all, in the literature devoted to the opening of the *Investigations*. Stern asks against this background: "Given that the motto is left out of the standard translations, what reason do we have to take it seriously as the opening words of the *Philosophische Untersuchungen*? Is the front matter really part of the book, and even if it is, how much does that matter?"[7] Concerning whether the line from Nestroy should even be counted as the genuine motto to the text of *Philosophical Investigations* (apart, that is, from the question concerning whatever role it should be accorded in understanding the book), Stern shows quite convincingly how Wittgenstein's manuscripts and typescripts make it clear that in fact the quotation from Nestroy deserves to be regarded as the motto to the book.

In taking up the question of whether or not the motto is important, Stern notes the possibility that "one could invoke a literary distinction here, and argue that the epigraph and preface, to be found on the preceding, roman numbered pages of the published book are part of the *paratext*, liminal material that is not really part of the book itself, and that the text begins on page 1 of the published book, not the first page of the typescript."[8] This possibility, though, raises perhaps an even larger question: "But how are we to understand the relationship between the text of the *Philosophical Investigations*, its paratext, and other texts, an issue that Wittgenstein interpreters have only occasionally given their full attention?"[9] In order to address this issue, Stern provisionally adopts a distinction drawn by Hans-Johann Glock between two ways of reading the *Investigations*, what Glock calls an "immanent" approach and a "genetic" approach.[10] Stern explains, "According to Glock, the immanent approach turns on two key assumptions: [1] that the 'author's intentions are irrelevant and [2] that an interpretation should only take into consideration what a reader can understand by looking at the text itself.' We might add: what the immanent reading rules out are extratextual intentions, not intentions as expressed in the text."[11] Stern goes on to point out that given the central role that the text plays on an immanent approach, it is initially surprising that supposedly immanent readers of the *Investigations* have devoted so little of their attention to the front matter of the book. On Stern's view, this becomes less puzzling once we recognize that, while it may seem natural to many to regard front matter as part of a text, one of the primary functions of the front matter (including the motto, should there be one) is to give the author a forum in which she can attempt to orient, or even manipulate, the reader in such a way that her work is read and received in accord with her own wishes. If this is true, then given what seems to be the immanent reader's general wariness of authorial intentions, we can see how it might be tempting for her to regard the front matter as extratextual and thus why purportedly immanent readers of Wittgenstein have overlooked the motto.

Drawing on the work of Gerard Genette, Stern argues against such an approach to Wittgenstein's text: "We ignore the motto—and the preface—at our peril, for they 'set the stage' just as much as the opening sections." But given a stubborn refusal to acknowledge the front matter (and perhaps anything outside a text that might pertain to authorial intentions), Stern points in addition to what Gerard Genette calls "the 'obvious fact' that the immanent reader, attending only to what is in the text itself, 'does not exist . . . and cannot exist.' The immanent reader, a familiar figure in the history of philosophy and modernist literary criticism, is an entirely fictional character, for in practice no one can bracket out everything they know or take for granted."[12]

Stern concludes, rightly, I think, that since one can't simply forget what one knows, it is simply better to acknowledge the fact that one knows it and that the information one gathers from the front matter to a text will, to some extent at least, inform one's reading of that text.[13] Indeed, there is every reason to think that Wittgenstein himself took front matter very seriously. This comes out clearly in two letters to C. K. Ogden concerning the front matter for the *Tractatus*. In the first letter, dated May 5, 1922, Wittgenstein writes in brackets, "Title, Dedication, Motto, Preface, No 1 etc." and adds, "This is the part I am responsible for and therefore must be left together." In the second letter, dated June 23, 1922, Wittgenstein appears to be responding to his publisher's idea to publish the German version of the *Tractatus* without the preface. He writes, "By the way: if I give to Messrs Kegan Paul all publication rights then they ought to print my preface in German too!!! *For the preface is part of the book.*"[14] All of this naturally leads one to expect that his selection of a motto for the *Investigations* would have been conducted with great care and, in fact, his reference to "Nestroy's magnificent saying" ("*das herrliche Wort Nestroys*") already in a letter to Schlick from September 18, 1930, makes it clear that his choice was far from casual.[15]

4.3

Wittgenstein's placing of the quotation from Nestroy's play at the beginning of his book can reasonably be taken as intended to guide the reader's attention into more than one channel of thought.[16] Baker and Hacker first note in their commentary, "In its original context it expresses such negative views on progress as would harmonize with W.'s own repudiation of this aspect, and this ideal, of European culture."[17] They immediately go on to speculate about what is clearly the main task of the motto:

> It remains, however, unclear what Nestroy's remark is intended to convey as a motto for *PI*. It might be suggested that it intimates that the advance made in *PI* over the philosophy of *TLP* is less substantial than it appears. This is unlikely. More probable is the hypothesis that the intention behind the motto echoes the end of the Preface to *TLP*: "the value of this work . . . is that it shows how little is achieved when these problems are solved."[18]

Toward the end of this chapter, I will return to some of the questions raised by this proposal. For now, I will simply mark a partial agreement with it by supposing it uncontroversial to believe that one natural way to understand the motto is to see

Wittgenstein as using it to signal *something* about the way in which we under-stand the relation between the *Investigations* and his first book, the *Tractatus*. This signal prompts us to keep the *Tractatus* in mind as we read the *Investigations*, something that we are encouraged to do again in the preface, where Wittgen-stein writes: "Four years ago I had occasion to re-read my first book (the *Tractatus Logico-Philosophicus*) and to explain its ideas to someone. It suddenly seemed to me that I should publish those old thoughts and the new ones together: that the latter could be seen in the right light only by contrast with and against the back-ground of my old way of thinking."

If one natural way to read the motto, then, is as some sort of expression of Witt-genstein's attitude to the way in which the *Investigations* compares with the *Tracta-tus*, or, more particularly, as an expression of his attitude toward the way in which it may (or may not) constitute progress over the *Tractatus*, then two important and connected questions are: "How did Wittgenstein conceive *specifically* of that prog-ress?" and "How might *we* conceive specifically of that progress?" I emphasize "spe-cifically" here because while the motto clearly suggests that Wittgenstein wants us to be careful about the way in which we understand the relation between the two books, it does not give us much more than that to go on. In other words, the motto issues some kind of caution to us, but beyond that we are left on our own to face some very large exegetical questions (questions with which we would have had to deal with or without the motto). But, at any rate, since it seems plausible to assume that Wittgenstein was concerned that the *Investigations*, including its relation to the *Tractatus*, would be variously misunderstood, the suggestion that the motto warns us to be wary of the way we take it to be progress seems especially appropriate.

How we understand the question of the progress that the *Investigations* makes beyond the *Tractatus*, and so how we conceive of their philosophical relation, is not only complicated by the fact that each book is difficult taken on its own. It is made more complicated by the fact that our understanding of the one is often intertwined with our understanding of the other. For example, it can seem natu-ral to read certain passages in the *Investigations* as vigorously attacking a theory of meaning that Wittgenstein held in the *Tractatus*. In that case, one must ask about the nature and object of the attack. Does one, for instance, see the attack as consisting of Wittgenstein showing how a theory of meaning he now advo-cates is more adequate than his old theory of meaning? Or does one instead see the *Investigations* opposing a Tractarian theory of meaning not with a new theory of its own but rather with a new *method* for dissolving philosophical problems, including problems left unsolved or even generated by his first book? Both are possibilities that have been explored a great deal over the last several decades (and they themselves comprise several subalternatives).[19]

Yet each of these possibilities shares the common assumption (and one that I obviously find dubious) that one of the targets of the *Investigations* is a theory of meaning that Wittgenstein espoused in the *Tractatus*. This indicates at least one further alternative for understanding the progression of Wittgenstein's thought, and this entails dropping the assumption that there is an actual theory of meaning in the *Tractatus* to criticize in the first place. Dropping this assumption will usually go with a way of reading the *Tractatus* and the *Investigations* in which neither book is intended as a piece of constructive or systematic philosophy and on which the two books share substantially *similar* goals.[20] One way to characterize those goals is to say that each of these books aims to show the illusory nature of attempts to construct philosophical theories that require the reader to occupy an external vantage point on language. Another way to put this point is to say that both in the *Tractatus* and in the *Investigations* Wittgenstein was concerned to show how emptiness in philosophy arises when philosophers, either explicitly or implicitly, imagine their work as presupposing nothing about human beings and their world. In addition, interpreters of Wittgenstein who tend to see the progress between his early and later work this way tend also to think that, to the extent that the goals of the two books do differ, this is more of a reflection of a significant change in Wittgenstein's understanding of philosophical method and not of a change in his theoretical or metaphysical ambitions. On this view, to the extent that the later Wittgenstein is critical of the *Tractatus*—and that he is critical of it is something no one really denies—such criticism is not directed in the first instance at the theories that the earlier book proffered but rather, as we saw in the last chapter, at the conception of method it embodied (and, in the end, at the way this method did in fact rely unknowingly on a sort of metaphysical theory).

As this very general sketch may suggest, it is not my intention to catalogue, let alone analyze and evaluate, the various positions and subpositions that comprise the debate concerning the continuity of Wittgenstein's thought. I shall simply state therefore that it is this last-mentioned alternative I find most compelling, that my understanding of the question of progress between the *Tractatus* and the *Investigations* has therefore been largely informed by those who have articulated this alternative, and that it is such an understanding of that progress that is taken for granted here and that shapes what I will say in the rest of the chapter and book about the concept of progress in Wittgenstein's later thought as that pertains to certain types of value judgments. Naturally, I hope my discussion of this other sense of progress in Wittgenstein's thought will make the assumption about the relation between the *Tractatus* and the *Investigations* seem more plausible. But the plausibility of much of what I say in this regard will to some extent rest on the original assumption concerning the nature of the continuity of Wittgenstein's thought. Consequently, the plausibility of what I say about each of the two ways for thinking about the concept of progress in his thought hangs together somewhat with what I say or assume about the other way. At any rate, the rest of the chapter will deal with this second way to think about progress in Wittgenstein.

4.4

There is little doubt among commentators today that the remarks on rule-following in the *Investigations* exhibit central features of the later Wittgenstein's treatment of meaning and intention. For my purposes here, moreover, these remarks are well suited to bring out an important consequence of the conception of philosophy ascribed to Wittgenstein in the last section. I will not, however, reconstruct or rehearse the arguments that take place in those remarks. Instead, I will rely for my orientation toward them on work carried out by some of the very same interpreters on whose work I rely for my overall understanding of the continuity and aim of Wittgenstein's philosophy.[21] Indeed, since their work on the remarks on rule-following has played an important role in the development of this overall understanding, this is not really a further assumption on my part (or not much of one, anyway).

Especially since the publication of Saul Kripke's *Wittgenstein on Rules and Private Language*, the remarks on rule-following have received much attention from many of the most capable philosophers writing on Wittgenstein.[22] Many commentators take these remarks as giving important expression to some version of a use theory of meaning that they take Wittgenstein to hold. The remarks are then seen as at once refuting certain deeply entrenched and widely held views about language (including some set of views that Wittgenstein is presumed to have held when he wrote the *Tractatus*) and as establishing Wittgenstein's own account of the ground of meaning, understanding, and normativity. Against this interpretative tendency to read the *Investigations* as a constructive work of philosophy, Warren Goldfarb writes,

> The rule-following considerations are not meant to yield a conclusive refutation of one or another sophisticated philosophy of language. Rather, they operate by examining what frames the first steps of a search for an account of meaning; and they are effective only insofar as what Wittgenstein provides . . . is a convincing portrayal of how such a project comes to have a hold on us. A better understanding of Wittgenstein's position thus requires far more clarity than we currently have about the sources of the inchoate demands we put on the notion of meaning and about the role such demands play in philosophical theorizing.[23]

John McDowell seconds Goldfarb's idea:

> There is indeed room to complain that Wittgenstein reveals a need for something but does not give it, or does not give enough of it. But what we might ask for more of is not a constructive account of how human interactions make meaning and understanding possible, but rather a diagnostic deconstruction of the peculiar way of thinking that makes such a thing seem necessary.[24]

This remark of McDowell's points to two related questions: what is the peculiar way of thinking that we might want a diagnostic deconstruction of, and what is the significance of this way of thinking for our understanding Wittgenstein's later philosophy? The "source of the inchoate demands we put on the notion of meaning" that Goldfarb speaks of in the passage cited above, is, I take it, something quite close to McDowell's "peculiar way of thinking," and in what follows I want to make it plausible to think that Wittgenstein's engagement with this peculiar way of thinking is in large measure intended as a philosophical response to what he takes to be one of the central organizing myths of modernity, what Charles Taylor has called the "rationalist" or "disengaged" view of human intelligence.[25] Taylor notes the following in this vein: "in speaking of the 'dominant' [disengaged] view I am not only thinking of the theories which have been preeminent in modern philosophy, but also of an outlook which has to some extent colonized the common sense of our civilization."[26] Essential to Wittgenstein's later philosophy are the distinctive ways he interrogates the accepted frameworks within which philosophical problems are posed. With Taylor's thought in mind, I want to urge that Wittgenstein understood this activity as necessarily involving an attempt to engage the philosopher as a person who comes to philosophy with a certain cast of mind that includes unexamined commitments from a particular cultural context.[27]

Part of what I want to do here should be seen as an attempt to develop my own inflection on Stanley Cavell's suggestion that the *Philosophical Investigations* is a book whose cultural teaching is *internal* to its structure and *not* a text in which we should necessarily expect to find its philosophy of culture expressed in cultural remarks per se. Cavell writes, on this question,

> Since I have in effect claimed that there is a perspective from which the *Philosophical Investigations* may be seen as presenting a philosophy of culture, I have implied that its attitude to its time is directly presented in it, as directly as, say, in Spengler, or as in Freud or Nietzsche or Emerson. Then the difficulty in articulating the difficulty of Wittgenstein's attitude is the difficulty of finding this perspective.[28]

In the next section, I try to articulate a way in which I find the remarks on rule-following to give expression to such a perspective. In particular, I want to count as part of the *Investigations*'s cultural teaching a perspective on ourselves with which Wittgenstein is trying to leave us vis-à-vis our relation to features of our culture such as the disengaged view in philosophy and to what he took to be its connection to that culture's dominant conception of progress.

4.5

At *Philosophical Investigations* §115, Wittgenstein speaks of a picture holding us captive, and his book is populated with images and idols of necessity that he thinks oppress us in philosophy. In the following two passages, John McDowell vividly retells the distorting picture of meaning that is on display in the remarks on rule-following.

> A succession of judgements or utterances, to be intelligible as applications of a single concept to different objects, must belong to a practice of going on doing the same thing. We tend to be tempted by a picture of what that amounts to, on the following lines. What counts as doing the same thing, within the practice in question, is fixed by its rules. The rules mark out rails along which correct activity within the practice must run. These rails are there anyway, independently of the responses and reactions a propensity to which one acquires when one learns the practice itself; or, to put the idea less metaphorically, it is in principle discernible, from a standpoint independent of the responses that characterize a participant in the practice, that a series of correct moves in the practice is really a case of going on doing the same thing. Acquiring mastery of the practice is pictured as something like engaging mental wheels with these objectively existing rails.[29]

> We can find this picture of genuine truth compelling only if we either forget that truth-bearers are such only because they are meaningful, or suppose that meanings take care of themselves, needing, as it were, no help from us. This latter supposition is the one that is relevant to our concerns. If we make it, we can let the judging subject, in our picture of true judgement, shrink to a locus of pure thought, while the fact that judging is a human activity fades into insignificance.[30]

In the case of rule-following (and judgment more generally), intractable difficulties seem to arise from the fact that none of our actual proceedings can meet the requirements for correctness that we imagine this picture imposes on us. But, as McDowell points out, the consequence of abandoning the idea that we might live up to the standards that the picture imposes on us seems in turn to be a slide into semantic nihilism: "If one is wedded to the picture of rules as rails, one will be inclined to think that to reject it is to suggest that, say, in mathematics, anything goes: that we are free to make it up as we go along."[31] McDowell goes on to argue that in our unfortunate recoil into skepticism, we overlook a "fully satisfying" perspective from which we are not haunted by the worries that attend the picture just given, where our choices seem limited to conceiving of ourselves as a "locus of pure thought" or to viewing our rational activities as ones where "anything goes." The perspective McDowell has in mind involves an appreciation of the significance of what in *Mind and World* he calls our acquisition of a second nature through the process of *Bildung*.[32]

The concept of *Bildung* encompasses the concepts of training, education, and cultural formation. That for Wittgenstein we *come to* an appreciation of *Bildung* as part of the dissipation of philosophical confusion entails that he thought that this confusion was itself at least in part a product of our having previously lacked precisely such an appreciation. It also naturally raises the issue of whether this lack of appreciation may itself have had something to do with a particular cultural formation. Most of the remainder of this chapter and the next are devoted to exploring a question that I see emerging naturally out of these considerations. If Wittgenstein thought that part of his effort to dissipate certain forms of philosophical confusion would lead to a better understanding of the connection between this confusion and our cultural and historical situation, then it seems reasonable to suppose that fostering such an understanding was itself an important motivation for his work. Why would he think doing this was important?

Perhaps the main intellectual requirement that the disengaged picture in philosophy makes on us is that we must envisage for ourselves a way to account for the rationality manifest in our various activities that is completely independent of those activities. In the particular case of following an arithmetical rule, the disengaged view requires us to imagine ourselves to be in possession of something that would satisfy the requirement that our understanding transcend all of our actual responses when we write out a numerical series. More specifically, we imagine that our understanding of the rule must be conceptually independent of those responses that we have previously accepted as being in accord with the rule and of all further possible moves we could give. When we are beholden to the requirement forced on us by the disengaged picture, acknowledging the conceptual interdependence of our understanding of the rule and our actions will at best seem like a compromise that practical necessity extracts from us; it will not appear to us to be in accord with rationality per se. Consider, in this context, the following exchange at *Investigations* §188 and §189.

> Here I should first of all like to say: your idea was that that act of meaning the order had in its own way already traversed all those steps: that when you meant it your mind as it were flew ahead and took all the steps before you physically arrived at this or that one.
>
> Thus you were inclined to use such expressions as: "The steps are *really* already taken, even before I take them in writing or orally or in thought." And it seemed as if they were in some *unique* way predetermined, anticipated—as only the act of meaning can anticipate reality.

In the interlocutor's response at §189, "But *are* the steps then *not* determined by the algebraic formula?" we can hear both puzzlement and perhaps his sense of the threat of skepticism. But this evokes merely the laconic reply, "The question contains a mistake."

The interlocutor's question contains a mistake because it derives its sense of urgency from the requirements placed on us by the disengaged view of rationality. But the sense of urgency behind the interlocutor's question can dissipate if we can see that view itself as illusory. Many commentators writing on Wittgenstein have pinpointed this requirement as one of the central targets in the remarks on rule-following. Goldfarb writes, "the demand, however, is for a fixing of the correct continuation that does not rely upon us or take for granted anything about us, at all. What Wittgenstein principally wants to suggest is that we do not have any real conception of what this comes to. We have, as Wittgenstein is wont to say, 'no model of it.' "[33] McDowell is close to Goldfarb on this point as well:

> The idea that the rules of a practice mark out rails traceable independently of the reactions of the participants is suspect even in this apparently ideal case (a numerical series): and insistence that wherever there is going on in the same way there must be rules that can be conceived as marking out such independently traceable rails involves a misconception of the sort of case in which correctness within a practice can be given the kind of demonstration we count as proof.[34]

Taylor's way of making this point is, I think, even better, because it explicitly calls our attention to the embeddedness of the rule in the practice.

> This reciprocity [between the rule and the practice that it guides] is what the intellectualist [disengaged] theory leaves out. In fact, what it shows is that the

"rule" lies essentially *in* the practice. The rule is what is animating the practice at any given time, and not some formulation behind it, inscribed in our thoughts or our brains or our genes, or whatever. That's why the rule is, at any given time, what the practice has made it.[35]

Of course, it is not that Taylor's point about the significance of practices is utterly missed by commentators. But a common way of construing the space Wittgenstein makes in his writings for the notion of a practice is to mistake it for an attempt to give a constructive theory of meaning. This is an interpretative tendency that McDowell is keen to counter. He writes,

> Readers of Wittgenstein often suppose that when he mentions customs, forms of life, and the like, he is making programmatic gestures towards a certain style of positive philosophy: one that purports to make room for talk of meaning and understanding, in the face of supposedly genuine obstacles, by locating such talk in a context of human interactions conceived as describable otherwise than in terms of meaning or understanding. But there is no reason to credit Wittgenstein with any sympathy for this style of philosophy. When he says, "What has to be accepted, the given, is—so one could say—forms of life," his point is not to adumbrate a philosophical response, on such lines, to supposedly good questions about the possibility of meaning and understanding or intentionality generally, but to remind us of something we can take in the proper way only after we are equipped to see that such questions are based on a mistake. His point is to remind us that the natural phenomenon that is normal human life is itself already shaped by meaning and understanding.[36]

McDowell is not alone in arguing for the inadequacies of interpretations of Wittgenstein that attribute to him constructive ambitions. In his well-known behaviorist interpretation of the remarks on rule-following, Saul Kripke finds Wittgenstein providing an "ersatz" account of meaning in terms of assertion conditions. Cora Diamond has criticized the way Kripke would have us understand Wittgenstein as providing an explanation of the meaning of such words as "agreement," "correctness," and "mistake" in abstraction from the particular roles those words have in our lives. Yet Diamond also warns us that even in our rejection of an overtly constructivist interpretation such as Kripke's, we need to be careful lest we fall into the same trap.

> How, then does the contrast [with Kripke's account in terms of assertion conditions] go with Wittgenstein's approach? Here is how not to put it: he says that

meaning is given, not by assertion-conditions, but by place-in-life. Rather, he thinks that, when we raise philosophical questions about meaning, we are for various reasons inclined not to attend to the place words have in our lives: to the very particular places. To give an account of meaning in terms of assertion-conditions is to remain with our eyes fixed in the wrong direction.[37]

If we fix our eyes in the direction that Diamond takes Wittgenstein to be trying to lead us, that is, to the surface level of our actual uses of rules, we get a quite different picture. In speaking of the surface level here, I mean that for Wittgenstein, meaning and understanding are not features of our life with rules that we need to dig *for*, as though they were something remote from us, below or behind what is plainly open to view in our various rule-following activities.[38] If we do this, we merely make it seem as though all sorts of problems for meaning and understanding arise. Wittgenstein's point, rather, is that we do not need to dig at all. What we need to do is to allow our philosophical attention to remain *at* the level at which we actually operate with rules in our lives and refuse to forfeit our right to use the term "correct" in every case merely because we take ourselves always to be able to imagine circumstances that might create problems for any given use of this term. And he hopes to help us along by drawing our attention to the profound differences between how we tend to regard these matters when doing traditional philosophy and how we stand to them when we are actually following rules in ordinary life, a life that is phenomenologically characterizable as one where our actual normal activities of following rules are remarkable for their unobtrusive yet pervasive success. The relevant difference between how rules show up for us when we step back from our activities of actual rule-following and ask ourselves what, in general, does following a rule consist in and how rules show up for us when we are engaged in following them is that in the former case it may be true to say that there is always a question whether someone understands, while in the latter case, in ordinary life, that is, there is usually no question at all.[39] This should not be taken as a covert argument for some kind of infallibilism; *going wrong* is clearly an important part of our rule-following activities. But we maintain our grip on this idea, too, when we keep meaning and understanding in view. Diamond writes,

> In fact, of course, we are not just trained to go "446, 448, 450" etc. and other similar things; we are brought into a life in which we rest on, depend on, people's following rules of many sorts, and in which people depend on us: rules, and agreement in following them, and reliance on agreement in following them, and criticising or rounding on people who do not do it right—all this is woven into

the texture of life; and it is in the context of its having a place in such a form of human life that a "mistake" is recognisably that.[40]

We saw earlier that the disengaged view demands that language operate presuppostionlessly, that it operate in all eventualities. But because we have no model for what it would look like for language to operate at that level, what seems to be our failure to find an account of meaning and understanding that fulfills the requirement of the disengaged view is not a genuine failure at all. For Wittgenstein, clarity comes in seeing that the level of the totality of contingencies was never one that we needed to be concerned with in the first place. (And, just to anticipate a possible concern taken up in my discussion of conservatism in chapter 5, this is connected to why our seeing the requirements of the disengaged view as illusory doesn't imply anything like a genuine loss of objectivity, rationality, or critical capacity.)

What has been said above about "correct" and "mistake" is no less true of Wittgenstein's use of the words "custom," "practice," and "form of life." For McDowell, Diamond, and other like-minded readers of Wittgenstein, we need to hear those words, too, as spoken from within the context of a form of human life that is already shaped by meaning and understanding. McDowell indicates what I take to be the right view of where Wittgenstein hopes the remarks on rule-following, and indeed in my opinion his later philosophy more generally, will leave his reader.

> Given a satisfying diagnosis, the inclination [to answer a philosophical question about meaning] should evaporate, and the question should simply fall away. There is no need to concoct substantial philosophical answers to them. The right response to "How is meaning possible?" or "How is intentionality possible?" is to uncover the way of thinking that makes it seem difficult to accommodate meaning and intentionality in our picture of how things are and to lay bare how uncompulsory it is to think that way.[41]

In coming to see the requirements that the disengaged view imposes on us as not compulsory, of course, we can come to see it for what it is: a picture that, having colonized our common sense, extracts commitments from us and perhaps more importantly blocks us from seeing others, blocks us especially in philosophy by opposing an examination of our rags (*Philosophical Investigations*, §52). But in addition to learning to let go of certain philosophical questions and learning to allow the inclination to ask them to evaporate, we can also be led to ask different questions not merely about the effects of the disengaged picture but about the sources it has in our lives, about what commitments on our part make it seem so compulsory. These questions may not strike us as immediately philosophical in themselves, but I believe that they are among the most important questions that Wittgenstein's philosophy intends to bring us to ask.

There is nothing wrong per se with understanding Wittgenstein's rule-following remarks specifically, and his later writings more generally, as having as their primary target the dissolution of philosophical puzzles concerning meaning and intentionality. But if we give an overly narrow construal of what hitting that target comes to, then we not only miss the true significance that, as McDowell puts it, "normal human life is itself already shaped by meaning and understanding," but we also miss the relevance of our having forgotten this. And so we never get around to an investigation of how it came about that we needed reminding.[42] As I have already argued, Wittgenstein's attempt to bring out the incoherence of the disengaged picture is of a piece with an attempt to bring out the way our rule-following practices are, as Diamond puts it, "woven into the texture of life." But if understanding Wittgenstein's remarks on rule-following requires that we really look to see how our rule-following practices are woven into the texture of our life with others, then it must also be true that integral to the aim of these and other related remarks is the hope that as we let go of the disengaged picture we will come to have a transformed understanding of ourselves, of the kind of creatures that we are. We are supposed to see our rule-following practices as making sense within specific contexts of a form of life. But to talk of "practice," "custom," and "form of life" in this way can immediately invoke other words such as "history" and "culture." To become aware of ourselves as embodying rule-following practices is ipso facto to become aware of ourselves as finite creatures who are embedded in a particular historical and cultural setting. Now, perhaps to some, talk of such an awareness must inevitably smack of a suspicious gesture at the subtle grasp of a thesis. But this suspicion is misplaced. The awareness that comes with the evaporation of the disengaged view is nothing that, for example, we should want to call "the engaged view."[43] Rather, Wittgenstein's work of assembling reminders (§127) in the *Investigations* is intended to help us to look (§66) at the multitude of ways in which our expressions find their place in our given form of life (§23) on the occasions of our various philosophical difficulties. And what we see when we look is not some kind of superlative fact or thesis that could do any philosophical work in advance of a need for the reminders and the looking. In fact, "to become aware of ourselves as finite creatures who are embedded in a particular historical and cultural setting" really only describes the acknowledgment of a truism.[44] (But the self-understanding achieved by acknowledging a truism can take on the feel of an earth-shattering insight.)

This brings new questions with it. What did Wittgenstein think about the relation between the kinds of philosophical questions that arise from the

disengaged view of ourselves and the historical-cultural setting we discover ourselves in when this role becomes clearer to us? If understanding the significance of
the involved, embedded nature of understanding is as closely tied to the dissipation of philosophical confusion as I am suggesting it is for Wittgenstein, then it
stands to reason that bringing this to light was an important aim of his writing.
Taylor connects the dominance of the disengaged view in philosophy with "the
hegemony of bureaucratic-technical reason in our lives."[45] I believe Wittgenstein
would agree with Taylor that the disengaged view of ourselves is not only endemic
to philosophy but is also what I above called one of the central organizing myths
of modernity. And, accordingly, I see taking the rule-following remarks in the
Investigations as calling into question the way in which this view finds its expression in philosophy as in turn providing support for the claim that Wittgenstein
was a philosopher of culture. If this is true, moreover, then it becomes very plausible to claim that Wittgenstein's cultural concerns should figure as an important
framework within which we engage those remarks, remarks that by nearly all
accounts occupy a central place in his later writings.

In the introduction, I wrote that part of the point of this chapter is to show
how it broadens our perspective on the nature of Wittgenstein's philosophy when
we see that two ways of thinking about the concept of progress in his thought
are actually woven together in his work. In section 4.2, I discussed one way for
thinking about the concept of progress that has been relevant here. In that way,
progress between the early and later Wittgenstein is not marked out by a more
successful achievement of constructive philosophical ambitions but rather by a
way of doing philosophy that more successfully deconstructs those ambitions,
that better shows up such ambitions to make philosophical progress empty.
Here I have been trying to bring out the way Wittgenstein's deconstruction of
the disengaged view in the remarks on rule-following can be seen as representing
an engagement with the concept of progress in a different sense. We can see this
if we can see that the disengaged view in philosophy is one reflection of a kind
of uncritical assumption about and mythological demand on rationality that has
often characterized our culture's thinking about progress in science, technology,
economics, politics, and morals.[46] We find these two ways for thinking about
progress in Wittgenstein's thought woven together by Wittgenstein himself in
the following excerpt from a 1930 sketch to what would later be published as the
foreword to *Philosophical Remarks*:

> It is all one to me whether the typical western scientist understands or appre-
> ciates my work, since in any case he does not understand the spirit in which
> I write.

Our civilization is characterized by the word progress. Progress is its form, it is not one of its properties that it makes progress. *Typically* it constructs. Its *activity* is to construct a more and more complicated structure. And even clarity is only a means to this end and not an end in itself.

For me on the contrary clarity, transparency, is an end in itself.

I am not interested in erecting a building but in having the foundations of possible buildings transparently before me.

So I am aiming at something different than are the scientists and my way of thoughts move differently than do theirs.[47]

This passage is not, however, the only place where I want to say that Wittgenstein allows the word "progress" to refer simultaneously to the two senses of progress that account for the ambiguity in the title of this chapter. I believe we also find the word "progress" doing "double duty," so to speak, in the motto for the *Philosophical Investigations*, a place that must be thought of as a highly significant point in Wittgenstein's authorship.

Returning then to the motto, recall that, in picking up earlier on an idea by Baker and Hacker, I indicated my sense that the motto is intended to convey to the reader a need for caution when reading the *Investigations* against the background of the *Tractatus* (and I went on to try to make clear at the outset how I understand that need in light of my own interpretative commitments). We saw, however, that while Baker and Hacker do make brief note of the motto's original context, a scene in Nestroy's play where a wide-eyed belief in historical and technological progress is clearly being ridiculed,[48] rather than exploring this direction, they immediately go on to assert, "It remains, however, unclear what Nestroy's remark is intended to convey as a motto for *PI.*" One wants to say to this that *of course* there are questions about the relevance of the motto for our understanding of the *Investigations*, including, though, questions about the significance of that original context. The brevity with which Baker and Hacker pass over that original context, however, betrays a conviction that it has little or nothing to contribute to that understanding, as though the fact that the motto refers us to such a context were, so to speak, merely decorative. And this effectively excludes the very possibility that in citing the words of an important Austrian dramatist and cultural critic, Wittgenstein may be signaling an idea that I have been trying to make plausible here on somewhat independent grounds: what the author of the *Philosophical Investigations* thought about what he calls in the preface the "darkness of these times," including what he thought about the concept of progress in a cultural-historical sense, was internally related to how he conceived of his own work in its composition, method, and style; in its relation to his earlier work; in the sort of transformation he hoped it might facilitate in those who read it, in particular, perhaps, in the transformation of their thinking about progress; and, of course, in light of the fact that he felt the work to have been written in a time where hardly anyone felt the need or saw the point of such a transformation.

5

THE TRULY APOCALYPTIC VIEW

5.1

I begin with two observations, one from a former colleague of Wittgenstein's, the other from a former student. Each observation records the perception of a difference between Wittgenstein's later work and that of other ordinary-language philosophers active in Great Britain around the same time. The first comment is by O. K. Bouwsma, who writes in the notes he made of his discussions with Wittgenstein in the late 1940s,

> W. talks about men as serious and deep. Perhaps it's just that these men strike Miss Anscombe as like magicians who with a certain trickery and sleight of hand expose the poor ninny philosophers whom they seize upon. The ninny philosophers may not have had the benefit of borrowed cleverness, but they were very earnest, they had problems to which they gave their lives and hard labor. These people have nothing to do but debunk. They are the hollow men sounding. It is not then that these people are mistaken in what they say. It is that they have nothing but this show they put on. What a clever boy I am![1]

Second is this recollection by Stephen Toulmin:

> Having spent the years 1946–47 as a research student at Cambridge, I went on a long visit to Oxford in the spring of 1948, and moved there at the end of the same year, taking up a University Lectureship in January 1949. The transition from Wittgenstein's Cambridge classes and "At Homes," to the style of philosophical disputations then current at Oxford, was a shock. For all its ingenuity

and discrimination, the "linguistic analysis" of Oxford in the 1950s seemed, by comparison with Wittgenstein, to lack any philosophical mainspring: it was like a nursery clock-face, equipped with all the necessary hands and figures, except that one was free to move the hands around just as one pleased. There was at this time, of course, much talk about Wittgenstein and his ideas outside Cambridge, and his name became something for people to swear by (or swear at). But to any-one who came straight from Wittgenstein's rooms at Trinity, both the Oxford philosophers who claimed him as a patron of linguistic philosophy and those opponents in London, like Karl Popper and Ernest Gellner, who belaboured him for trivialising philosophy seemed, equally, to be quarrelling over a lay fig-ure. The real man, the real philosopher, had escaped them.[2]

I take it that the felt contrast that each of these observations is meant to regis-ter arises from something like a sense that an apt response to philosophy pursued under the pretence of disinterested inquiry is disinterest. Wittgenstein himself makes an issue of his philosophical motivations at *Philosophical Investigations* §118, where he writes,

> Where does our investigation get its importance from, since it seems only to destroy everything interesting, that is, all that is great and important? (As it were all the buildings, leaving behind only bits of stone and rubble.) What we are destroying is nothing but houses of cards and we are clearing up the ground of language on which they stand.

Wittgenstein, in telling us that he is only destroying houses of cards, may help to assuage the fear that his philosophical motivations are malicious. But it does not actually answer the question he originally raises.[3] Consider against this backdrop a remark from 1947 that provides a dramatic but fairly typical example of the sen-timents one finds expressed in manuscripts and discussions spanning many years:

> The truly apocalyptic view of the world is that things do *not* repeat themselves. It isn't absurd, e.g., to believe that the scientific and technological age is the begin-ning of the end for humanity; that the idea of Great Progress is a bedazzlement, along with the idea that the truth will ultimately be known; that there is nothing good or desirable about scientific knowledge and that humanity, in seeking it, is falling into a trap. It is by no means obvious that this is not how things are.[4]

This chapter deals with the question of the purpose of Wittgenstein's later work by showing how a substantial number of remarks in which he addresses cultural-historical topics bring out the importance of the quite specific connections he saw between the philosophical problems with which he grappled in his later philosophy and the historical-cultural context in which those problems arose. A grasp of the significance of the ideas expressed in this material is integral to a proper understanding of a central strand in the continuity of Wittgenstein's thought, and bringing out these connections serves to put much of that material into a coherent conceptual framework.

In this chapter, I try to assess the relation of Wittgenstein's cultural concerns to his engagement with metaphysics, in particular with the conception of rationality underlying the view of rules as rails. My first step in this assessment consists of a brief summary of Spengler's influence on Wittgenstein. I will then show that Wittgenstein's development of Spengler's thought is an important connecting link between, on the one hand, his thinking about the kind of mythological conceptions of rationality that underlie the view of rules as rails and, on the other, his concerns about culture and history. Particularly important for this analysis will be my discussion of Wittgenstein's understanding and employment of the concept of a *Betrachtungsform* ("form of observation" or "form of contemplation") and a few closely related concepts. After the nature of Spengler's influence on Wittgenstein has been clarified, I offer an interpretation that brings out what I believe to be the significance of the connection in his later thought between his philosophical activity and his views about the modern West. I then take up briefly the question of how these issues intersect with Wittgenstein's attitude toward and engagement with religion. Last, I address the question of whether the perspective on progress and decline that I have articulated entails a kind of political conservatism, especially when taken together with some of Wittgenstein's stated views on modern civilization.

5.2

In the midst of reflections on Jewishness and originality recorded in 1931, we find Wittgenstein making the following comment on his own thought:

> I think there is some truth in the idea that I am really only reproductive in my thinking. I think I have never *invented* a line of thinking but that it was always provided for me by someone else & I have done no more than passionately take it up for my work of clarification. That is how Boltzmann, Hertz, Schopenhauer, Frege, Russell, Kraus, Loos, Weininger, Spengler, Sraffa have influenced me.[5]

The appearance of Oswald Spengler's name on this list of those thinkers whom Wittgenstein acknowledges as sources of influence no doubt came as a surprise to many readers. In fact, however, as is shown by the following remark written in 1942 in the context of a discussion of mathematics, Spengler's thought had a lasting significance for Wittgenstein: "I just want to say: These people should not arrive at the view that they are making mathematical discoveries—but rather only physical discoveries. [How much indeed I am influenced by Spengler in my thinking.]"[6] Of course, to acknowledge influence is to say very little about its nature. To get clearer about this issue, therefore, I first want to summarize the main lines of a helpful account of this influence given by Rudolf Haller.

Haller maintains that it was not so much the *content* of Spengler's philosophy to which Wittgenstein was attracted but rather its *method*, which Haller characterizes as that of a "Gestalt analysis of history" or the "method of descriptive morphology."[7]

> The procedure for comparative research is to determine the archetypal forms taken by the passage of history, and to derive from them—per analogiam— statements that render the future predictable. Of course, these would not be the kinds of predictions that forecast the appearance of certain individual figures or the occurrence of particular events, but rather foretell the direction to be taken by the development of history: these are the content of morphological prognosis.[8]

Passages such as the following one from 1930 (which I have already quoted in the conclusion to part 1, on 99) certainly support the contention that Spengler's Gestalt analysis of history resonated strongly with Wittgenstein:

> Reading Spengler, *Decline* etc. and finding, despite much that is irresponsible in specifics, *many* genuinely significant thoughts. Much, perhaps most of it, touches on what I myself have often thought. The possibility of several self-contained systems which, once one has them, look as though one were a continuation of the other. And all of this also connects with the thought that we really don't know (or consider) how much can be taken from or given to humans.

We can perhaps see the influence of Spengler's method of descriptive morphology in Wittgenstein's criticisms of Sir James Frazer's anthropological study of magic. Many of these remarks were written just over a year after the above passage, where Wittgenstein writes that he is currently reading Spengler. An interesting fact that Haller points out is that most of *Philosophical Investigations* §122, a well-known remark on philosophical method, was taken from these same remarks on Frazer. In the original manuscript, the remark reads as follows:

> The concept of a perspicuous representation is of fundamental significance for us. It denotes the form of our representation (*Darstellungsform*), the way we look at things. (A kind of "World-view" as it is apparently typical of our time. Spengler.)
>
> This perspicuous representation imparts the understanding which consists precisely in the fact that we "see the connections." Hence the importance of finding *connecting links*.[9]

Wittgenstein brings the idea of a perspicuous representation to bear in his objections to Frazer's practice of understanding the magical rituals of his subjects as protoscientific theories. Doing so leads Frazer to see a seamless conceptual development from these practices to the theoretical activities comprising our modern scientific world view. Wittgenstein maintains, against Frazer, that such an interpretation distorts the anthropological record.

> But an hypothetical connecting link should in this case do nothing but direct the attention to the similarity, the relatedness, of the *facts*. As one might illustrate an internal relation of a circle to an ellipse by gradually converting an ellipse into a circle; *but not in order to assert that a certain ellipse actually, historically, had originated from a circle* (evolutionary hypothesis), but only in order to sharpen our eye for a formal connection.[10]

Wittgenstein thought Frazer's work was marred by modern prejudices, manifest in his inability to imagine how these magical practices might have shown up to these people, how they made sense to them in ways that most likely differed fundamentally from our modern scientific ways of conceptualizing the world: "The very idea of wanting to explain a practice—for example, the killing of the priest-king—seems wrong to me. All that Frazer does is to make them plausible to people who think as he does. It is very remarkable that in the final analysis all these practices are presented as, so to speak, pieces of stupidity."[11] In his failure to recognize that the capacity to set observations of nature into a scientific explanatory *Betrachtungsform* is not a given but rather a historically conditioned *achievement* involving specific intellectual and moral commitments, Frazer is blind to the possibility of others who may not have attained to or may not as of yet developed an interest in doing so.[12] According to Wittgenstein, this blindness underlies Frazer's inclination to explain magical practices as primitive theories. Moreover, Frazer's failure to see the significance of the fact that his understanding and that of the subjects of his research are each situated within their respective historical horizons leads him to set his "data" of their practices and that of his own modern scientific outlook into an overarching *Betrachtungsform* of progress. Wittgenstein writes, "The historical explanation, the explanation as an hypothesis of development, is only *one* way of assembling the data—of their synopsis. It is just as possible to see the data in their relation to one another and to embrace them in a general picture without putting it in the form of an hypothesis about temporal development."[13] Wittgenstein thus thought Frazer displayed a certain kind of modern parochialism in assuming that the different magical practices he writes about line up in any obvious way with scientific hypotheses and so too in assuming that there is any straightforward sense in which the refined theories of modern science constitute progress over those practices.[14]

Haller does not claim that Wittgenstein merely appropriates Spengler's method but rather that he modifies and employs it in a way not always clearly traceable to its source.[15] As Haller also makes clear, Wittgenstein not only appropriates aspects of Spengler's method, but "He reproaches Spengler for repeatedly making the mistake of extending the scope of statements true of the archetype of contemplation to the objects of contemplation."[16] Haller is pointing to an idea that is central to the later Wittgenstein's method, what we might call the idea of a "descriptive morphology" of language games. According to Wittgenstein, when particular examples ("prototype" [*Urbild*] or "paradigm" [*Paradigma*]) shape the way we think and talk about things, when they provide the form of our language game, then statements about these examples are not ordinary assertions but rather grammatical remarks that present to us the form of our discussion.[17] If we are clear about the role of these examples in our discussion, then we shall not be tempted to construe such grammatical remarks as necessary *truths*, nor shall we be puzzled when our ordinary assertions about the objects of our discourse seem to lack the *necessity* that belongs to the grammatical remarks that hold only of the examples. This is the main point of an observation recorded by Wittgenstein in 1937, much of which would later appear in modified form as *Philosophical Investigations* §131:

> The only way for us to avoid prejudice—or vacuity—in our claims, is to posit the ideal as what it is, namely an object of comparison [*Vergleichsobjekt*]—a measuring rod as it were—within our way of looking at things, and not as a preconception to which everything must conform. This namely is the dogmatism into which philosophy so easily degenerates. But then what is the relation between an approach like Spengler's and mine? Injustice in Spengler: The ideal doesn't

lose any of its dignity if it is posited as the principle determining the form of one's approach [*Betrachtungsform*]. A good unit of measurement.[18]

These considerations make it highly plausible that some of the most characteristic ideas of Wittgenstein's post-*Tractatus* writings were, in part, a result of his having reflected over many years on themes he found in Spengler. This, then, is his reason for including Spengler among those whose thinking he seized upon for his "work of clarification."

5.3

While Haller's account certainly helps to clarify the nature of Spengler's influence on Wittgenstein, there is an important point on which it could well be misleading.[19] This point pertains to the way in which, by Wittgenstein's lights, Spengler had fallen into confusion over what it means to take an evaluative standpoint toward one's own historical epoch. In the sketch for the foreword to *Philosophical Remarks*, Wittgenstein writes,

> This book is written for those who are in sympathy with the spirit in which it is written. This is, I believe, different from that of the prevailing European and American civilisation. The spirit of this civilisation, the expression of which is the industry, architecture, music, of present day fascism and socialism, is a spirit that is alien and uncongenial to the author. This is not a value judgement.[20]

With the above passage in mind, Haller confidently asserts,

> In the sketch of a preface to the *Philosophical Remarks* Wittgenstein clearly counts himself among the many *Kulturkritiker* close to Spengler, who, building upon the opposition between culture and civilisation, fall upon the civilisation of western Europe with Nietzschean ridicule.
> Wittgenstein's contempt for this form of life, and his preference for the traditional one, become clearly visible against the background of this opposition, although he hadn't wanted to pass *any* value judgments at all. There is, however, no question that the two thinkers met in their evaluations of the intellectual and spiritual situation of the time![21]

Spengler's evaluation of our modern intellectual and spiritual condition is what I would describe as a "metaphysically pessimistic" one. Spengler took his analysis of cultural decline in the West for something like an unconditioned description of a factual state of affairs, a state of affairs that he thought had come about as part of the inevitable process of birth, growth, and decay of the life of a culture. We read, for example, in *Decline of the West*,

> For every Culture has its own Civilization. . . . The Civilization is the inevitable destiny of the Culture. . . . Civilizations are the most external and artificial states of which a species of developed humanity is capable. They are a conclusion, the thing-become succeeding the thing-becoming, death following life, rigidity following expansion. . . . The transition from Culture to Civilization was accomplished for the Classical world in the fourth, for the Western in the nineteenth century.[22]

There is no shortage of biographical and textual evidence to support the claim that Wittgenstein tended to take a dark view of the modern world. To claim as Haller does, however, that "there is no question . . . that [Wittgenstein and Spengler] met in their evaluations of the intellectual and spiritual situation of the time" makes it seem as though Wittgenstein shared Spengler's metaphysically pessimistic outlook as well. And this gives us a distorted impression of what Wittgenstein actually thought.

To see why this is so, consider again a passage I discussed in the previous chapter, which comes from the same sketch to a foreword for *Philosophical Remarks* as the passage quoted above to which Haller refers: "Our civilization is characterised by the word progress. Progress is its form, it is not one of its properties that it makes progress. Typically it constructs. Its activity is to construct a more and more complicated structure. And even clarity is only a means to this end and not an end in itself." Now consider this description by Rush Rhees of Wittgenstein's participation in a discussion following the reading of a paper by a Professor Farrington on "Causal Laws of History," given in the 1940s:

> In the discussion Wittgenstein said that when there is a change in the conditions in which people live, we may call it progress because it opens up new opportunities. But in the course of this change, opportunities which were there before may be lost. In one way it was progress, in another it was decline. A historical change may be progress and also be ruin. There is no method of weighing one against the other to justify you in speaking of "progress on the whole."
>
> Farrington did not see how progress could also be ruin. What would be an example of this?

Wittgenstein: "Why just what you described when you said that the mining of iron and coal made it possible for industry to develop and at the same time scarred the valley with slagheaps and old machinery."

Farrington thought this was not a reason against saying that there has been progress on the whole. "With all the ugly sides of our civilisation, I am sure I would rather live as we do now than have to live as the cave man did."

Wittgenstein: "Yes of course you would. But would the cave man?"[23]

In using the word "form" above to describe the way the word "progress" characterizes our civilization, I read Wittgenstein in effect to be saying that he sees progress functioning as our modern *Betrachtungsform*.[24] This means that for him, the notion of progress shapes the way we tend to think and talk about things; it defines, if you like, our *Weltanschauung*. According to Wittgenstein, moreover, we fall into metaphysical confusion when we fail to distinguish the language that delineates the conceptual form of our discourse, its *Betrachtungsform*, from an unconditioned assertion of fact. This point is put succinctly in this remark from 1947: "Philosophical investigations: conceptual investigations. The essence of metaphysics: that the difference between factual and conceptual investigations is unclear to it. The metaphysical question always has the appearance of being a factual one, although the problem is a conceptual one."[25]

Such considerations, I take it, are the basis for his voicing skepticism toward speaking about "progress on the whole" in the conversation recorded by Rhees. For that way of putting things often goes hand in hand with a failure to recognize this distinction. To portray Wittgenstein, then, as sharing Spengler's metaphysical pessimism about cultural decline unnecessarily has him committing the very "injustice" of which he accuses Spengler in the passage quoted at the end of the last section, and it makes it seem as though he contradicts his own diagnosis of unclarity in Spengler's thought that he offers in the following remark from 1931:

Spengler could be better understood if he said: I am *comparing* different periods of culture with the lives of families; within the family there is a family resemblance, while you will also find a resemblance between members of different families; family resemblance differs from the other sort of resemblance in such and such ways, etc. What I mean is: we have to be told the object of comparison (*Vergleichsobjekt*), the object from which this way of viewing things is derived, so that prejudices do not constantly slip into the discussion. Because then we shall willy nilly ascribe what is true of the prototype of the approach (*Urbild der Betrachtung*) to the object to which we applying the approach as well; and we claim "*it must always be . . .*"

This comes about because we want to give the prototype's characteristics (*Merkmalen des Urbilds*) a foothold in the approach. But since we confuse prototype and object we find ourselves dogmatically conferring on the object properties which only the prototype necessarily possesses. On the other hand we think the approach (*Betrachtung*) will lack the generality we want to give it if it really holds only of the one case. But the prototype must just be presented for what it is; as characterising the whole approach and determining its form. In this way it stands at the head and is generally valid by virtue of determining the form of approach (*Form der Betrachtung*), not by virtue of a claim that everything which is true only of it holds for all the objects to which the approach is applied.

One should *thus* always ask when exaggerated dogmatic claims are made: What is actually true in this. Or again: In what case is that actually true.[26]

This is all to say that if Wittgenstein had actually shared what I am calling Spengler's metaphysical pessimism, it would have amounted to his committing the same mistake for which he repeatedly reproaches Spengler and that he considers characteristic of philosophical confusion. We should therefore be as suspicious of ascribing to him a belief about the idea of "decline on the whole" as he was of accepting the idea of "progress on the whole."

5.4

Yet cultural decline *is* an important theme for Wittgenstein. What we need is a better understanding of the role that it and related themes play in his thinking. We read earlier in remarks by Bouwsma and Toulmin that each shared a distinct impression that philosophical activity had a radically different significance for Wittgenstein than it did for many of his contemporaries. I would contend that Wittgenstein's concerns with the connection between culture and philosophy comprise a very substantial part of such impressions. In order to be clearer about this question, I believe we need to recognize two conceptually distinct levels at which these concerns may be at work in his outlook.

As we just saw, Wittgenstein was prepared to call progress the dominant form of our civilization, and he believed that the role of this form in our thinking remained largely obscure. Wittgenstein himself, however, was attracted to the concept of decline and was prepared to let it shape much of his own thinking about the contemporary West.[27] Now, his views on such matters could give rise to certain objections that might take the form of questions such as "How does he *know* that progress characterizes our civilization?" or "How does he *know* that in fact we are in decline?" or, perhaps even more forcefully, "How could he or anyone *possibly* know about such things?" A short answer to these questions is that Wittgenstein need not be understood as making knowledge claims in these cases. Instead, he can be understood to be doing something more akin to offering an *interpretative framework* that, in his view, makes sense of certain phenomena by providing a "perspicuous representation" of them. As passages such as this one make clear, Wittgenstein saw this kind of activity as importantly different from, and in some sense even prior to, acquiring knowledge or stating facts.

> What, however, does a conceptual investigation do? Is it a natural history of human concepts?—Now, natural history describes, let's say, plants and animals. But could it not be the case that plants had been described in all particulars, and now someone comes along who sees analogies in their structure which one had not seen before? That is, that *he establishes a new order in these descriptions*. He says, for example: "Don't compare this part with this, but rather with that!" (Goethe wanted to do something like this.) And in doing so he need not speak of ancestry, though the new arrangement could give scientific investigation a new direction. He says "Don't look at it this way!"—and now that can have various advantages and consequences.[28]

Articulation of such an interpretative framework, moreover, is given by providing examples:

> If we were asked about the essence of punishment, or about the essence of revolution, or about the essence of knowledge, or of cultural decay, or the sense for music,—then we would not try to specify something that all of the cases had in common,—that which they all are intrinsically—that is to say an ideal that is *embodied* in all of them; but rather examples, as it were, foci of variation.[29]

Furthermore, Wittgenstein was aware that the inclination to assemble the facts one way instead of another, to have one's discourse shaped by *this* prototype, to provide these examples and not those, *already* presupposes specific commitments. This point emerges somewhat haltingly in this exchange with Rush Rhees recorded during a 1938 lecture course on aesthetics, in which Rhees asked Wittgenstein some question about his "theory" of deterioration.

> Do you think I have a theory? Do you think I'm saying what deterioration is? What I do is describe different things called deterioration. I might approve deterioration—"All very well your fine musical culture; I'm very glad children don't

learn harmony now." [Rhees: Doesn't what you say imply a preference for using "deterioration" in certain ways?] All right, if you like, but this by the way—no, it is no matter. My example of deterioration is an example of something I know, perhaps something I dislike—I don't know. "Deterioration" applies to a tiny bit I may know.[30]

The point is more clearly formulated in this later remark from 1949: "My own thinking about art and values is far more disillusioned than would have been *possible* for someone 100 years ago. However that does not mean that it is more correct on that account. It only means that there are examples of decline in the forefront of my mind, which were not in the *forefront* for those people then."[31] I do not mean to suggest that Wittgenstein believed description to be impossible in philosophy but only that there is no reason to believe that he considered his motivations for engaging in various types of philosophical description to be morally and aesthetically neutral. Wittgenstein clearly does have an open distaste for many of modernity's realities, and surely this is true in part because he regards them as destructive of particular values, institutions, and practices that he cherishes. Yet although Wittgenstein shows little sympathy for much of the modern West, this should not be understood to mean that he believed he occupied a position from which it made sense to render an unconditional judgment that, on the whole, the practices and values of the present age are corrupt. As we have seen, he is suspicious of the very idea of such an unconditioned assertion "on the whole."[32] The type of nonmetaphysical cultural pessimism that I am here attributing to Wittgenstein simply amounts to the coherent mourning of the passing of one set of substantive values and practices and the emergence in its place of another set that one judges to be inferior by comparison.

But I want to argue, in addition, that Wittgenstein's concern with cultural decline should not only be understood in these terms. In the previous chapter, I claimed that the attempt in the remarks on rule-following to make manifest the incoherence of a certain mythology of rationality is of a piece with bringing out the philosophical significance of our acquisition of a second nature via a process of training, education, and cultural formation (*Bildung*). Since this attempt will necessarily foreground how the kind of understanding transmitted in this process is constituted largely by inherited shared practices, Charles Taylor calls the task of overcoming the "irresistibly monological" view of rationality that is essential to this mythology the "inherently holistic" thrust of Wittgenstein's philosophy.[33]

The background understanding we share, interwoven with our practices and ways of relating, isn't necessarily something we partake in as individuals. That is, it can be part of the background understanding of a certain practice or meaning that it is not mine but ours; and it can indeed be "ours" in a number of ways: as something intensely shared, which binds a community; or as something quite impersonal, where we act just as "anyone" does. Bringing in the background allows us to articulate the ways in which our form of agency is nonmonological, in which the seat of certain practices and understandings is precisely *not* the individual but one of the common spaces between.[34]

Noticing that the picture of rationality manifest in the view of rules as rails also carries with it an inherently atomist conception of human agency that blots out the common spaces between us allows me to point out the second, and I think more profound, level where we ought to see the relevance of Wittgenstein's cultural concerns for motivating his later work. It also lets me connect my discussions of this and the previous chapter with what I have said earlier about the *Tractatus* in such a way that helps to fill in an important line of continuity in Wittgenstein's work in philosophy.

I have claimed that the ethical point of the *Tractatus* is to be found in that book's attempt to reawaken a sense of wonder in the reader (which Wittgenstein variously characterizes as "wonder at the existence of the world," "wonder at the existence of language," and to which I added "wonder at the fit between language (or mind) and world"). I have also argued that at the heart of the book's ethical point are a set of cultural concerns that were a constant in Wittgenstein's self-understanding as a philosopher. If these claims are true, it should be possible to say something about how these concerns inform his later thought. Now, as I think comes through in this remark from 1947, the task of fostering an openness to wonder remained an integral part of Wittgenstein's understanding of philosophy throughout his life.

> The mathematician too can of course marvel at the miracles (the crystal) of nature; but can he do it, once a problem has arisen about what he sees? Is it really possible as long as the object he finds awe-inspiring or gazes at with awe is shrouded in a philosophical fog?
>
> I could imagine someone admiring trees, & also the shadows, or reflections of trees, which he mistakes for trees. But if he should once tell himself that these are not after all trees and if it becomes a problem for him what they are, or what relation they have to trees, then his admiration will have suffered a rupture, that will now need healing.[35]

And Norman Malcolm reports his belief that "a certain feeling of amazement that *anything should exist at all*, was sometimes experienced by Wittgenstein, not only during the *Tractatus* period, but also when I knew him."[36] Still, what I think strikes many readers as the generally more secular spirit animating *Philosophical Investigations* (contrasted with Wittgenstein's willingness to employ more overtly religious terms in the *Tractatus*) seems to justify Stanley Cavell's choice of the more secular-sounding term "surprise" when be claims that

> what motivates Wittgenstein to philosophize, what surprises him, is the plain fact that certain creatures have speech at all, that they can say things at all. No doubt it is not clear how one might go about becoming surprised by such a fact. It is like being surprised by the fact that there is such a thing as the world. But I do not say that Wittgenstein's thoughts demand that you grasp these surprises before you begin studying those thoughts. On the contrary, I believe that such experiences are part of the teaching which those thoughts are meant to produce.[37]

If I imagine his meaning "surprise" at the extreme end of that word's register, then I want to say that what Cavell says here is just right. Although I won't claim that the theme of wonder per se can be located in the pages of the *Investigations*, I want to try to justify, so to speak, nudging Cavell's word choice from "surprise" over to something stronger, partly by developing one of his own thoughts, in order to show how something *essentially preliminary* to wonder can be located in the *Investigations*.[38] And I want to show how this is an interesting fact about that book and what it means in the overall context of Wittgenstein's authorship.

When I wrote in chapter 3 that the metaphysical assumptions about language built into the method of the *Tractatus* preclude its reader from attaining to the very same authentic relation to language that it was supposed to help him secure, I emphasized that this was because of a certain obtuseness in the book's understanding of language, manifest in its distance from the particular ways in which we try to make sense with what we say. I could have also said that the *Tractatus* leaves almost entirely out of view what we've read Taylor describe above as the "common spaces in between." The *Investigations* are, of course, famous for Wittgenstein's insistent calling attention to the diversity of linguistic use and for (self-)criticism of the philosopher's tendency to nourish his thinking with only one kind of example.[39] But the point of his doing so is not merely to show us both that our philosophy suffers from an incomplete taxonomy of speech acts[40] but from a sense that the resolution of philosophical problems requires the cultivation of an appreciation of the myriad purposes that our linguistic forms can serve and how these purposes are woven together in the complicated context of significance he calls a form of life.[41]

A form of life is constituted by common matters of concern that inform the shared actions and practices that let us open up a common world, a common world, furthermore, in terms of which we understand ourselves and our common matters of concern. Recall that as part of the dialectic in the remarks on rule-following, a demand is made on us to imagine the intelligibility of developing a numerical series according to a rule completely independently of our responses to the relevant features of a particular context and completely independently of the overall relevance or significance that such an activity as rule-following has in our lives. This is the demand that the disengaged picture of rationality forces on us. But rather than leading to skepticism about the rationality of this activity, our losing our grip on the rationality of what should be this paradigmatically rational activity as a consequence of trying to meet the requirements of the picture is supposed to let us come to see the picture itself as nothing more than an empty mythology (albeit, a powerful one). But to show that rule-following and our uses of words more generally cannot be understood apart from what shows up as relevant to us lands us in the conclusion that speaking is unintelligible apart from what shows up as important to us. Cavell thus writes,

> What we seem headed for is an idea that what can comprehensibly be said is what is found to be worth saying. This explicitly makes our agreement in judgment, our attunement expressed through criteria, agreement in valuing. So that what can be communicated, say a fact, depends upon agreement in valuing, rather than the other way around. This is what our speech acts come to or come from.[42]

The centrality of practices, attunements, or forms of life in Wittgenstein's later philosophy may sound like a recipe for antirealism and so may appear to deprive the world of its objectivity. To see why this is not so, I want to go back to this passage from McDowell that I quoted in chapter 4 (118).[43]

> When [Wittgenstein] says, "What has to be accepted, the given, is—so one could say—forms of life," his point is not to adumbrate a philosophical response, on such lines, to supposedly good questions about the possibility of meaning and understanding or intentionality generally, but to remind us of something we can take in the proper way only after we are equipped to see that such questions are based on a mistake. His point is to remind us that the natural phenomenon that is normal human life is itself already shaped by meaning and understanding.

McDowell's primary point here is that it is a mistake to interpret Wittgenstein's invoking of terms like "form of life" as part of a constructive, theoretical response to a genuine problem. But I want to focus on something implicit in McDowell's overall therapeutic point and apart from which I don't believe that point can really be made: to talk of normal human *life* as *already* shaped by meaning and understanding is also to imply the existence of the world in which that normal human life is lived, a world without which there can be no talk of normal human life, a world that (normally) neither forces its meanings on us (realism) nor on which we force our meanings (antirealism). There is nothing wrong with taking the appreciation of common spaces, attunements, and forms of life as aimed at bringing about a peace of mind we find when our minds are no longer bothered by questions like "How can a mere sign tell me what I am supposed to do now?" But my suggestion here is that Wittgenstein would have wanted these considerations to draw us further. Explaining what I mean by this will let me make my point about locating something essentially preliminary to wonder in the *Investigations*.

In one sense, I am trying to describe a way of reading the *Investigations* as in essence having the same ethical point as the *Tractatus*. But I am also trying to bring out that the *Investigations*'s travels "over a wide field of thought criss-cross in every direction"[44] should be understood as a step back from or, perhaps better, a slowing up in the attempt to achieve that ethical aim. Even if we don't read the *Investigations*'s discussions of ostensive definition, universals, private language, the nature of language, the nature of philosophy, rule-following, and so on as landing us in some form of antirealism, the perspective on our mind-world predicament it leaves us with is hard to occupy and harder to assimilate in our times. I think this is largely because this perspective doesn't just involve some select subset of procedures in which our confidence is (or at any rate, used to be) high but implicates our whole complicated background of practices and commitments, where the soft spots seem to outnumber the hard. If there is necessity here, it does not really pertain to any one particular concept or practice that is necessary for opening up a world. Rather, we seem saddled with the necessity of there being a conventional (rational) animal with attunements and common spaces.[45] The problem is, of course, that accepting our being at the same time agents and victims of the world's intelligibility seems to defy explanation in the way we want our explanations to work. But instead of seeing the fit between mind and world (and so meaning) as a "phenomenon" for which we have so far failed to find a scientific explanation, I am claiming that for the later Wittgenstein no less than the early, "the existence of language" is the terminus we moderns are left to acknowledge, and even, perhaps, to regard as miraculous.[46]

If we connect these considerations to the disengaged view of rationality under attack in the remarks on rule-following, we can say that a mythology of what it is to be a rational agent blocks us not only from recognizing the broader range of commitments that give our forms of speech the contours they have but also blocks us from even acknowledging what can be the legitimate motivations behind taking the disengaged stance of instrumental reason itself.[47] As Taylor notes, "Another possibility is systematically blocked out: an articulation of things which would lay out their meanings for us (and hence where the discourse would not be that of science) but where the meanings would not be merely human-centered (and hence the discourse would not be one of self-expression.)"[48] Instead, the world shows up as a disenchanted "how things are anyway." We enter into a vicious circle where it becomes nearly impossible to teach the habits of thought required for responding to features of our lives and world not envisaged from the disengaged stance and where the world increasingly loses any power to evoke those responses in us. More than other virtues, reverence as a capacity for wonder suffers here, because in a certain sense it is a "metavirtue" that concerns our response to the whole of our life and world and, moreover, that depends on our recognizing there being a certain "subset" of virtues and values that lie at the basis of the world's being intelligible for us. So the mythology of rationality manifested concretely in the hegemony of certain construals of technology and natural science that dominate modernity blocks the very attitude that Wittgenstein thought characterized the highest way of living for human beings, individually and collectively.

A mark of Wittgenstein's later thought, then, is the idea that "authentic" clarity in philosophy is inseparable from our acceptance that the meaning of our words is in a certain sense dependent on what shows up as mattering to us. (And a major goal of his later writing is to find a way of making this acceptance as intellectually palatable as possible.) If I am right, moreover, the hope of reawakening wonder and reverence for the world and our place in it was something he saw as the most important reason for working toward that clarity throughout his philosophical life. More generally, success in this project assumes that at any time a culture has enough (and how many is enough is probably impossible to tell) members who can learn and assimilate the virtues required to respond to and articulate what matters to its members in a way that matters. But I think that the observation that nothing guarantees that a culture's reserves of such a capacity are limitless would have struck Wittgenstein as just right.

> If we formulate the idea that valuing underwrites asserting as the idea that interest informs telling or talking generally, then we may say that the degree to which you talk of things, and talk in ways, that hold no interest for you, or listen to

what you cannot imagine the talker's caring about, in the way he carries the care, is the degree to which you consign yourself to nonsensicality, stupefy yourself. (Of course your lack of interest may be your fault, come from your own commitment to boredom.) I think of this consignment as a form not so much as dementia as of what amentia ought to mean, a form of mindlessness. It does not appear unthinkable that the bulk of an entire culture, call it the public discourse of the culture, the culture thinking aloud about itself, hence believing itself to be talking philosophy, should become ungovernably inane. In such a case you would not say that the Emperor has no clothes; in part because what you really want to say is that there is no Emperor; but in greater part because in neither case would anyone understand you.[49]

What I meant when I spoke above of a deeper level to Wittgenstein's concern with cultural decline comes to this: Wittgenstein's complaint against contemporary Western civilization does not primarily concern its content so much as its *lack* of content.[50] This amounts to much more than mere disdain for the actual values and practices of contemporary technological culture. Putting my point in terms borrowed from Heidegger, Wittgenstein is not concerned with cultural decay as mere "destruction," as an unfortunate yet, as it were, "merely empirical" event to which we bear witness.[51] Rather, I think he also envisioned a kind of spreading "devastation" wrought by the very unfolding of the internal logic of the West's current set of dominant practices such that no genuine and significant public possibilities for action show up for those who lead their lives within the field of those practices. It is such a concern that I take him to be voicing in the sketch for a foreword to *Philosophical Remarks*, which I quoted from earlier:

> Culture is like a great organisation which assigns to each of its members his place, at which he can work in the spirit of the whole, and his strength can with a certain justice be measured by his success as understood within that whole. In a time without culture, however, forces are fragmented and the strength of the individual is wasted through overcoming of opposing forces and frictional resistances; it is not manifest in the distance travelled but rather perhaps in the heat generated through the overcoming of frictional resistances. But energy is still energy and even if the spectacle afforded by this age is not the coming into being of a great work of culture in which the best contribute to the same great end, so much as the unimposing spectacle of a crowd whose best members pursue purely private ends, still we must not forget that the spectacle is not what matters.
>
> Even if it is clear to me then that the disappearance of a culture does not signify the disappearance of human value but simply of certain means of expressing

this value, still the fact remains that I contemplate the current of European civili-sation with no sympathy, without understanding its aims if any. So I am really writing for friends who are scattered throughout the corners of the globe.[52]

Despite what appears to be the striking gap between the themes taken up in this passage and those addressed in the text of *Philosophical Remarks*, Wittgenstein had conceived of the work as being concerned with a fragmentation of forces characteristic of our time and, as he says in the foreword to the published work, as written in a spirit "different from the one that informs the vast stream of European and American civilisation in which all of us stand."[53] I think no less is true of *Philosophical Investigations*, where a central philosophical aim is the overcoming of a fragmenting mythology of rationality, a mythology that perhaps paradoxically gets transmitted along with our contemporary *Bildung* yet, in being passed off as mere common sense, blocks an appreciation of our shared life with language and, with that, the possibility of wonder. In the preface to that book, Wittgenstein expresses his hope that his work might, even "in the darkness of this time . . . bring light into one brain or another." But since, as we saw above, he took the dominant form of our civilization to be an empty, metaphysical conception of progress that is tied to the mythology of rationality and since "the main point about progress is that it always seems greater than it really is," this was of course "not likely."[54]

5.5

My emphasis above on the relation between Wittgenstein's thought and cultural decline should not be taken to imply that I believe that he had no philosophical interest in the individual. On the contrary, throughout his life he retained a deep interest in the individual person as a locus of philosophical concern. His words in the sketch for a foreword to *Philosophical Remarks* concerning the plight of the individual in an age without culture suggests to me that a sharp distinction between the plight of the individual and the state of the culture would be some-thing he would have regarded as artificial. The two are intimately intertwined in his thought. In chapter 4, I focused on how the view of rules as rails is implicated in sustaining a metaphysical conception of progress that Wittgenstein thought characterizes our culture's self-understanding. In this chapter, my focus has been on how Wittgenstein sees this same view of rationality as implicated in block-ing us from the possibility of an experience of genuine shared commitments. Put-ting these two ideas together yields the conclusion that Wittgenstein thought that a culture whose form is a metaphysical conception of progress, if not entirely leveling and nihilistic, is no more than an "unimposing spectacle" where "the strength of the individual is wasted through overcoming of opposing forces and frictional resistances." In the final two sections of this chapter, I briefly consider the relevance of Wittgenstein's attitude toward religion for my discussion and some possible political implications of what I have said here about his later thought.

In the previous section, I tried to give a partial articulation in broadly non-confessional terms of the relations between meaning, value, virtue, and openness to wonder in Wittgenstein's later philosophy. Nevertheless, for Wittgenstein, these issues were also connected to his lifelong reflections on religion and the possibility of a religious commitment in more traditional terms. Anyone who really knew Wittgenstein well recognized not only that the subject of religion had enormous significance for him but also that his own relation to religion was difficult and hard to pin down. The ambiguity of the place of religion in Wittgenstein's life and in his attitude toward it comes out nowhere more succinctly than in Drury's oft discussed recounting of Wittgenstein's telling him that "I am not a religious man but I cannot help seeing every problem from a religious point of view."[55] My discussions in chapter 2 and immediately above of the importance of wonder for understanding Wittgenstein's thought account for a great deal of what I take to be the relevance of "religious point of view" in this statement (although I realize that my willingness to allow the expression "religious" to be used in this way is likely to arouse strong opposition from different quarters). In any case, it's also true that Wittgenstein spent an enormous amount of energy reading, reflecting, writing, and discussing religion in its confessional, denominational, and especially Christian modes. Although it's clear that he had great respect for Catholicism (he even seems to have contemplated becoming a priest at some point),[56] if I had to characterize his own engagement with religion, I would say that his attitude tended more toward certain strands of Protestantism, even toward something akin to pietism.[57] But there are important qualifications and details needed in order to make this characterization clearer and to relate it to my discussion above.

Paul Engelmann described in his memoir a feature of his outlook on life that he felt most attracted Wittgenstein to him and that Wittgenstein shared:

In me Wittgenstein unexpectedly met a person who, like many members of the younger generation, suffered acutely under the discrepancy between the world as it is and as it ought to be according to his lights, but who tended also to seek the source of that discrepancy within, rather than outside, himself. This was an attitude which Wittgenstein had not encountered elsewhere and which, at the same time, was vital for any true understanding or meaningful discussion of his own spiritual condition.[58]

I think Engelmann's perceptive observation of his friend from the time of World War I not only pinpoints what would be a lasting character trait but also provides a helpful way to think about his relation to religion from that period until his death.[59] One of the most important possibilities Wittgenstein saw in religion, one of the most important of his needs that he hoped it would fulfill, was its potential to allow him to heal his relation to the world.[60] This attitude to religion as fundamentally involving inner individual change, combined with his general alienation from his fellows, no doubt made institutionalized religion, especially more communal and liturgical traditions, difficult for him to take part in. Jim Klagge puts this point nicely:

> For Wittgenstein . . . religion has two aspects, the inner aspect—one's spiritual relationship to God—and the outer aspect—one's participation in ceremony, obedience and loving behavior. Not surprisingly, Wittgenstein's engagement with religion consisted almost entirely of the former. The latter was lost on, or more difficult for, an exile without a community. Thus, I believe, we get Wittgenstein's ambiguous attitude towards religion in his own life.[61]

An exchange from around 1930 that Drury relates captures this aspect of Wittgenstein's attitude to religion especially well:

> Drury: "Isn't it important that there should be ordained priests to carry on this tradition? That was my idea in wanting to be ordained."
> Wittgenstein: "At first sight it would seem a wonderful idea that there should be in every village someone who stood for these things. But it hasn't worked out that way at all. For all you and I can tell, the religion of the future will be without any priests or ministers. I think one of the things you and I have to learn is that we have to live without the consolation of belonging to a church. If you feel you must belong to some organization, why don't you join the Quakers?"
> The very next morning he came to see me, to say that he had been quite wrong to suggest my becoming a Quaker. I was to forget that he ever mentioned it. "As if nowadays any one organization was better than another."
> Wittgenstein: "Of one thing I am certain. The religion of the future will have to be extremely ascetic; and by that I don't mean just going without food and drink."[62]

Wittgenstein's abhorrence of systematic theology would no doubt have distanced him even further from Catholic and much Protestant thought. A remark recorded by Drury is fairly typical of his attitude: "The symbolisms of Catholicism are wonderful beyond words. But any attempt to make it into a philosophical system is offensive."[63] Indeed, he tended to think that Christianity had nothing to do with the truth of its propositions at all.

> Christianity is not based on a historical truth; rather, it offers us a (historical) narrative and says: now believe! But not, believe this narrative with the belief appropriate to a historical narrative, rather: believe, through thick and thin, which you can do only as the result of a life. *Here you have a narrative, don't take the same attitude to it as you take to other historical narratives!* Make a *quite different* place in your life for it.—There is nothing *paradoxical* about that!"
>
> Queer as it sounds: The historical accounts in the Gospels might, historically speaking, be demonstrably false and yet belief would lose nothing by this: *not*, however, because it concerns "universal truths of reason"! Rather, because historical proofs (the historical proof-game) is irrelevant to belief. This message (the Gospels) is seized on by men believingly (i.e. lovingly). *That* is the certainty characterizing this particular acceptance-as-true, not something else.
>
> A believer's relation to these narratives is *neither* the relation to historical truth (probability), *nor yet* that to a theory consisting of "truths of reason." There is such a thing.—(We have quite different attitudes even to different species of what we call fiction!).[64]

Clearly, much of this remark pertains to questions specifically associated with Christianity (and perhaps to other so-called historical religions). Still, I think that the central idea in what Wittgenstein says here about Christianity characterized his entire view of religion, namely, that in its essence it is not concerned with claims to historical truth or about the "furniture of reality." Instead, religion concerns the fundamental transformation in one's life that can come about when, as he puts it, one makes a quite different place in one's life for religious discourse. He thought of that different place as the grammar of one's experience of the world.[65]

> It appears to me that a religious belief could only be (something like) a passionate committing oneself to a system of coordinates. Hence although it's *belief*, it's really a way of living, or a way of judging life. It's passionately taking up *this* interpretation. And so instruction in a religious faith would have to be portraying, describing that system of reference and at the same time appealing to the conscience. And these together would have to result finally in the one under

instruction himself, of his own accord, passionately taking up that system of reference. It would be as though someone were on the one hand to let me see my hopeless situation, on the other depict the *rescue-anchor*, until of my own accord, or at any rate not led by the hand of the *instructor*, I were to rush up and seize it.[66]

In chapter 2, I criticized one part of Conant's and Kremer's interpretations of the *Tractatus* when I argued for a serious disanalogy between the writings of St. Paul, St. Augustine, and Kierkegaard, on the one hand, and the *Tractatus*, on the other. My argument was that the relevant difference is that, unlike the works of these three other writers, the *Tractatus* makes no attempt to point to something outside the self, a paradigm figure like Jesus for example, that might confer the kind of justification the self requires but cannot provide for itself out of its own resources. Of course, there is no mention in the *Investigations*, either, of anything like a concrete religious figure. But that book's emphasis on learning and on the multiplicity of language games, including its emphasis on the way in which models or paradigms can function in those language games, makes it much easier to think about the role of religious instruction in our overall thinking about thought and language. I mention this because I think the passage quoted above shows many of these characteristic marks of Wittgenstein's later philosophy as they relate specifically to religious discourse. Apart from whether this is the proper attitude for seizing or being seized by a religious symbol system, and apart from whether it correctly describes the way things look to participants from within a religious practice, I think Wittgenstein saw religions as essentially grammars of wonder, and so as holding out the promise of sustaining an openness to wonder, not least by providing a vehicle for its expression.[67] Religions were "systems of coordinates" for giving direction to a life fundamentally characterized above all by reverence, which Wittgenstein felt was the highest kind of human life to lead.

Wittgenstein was never successful in making the grammar of Christianity his own, and until the end of his life he often experienced the absence of a religious commitment in his life as the ache of an unmet need and the failure of an unfinished task.[68] There is no question of my attempting an explanation of this failure. But I do want to draw attention to a feature of Wittgenstein's personal struggles with religion that seems relevant in light of my discussion above. This concerns a way in which his own engagement with Christianity goes to some extent against the grain of the sometimes robust "Aristotelian" strands running through much of his later thought, including through much of what he said and wrote about religion itself.[69] I mean that turning purely inward in the pursuit of personal transformation seems to ignore the social context necessary for acquiring the virtues needed to adopt a grammar of wonder. I should make clear that what I am saying here is not dependent on taking a "communitarian" reading of rule-following or a behaviorist interpretation of the remarks on private language and then applying these readings to Wittgenstein's religious pursuits. Nor do I mean to suggest the necessity or superiority of more communal or liturgical forms of religious life and worship. I am not quarrelling here with the mere idea that a competent mastery of a religious practice might allow someone to "go on by himself," as it were. But without instruction in a way of life informed by a grammar of wonder, it's questionable how much friction an individual will be able to generate, especially during a time of the "fragmentation of forces."[70] If culture is the home of wonder or, at any rate, of the wonder language game, then speaking ethical nonsense has its conventions too; even Augustine needed a tradition. On the other hand, if Wittgenstein recognized his situation all along, then there is something of the tragic in his having felt an infinite need while knowing he was incapable of entering into a way of life that could heal it.

> Tradition is not something that anyone can pick up, it's not a thread that someone can pick up, if and where he pleases; any more than you can choose your own ancestors.
>
> Someone who has no tradition and would like to have one, is like an unhappy lover.
>
> The happy lover and the unhappy lover both have their own particular pathos.
>
> But it is harder to be good unhappily in love than happily in love.[71]

5.6

It may seem obvious to some readers that the directions in Wittgenstein's thinking that I have been tracing out here justify the impression some have had that his work expresses or supports a form of political and social conservatism. Recall from chapter 4 something Baker and Hacker say of the motto to *Philosophical Investigations*: "In its original context it expresses such negative views on progress as would harmonize with W.'s own repudiation of this aspect, and this ideal, of European culture." The wording and lack of elaboration leads me to suspect that it is simply being taken for granted here that the motto is an expression of Wittgenstein's endorsement of the antiprogressive views he finds espoused in Nestroy's play, views we can assume "harmonize" with his own.[72] There is certainly no shortage of remarks or recorded conversations that might be seen as forming the basis for such an assumption.[73] Nevertheless, I want to close by giving some reasons for not making it.

A first step in defusing any "charge" of conservatism against Wittgenstein is simply to admit the obvious fact that he was attracted to the thought of many writers who, in one way or another, can fairly be classified as conservative.[74] But interest, attraction—even applause—should not be confused with endorsement.[75] To do so is to forget just how much creative and intellectual achievement comes about through very complicated pathways of appropriation. For example, despite that Wittgenstein includes the name of the archconservative Spengler among those whose work influenced him, there is no reason to conclude from this that he merely adopted Spengler's philosophical or political views. There are, on the other hand, many good reasons for thinking that Wittgenstein nearly always introduced profound modifications into whichever line of thinking he took up for his work of clarification.

Yet this point alone may not dispel the notion that the work of conservative thinkers like Spengler was not merely fodder for Wittgenstein's thought, and it will not necessarily remove the widespread impression that Wittgenstein shared too much of their conservative spirit for this to be the case. So the conclusion can still be drawn that Wittgenstein was a political conservative of one kind or another.[76] But we need not draw this conclusion if it is possible to embrace the spirit of someone's thought, all the while rejecting the content, in this case the politics, of that thought. A story about Dostoyevsky's work as the publisher of the political and literary magazine *Time* may help illustrate what I mean.

> Throughout the nineteenth century a fierce debate raged in Russia between westward-looking reformers and czarist conservatives. At issue were the condition of the serfs, the authority of the czar. In his editorial for the opening issue of *Time* in 1861, Dostoyevsky makes the strange claim that what will distinguish his paper from others is that, unlike his political opponents, he is really convinced of what he is saying, even if it may sound as though taken from a "copybook of maxims." In the following editorials he goes on to attack the ideas of Westernized liberals, while sympathizing with their generous spirit, and to support the conservative ideas of the czarist camp while attacking their reactionary harshness.... No idea can be judged without consideration of the mentality that anchors it in reality.[77]

Without denying the difficulties we may have in assimilating Dostoyevsky's attitude toward political questions, the important thing in the present context is the possibility that Wittgenstein conceived of his own position in structurally the same way. In a passage from the sketch for a foreword to *Philosophical Remarks* quoted in chapter 4 (122–23), Wittgenstein states that it is the *spirit* in which he writes that is different from that of the typical Western scientist. Earlier in the same sketch, one reads that it is the *spirit* of American and European civilization that is unsympathetic and alien to him.[78] I take it that what attracted Wittgenstein to certain conservative thinkers was a certain sensitivity to history, practice, and tradition. And he made no secret of the disdain he felt for those in whom he found such sensitivity lacking.[79] But these considerations make it possible to postpone the question of whose (if anyone's) actual policies Wittgenstein endorsed and so make it unnecessary to think that he was a political conservative.[80]

In the broader context of my discussion, however, the main reason for opposing the idea that what I have said automatically licenses an ascription of some kind of political conservatism to Wittgenstein is that this ascription has little basis if the "ideal" of European (and American) culture that he "repudiates" is a *metaphysical* conception of progress and, indeed, one that is symptomatic of a confusion: that the validity of our (nongrammatical) ordinary assertions about progress can be secured, as it were, completely independently of any of our actual determinations of what counts as progress. This confusion is in fact no more than a recapitulation of the mythological demand on rationality critiqued in the rule-following remarks, the demand that our understanding of the rule be conceptually independent, both of those responses that we have previously accepted as being in accord with the rule and of all further possible moves we could give. An important consequence of these considerations is that we should realize that there is nothing mysterious or inherently wrong with using the word "progress" or, for that matter, its opposite, "decline." (And had Wittgenstein taken the latter to be the form of our civilization, identical considerations would apply to it.) We read at *Investigations* §116: "What *we* do is to bring words back from their metaphysical to their everyday use." I believe that Wittgenstein hoped one of the true marks of progress in the *Investigations* would be its ability to clarify our relationship to the *Betrachtungsform* "progress," thus allowing us to see how a lack of clarity distorts our view in and, even more importantly, out of philosophy. In the present context, this means helping us to see how the everyday, nonmetaphysical uses of "progress," "decline," and related terms can do all the work we need for them to do in the arenas of politics and social criticism.[81]

6

THE FATE OF METAPHYSICS

Are we dealing with errors and difficulties that are as old as language?
Are they, so to speak, sicknesses that are tied to language, or are they of a
special nature, characteristic of our civilization?

6.1

I take it to be a central task of Wittgenstein's philosophy to undermine certain mythological conceptions of rationality that tend to hold us captive in philosophy, and I have been arguing that one of his primary motivations for attempting this task is his sense of the corrosive effect that such conceptions have on a society uncritically beholden to them.[1] This last chapter explores a related question: how did Wittgenstein understand our relation to the philosophical problems that arise from these mythological conceptions once we have a clearer picture of the connections between the mythology and the problems? More specifically, I discuss the suggestion, made independently by John McDowell and Stanley Cavell, that Wittgenstein believed the problems of philosophy to be so fundamentally rooted in our humanity that any freedom from metaphysical quandaries one may enjoy can at best be temporary.[2]

An immediate reason for being suspicious of the idea that McDowell and Cavell attribute to Wittgenstein is that it can seem to involve some fairly hefty knowledge claims about human nature. While this suspicion may be invited by how Cavell and McDowell have expressed themselves on this matter, it may in fact be directed at a straw man. Read more charitably, Cavell and McDowell need not be understood as offering straightforward knowledge claims but rather as putting forth an interpretation of a striking phenomenon: the tenacity of metaphysical problems.[3] But quite apart from the overall validity this view may have as an interpretation of the relation between human beings and metaphysics, there is the question of whether it is what Wittgenstein actually held. My aim here, therefore, is not to offer a particular competing diagnosis according to which what actually accounts for the "will to philosophy" in us is transient. Nor do I argue that Cavell's and McDowell's interpretations are actually *inconsistent* with, for example, the text of *Philosophical Investigations*.[4] Rather, I wish simply to argue that there are good reasons for doubting Cavell's and McDowell's positions and for believing that Wittgenstein believed it possible to abandon metaphysics.[5] After providing an overview of Cavell's and McDowell's views on this issue, I try to make the case for thinking that Wittgenstein believed it possible to let go of the Western metaphysical tradition as one perhaps necessary step in a process of a cultural transformation that was deeply important to him.

6.2

McDowell's view is presented toward the end of *Mind and World*, in a passage that I give here in its entirety.

> In the lecture I credit Wittgenstein with the aspiration of seeing through the apparent need for ordinary philosophy. This needs to be taken with care. I do not mean to suggest that Wittgenstein seriously contemplates a state of affairs in which ordinary philosophy no longer takes place. The intellectual roots of the anxieties that ordinary philosophy addresses are too deep for that. This point comes out dramatically in the multiplicity of voices in Wittgenstein's later writing, its dialogical character. The voices that need to be calmed down, recalled to sobriety, are not alien voices; they give expression to impulses he finds, or at least can imagine finding, in himself. When he writes, "The real discovery is the one that makes me capable of stopping doing philosophy when I want to" (*Philosophical Investigations*, §133), we should not take him to be envisaging a post-philosophical culture (an idea that is central to Rorty's thinking). He is not even envisaging a future for himself in which he is definitely cured of the philosophical impulse. The impulse finds peace only occasionally and temporarily.
>
> But I do not think it follows that there can be no role, in a style of thinking that is genuinely Wittgensteinian in spirit, for the sort of diagnostic move I propose in the lectures. What I suggest is that our philosophical anxieties are due to the intelligible grip on our thinking of a modern naturalism, and we can work at loosening that grip. It is a way of making this suggestion vivid to picture a frame of mind in which we have definitely shrugged off the influences on our thinking that lead to philosophical anxieties, even if we do not suppose we could ever have such a frame of mind as a permanent and stable possession. Even so, this identification of a source for our apparent difficulties can be one of our resources

for overcoming recurrences of the philosophical impulse: recurrences that we know there will be.[6]

Something in what McDowell says here that presents a slight complication for my discussion can be brought into focus by juxtaposing these two fragments: "I do not mean to suggest that Wittgenstein seriously contemplates a state of affairs in which ordinary philosophy no longer takes place. The intellectual roots of the anxieties that ordinary philosophy addresses are too deep for that" and "What I suggest is that our philosophical anxieties are due to the intelligible grip on our thinking of a modern naturalism, and we can work at loosening that grip." It is unclear, to me at least, to what extent McDowell is speaking only for himself when he connects the issue of our relation to philosophical anxieties to the specific idea of modern naturalism or whether he means to attribute such a view to Wittgenstein as well. My discussion of this section is meant to deal with these possibilities taken jointly. On the other hand, McDowell may hold that Wittgenstein's view is more general: that, for instance, he would consider modern naturalism as merely one particularly virulent manifestation of an even more deeply rooted and permanent intellectual tendency in human beings (whatever name we eventually choose to give this deeper tendency). I will deal with this sort of possibility in the next section, when I discuss Cavell's view.

What McDowell says in the long quotations above could be taken as suggesting that our deeply rooted philosophical anxieties only *began* with the advent of modern naturalism. This would simply be a consequence of his claim that philosophical anxieties result from the grip of naturalism on our thinking and the fact that modern naturalism itself can be roughly determined to have originated during a particular historical period. These imply that the philosophical anxieties that come from modern naturalism would themselves have their origins in the same period. But it seems to me unlikely that McDowell can mean this, since it has the perplexing result that before the modern period there were no philosophical anxieties, or at least no very deep ones. More charitably, perhaps, McDowell could be taken to mean that while there certainly were deeply rooted philosophical worries before there was anything recognizable as modern naturalism, only after the establishment of modern science, when naturalism became common sense for a large segment of the educated classes, did these anxieties become so deeply anchored in our thinking that nothing could uproot them for good. Yet this reading still raises the troubling question as to how an intellectual outlook could at once be so clearly historical in its origins yet be too deeply rooted to pass away. How is it possible that a movement of thought like modern naturalism could be so extraordinary that it has somehow effected a permanent shift in our mentality?

I am not disputing the idea that much of Wittgenstein's work grapples with questions closely related to the specific problematic of modern naturalism that McDowell diagnoses in *Mind and World*. Several passages that I have already quoted, such as these two (chapter 2, p. 51) make explicit that he saw a close connection between modern naturalism and philosophical confusion: "That is the fatal thing about the scientific way of thinking (which today possesses the whole world), that it considers every disquietude to be a question and is surprised not to be able to answer it" and "What is insidious about the causal approach [*kausalen Betrachtungsweise*] is that it leads one to say: 'Of course, that's how it had to happen.' Whereas one ought to say: It may have happened *like that*, and in many other ways."

In these and many other remarks, Wittgenstein is clearly bemoaning what he takes to be our modern fascination with scientific method, a method that accounts for things by subsuming diverse phenomena under general causal laws. The astonishing success and power of this method for the purposes of explaining certain phenomena can then seduce us into seeing everything this way, and we are "surprised" when other phenomena ("disquietudes") resist being understood in naturalistic terms. At one point in the *Blue Book*, Wittgenstein even goes so far as to voice the idea that the undue influence of science in philosophy is the very source of philosophical confusion: "Philosophers constantly see the method of science before their eyes, and are irresistibly tempted to ask and answer questions in the way science does. This tendency is the real source of metaphysics, and leads the philosopher into complete darkness."[7] Yet even if metaphysics *cum* naturalism virtually became common sense for many in the modern West, it seems highly implausible to suggest that Wittgenstein believed philosophers enjoyed a merely casual relation to the problems of philosophy before the modern period. In fact, this last remark is a description of only one of *four* "tendencies" that Wittgenstein connects with the "craving for generality" characteristic of metaphysical confusion.[8] In truth, moreover, the craving for explanation of a non-naturalist sort by rationalists such as Plato, Descartes, Leibniz, or Frege is closer in spirit to modern naturalism than one might suspect; rationalists no less than modern naturalists accept a certain dichotomous view of nature and rationality that, if McDowell is correct in *Mind and World*, is one of the central targets of Wittgenstein's later philosophy. (I don't take this to imply that Wittgenstein would consider the craving for theory in, say, Plato, to be any more part of our constitution than he would scientism or naturalism.) More to the present point, even the above remark from the *Blue Book* does not support the conclusion that Wittgenstein thought that modern naturalism had any sort of permanent grip on our thinking.

Indeed, the long quotation in chapter 2 (56–57), where Wittgenstein attacks Ernst Renan, strongly suggests that the contrary is true. I think an upshot of what Wittgenstein says there is that it is a kind of superstition to suppose that the craving for causal explanations manifest in modern naturalism has become a permanent feature of the modern psyche and that a reawakening to a kind of wonderment free of that craving is forever closed off to us. Thus, if it is correct for McDowell to read Wittgenstein as identifying modern naturalism as the source of philosophical anxieties, then there would seem to be a serious problem with the further claim that Wittgenstein believed that the roots of these anxieties ran so deep as to make a genuine abandonment of the metaphysical tradition impossible, since the marvel and awakening of which he writes in this passage suggests to me that he thinks we can do much more than merely "loosen" the hold that scientifically inspired modern naturalism exercises over us.

Of course, if McDowell holds that Wittgenstein thought that the fixed roots of our philosophical anxieties actually *go deeper* than, and therefore should not be identified with, modern naturalism, then these last considerations alone do not tell against his interpretation. But other considerations do, which I can now take up by turning to Cavell.

6.3

The gist of Cavell's view can be gotten if we look at some passages taken from works in which he has articulated that view over many years. We read in an essay from the early 1960s,

> For Wittgenstein, philosophy comes to grief not in denying what we all know to be true, but in its effort to escape those human forms of life which alone provide the coherence of our expression. He wishes acknowledgment of human limitation which does not leave us chafed by our own skin, by a sense of powerlessness to penetrate beyond the human conditions of knowledge. The limitations of knowledge are no longer barriers to a more perfect apprehension, but conditions of knowledge *überhaupt*, of anything we should call "knowledge."[9]

This view is given further elaboration by Cavell some years later in *The Claim of Reason*:

> The coincidence of soul and body, and of mind (language) and world *überhaupt*, are the issues to which Wittgenstein's notion of grammar and criteria are meant

to speak. The *practical* difficulty of pegging the mind to the world, and especially to the social-political world, the world of history; and the psychological difficulty of it in the world of religion; are main subjects of modern literature and of certain existentialisms. The gap, or distorted relation, between intention (or wish or feeling) and its execution, and between execution and consequence, is what the sense of "absurdity" is a response to. But then how does the gap or distortion appear, and how can it be closed? In Wittgenstein's view the gap between mind and the world is closed, or the distortion between them straightened, in the appreciation and acceptance of particular human forms of life, human "convention." This implies that the *sense* of gap originates in an attempt, or wish, to escape (to remain a "stranger" to, "alienated" from) those shared forms of life, to give up the responsibility of their maintenance.[10]

When I read these passages in isolation, I want to give each of them full-throated approval, both to what their words seem to say about Wittgenstein's understanding of the logic of philosophical confusion, that it arises from attempts to escape from human forms of life and human conventions, and to what the words in each seem to say about Wittgenstein's view of the alleviation of this confusion: the acknowledgment, appreciation, and acceptance of those same forms of life and conventions the philosopher wishes to escape from. Yet the real significance that the terms "forms of life," "convention," and the "human" have within the broader context of Cavell's argument point to what I think are some deep problems in his interpretation of Wittgenstein's understanding of the nature and origins of philosophical problems.

Cavell (rightly) tries to make a space for a use of the term "convention" that is outside of the traditional philosophical opposition marked by "arbitrary" and "logically necessary"; his way of doing this is to locate the relevant sense of "convention" in human nature itself, a use of "convention" meant to underscore that while our natural reactions cannot correctly be said to be guided by logical necessity, neither can they be correctly described as arbitrary.

The conventions we appeal to may be said to be "fixed," "adopted," "accepted," etc. by us; but this does not now mean that what we have fixed or adopted are (merely) the (conventional) *names* of things. The conventions which control the application of grammatical criteria are fixed not by customs or some particular concord or agreement which might, without disrupting the texture of our lives, be changed where convenience suggests a change. (Convenience is *one* aspect of convention, or an aspect of one kind or level of convention.) They are, rather, fixed by the nature of human life itself, the human fix itself, by those "very general facts of nature" which are "unnoticed only because so obvious", and, I take it, in particular, very general facts of *human* nature.[11]

Cavell also believes that commentators of the *Investigations* have too often overemphasized the notion of a social practice for their understanding of what Wittgenstein means by the term "form of life" (*Lebensform*), and so they have neglected the importance that our common human biology plays in the book.

> The idea (of a form of life) is, I believe, typically taken to emphasize the social nature of human language and conduct, as if Wittgenstein's mission is to rebuke philosophy for concentrating too much on isolated individuals, or for empha- sizing the inner at the expense of the outer, in accounting for such matters as meaning, or states of consciousness, or following a rule, etc.; an idea of Witt- genstein's mission as essentially a business of what he calls practices or conven- tions. Surely this idea of the idea is not wrong, and nothing is more important. But the typical emphasis on the social eclipses the twin preoccupation of the *Investigations*, call this the natural, in the form of "natural reactions" (185), or in that of "fictitious natural history" (230), or that of "the common behavior of mankind" (206). The partial eclipse of the natural makes the teaching of the *Investigations* much too, let me say, conventionalist, as if when Wittgenstein says that human beings "agree in the language they use" he imagines that we have between us some kind of contract or an implicitly or explicitly agreed upon set of rules (which someone else may lack). Wittgenstein continues by saying: "That [agreement in language] is not an agreement in opinions but in form of life" (241). A conventionalized sense of form of life will support a conventional- ized, or contractual, sense of agreement. But there is another sense of form of life that contests this.
>
>   Call the former the ethnological sense, or horizontal sense. Contesting that there is the biological or vertical sense.[12]

Two more points need filling in before I am finished with this sketch of Witt- genstein's view of the nature of skepticism according to Cavell. First, for Cavell, the "wish" or "effort" to escape our human form of life not only figures centrally in Wittgenstein's diagnosis of philosophical confusion. Cavell sees it as an impulse that itself originates *in* our form of life, in our human nature: "Philosophy, the desire for thought, running out of control . . . has become an inescapable fate for us, apparently accompanying the fate of having human language."[13] "I mean to say that it is human, it is the human drive to transcend itself, make itself inhuman, which should not end until, as in Nietzsche, the human is over."[14]

Finally, at times at least, Cavell seems prepared to attribute this view of the origins of philosophical confusion to Wittgenstein. What he says in this passage from "Declining Decline: Wittgenstein as a Philosopher of Culture" perhaps suggests a certain reticence about making any such attribution: "Why intellectual bewitchment takes the forms it takes in the *Investigations* we have not said— Wittgenstein speaks of pictures holding us captive, of unsatisfiable cravings, of disabling sublimizings. He does not, I think, say very much about why we are victims of these fortunes, as if his mission is not to explain why we sin but to show us that we do, and its places."[15] Nevertheless, whatever uncertainty Cavell may have concerning Wittgenstein's thoughts on the etiology of philosophical bewitchment is not strong enough in the end to prevent the occasional diagnosis on Wittgenstein's behalf from appearing in various of his works, even if he does not make it the centerpiece of his interpretation.[16] The suggested idea is that Wittgenstein held that metaphysical puzzlement is the inevitable result of our human urge to transcend the fundamental fact of our human finitude, more specifically, that he saw the problems of philosophy as arising out of our human life with language. We read in *The Claim of Reason*: "Disappointment over the failure (or limitation) of knowledge has, after all, been as deep a motivation to the philosophical study of knowledge as wonder at the success of knowledge has been. In Wittgenstein's work, as in skepticism, the human disappointment with human knowledge seems to take over the whole subject."[17] In "Declining Decline," Cavell writes, "What I am here reporting as my impression of [Wittgenstein's] Spenglerian valence . . . means that I think the griefs to which language repeatedly comes in the *Investigations* should be seen as normal to it, as natural to human natural language as skepticism is."[18] And, in "The Argument of the Ordinary," after identifying what he terms the "argument of the ordinary" as "fundamental to the *Investigations*," Cavell goes on to assert: "The human capacity—and the drive—both to affirm and to deny our criteria constitutes the argument of the ordinary."[19]

6.4

It is not my task here to examine all of the reasons that lead Cavell to attribute to Wittgenstein the views I describe above or for apparently holding those views himself (even if I realize that a fuller understanding of what his position involves might require more investigation into why he holds them). I merely want to show that there are prima facie good reasons for doubting that Wittgenstein held some of the views on the nature of philosophy that we've seen Cavell attribute to him. I start with the significance of practices, customs, forms of life, and related notions in Wittgenstein's later thought.

I would like to believe that my disagreement with Cavell on this matter is mostly a matter of emphasis; I certainly do not wish to deny, for instance, the "twin preoccupation" that *Philosophical Investigations* exhibits with our natural history. Yet for all that, it seems to me that Cavell fails to understand the significance that practices have for Wittgenstein's thought and that this is perhaps in part because of a superficial understanding of the possible depth of practices themselves. If Wittgenstein understood practices, social conventions, and customs to be as contractual and explicit as Cavell describes them, then a sympathetic interpreter could certainly be tempted to avoid overemphasizing the role they play in Wittgenstein's thought. Conventions that human beings establish by means of explicit agreements could not account for a fraction of the agreement in judgments that is so important for the later Wittgenstein's philosophy. But even if some conventions are contractual, and even if no practice can rival the biological in its claim to depth, I believe that there is no good reason for thinking that all practices are contractual and no good reason for thinking that Wittgenstein thought this was so. To take just one example, I find it extremely strained to use "contractual" to describe most (or probably all) cultures' practices for standing the correct distance from a person with whom one is conversing.[20] But perhaps Cavell would argue that though such an example shows that a practice need not be contractual, it was nevertheless Wittgenstein's view that nothing really fundamental in human life could rest on practices. These, after all, are what are referred to by the merely "horizontal" sense of "form of life" and concern merely "the arrangements a particular culture has found convenient, in terms of its history and geography, for effecting the necessities of human existence."[21] In criticizing Kripke's interpretation of Wittgenstein as too conventionalist, Cavell writes,

> Kripke speaks of our "achieving agreement in our criteria" but that suggests to me a rejection of Wittgenstein's idea of agreement, or let me say a contractualizing or conventionalizing of it. On Wittgenstein's view, the agreement criteria depend upon lies in our natural reactions. We may laugh and cry at the same things, or not; some experience may throw us out of, or into, agreement here, but the idea of *achieving* agreement in our senses of comedy or tragedy seems out of place. When the child starts to walk, she or he walks, tentatively, as I do; we agree in walking; but we have not achieved this agreement, come to agree; it makes more sense to say that we have each come to walk.[22]

Kripke's talk of "achieving agreement" is indeed misplaced, and Cavell is correct to criticize it. But Kripke's own superficial understanding of what agreement comes to cannot by itself be taken to impugn the possibility of a much more basic role in our lives for practices (including practices that concern our senses of comedy and tragedy). Nor can such a narrow understanding be taken as the basis for an assessment of the idea that Wittgenstein felt that our distorted relation to practices is centrally implicated in generating and sustaining philosophical confusion. Consider in this vein this passage from one of the manuscripts from which much of *On Certainty* is taken (much of which, by the way, I find difficult to square with Cavell's claims):

> Assertion: "I know that the bottle stood there."—"How do you know that?"—"I saw it there."—Now if the assertion is: "I know that he was happy," and it is asked "How do you know that?"—What is the answer? It is not simply the description of a physical state of affairs. It is relevant, for example, that I know the person concerned. If a film could be shown in a courtroom, in which the whole scene was replayed, his demeanor, his gestures, his voice, sometimes that could be very convincing. At least if he is not an actor. But it works only if those who are judging the scene belong to the same culture. I wouldn't know, for example, how genuine joy looked with Chinese.[23]

The message to take from this passage is not that Wittgenstein wants to instigate skeptical worries about joy. He is not suggesting here that, alas, in the end we can at best have an opinion that someone is joyful, that someone is a soul, because our understanding that someone is joyful or is a soul rests on (contractual) practices and that these could never provide us with certainty. Nor is he suggesting that our felt certainty that someone feels joy rests on a prior agreement, as though we were to define joy by saying "Joy shall be defined by these movements and no others." The message to draw, rather, is that even something as fundamental as our attitude toward someone's being a soul filled with joy may rest to some degree on our sharing with that person something beyond our common natural history. But since on Cavell's understanding, anything but a biological sense of "conventional" comes close to meaning "convenient," too much emphasis on the role that practices play in Wittgenstein's thinking would leave it unable to do genuine justice to skepticism, especially to skeptical problems connected to our relation to others.

I want to explore some of my differences with Cavell on these matters just a bit further. To do that, we have to consider a claim by von Wright to which Cavell responds in "Declining Decline." Von Wright writes, "Because of the interlocking of language and ways of life, a disorder in the former reflects a disorder in the lat-ter. If philosophical problems are symptomatic of language producing malignant outgrowths which obscure our thinking, then there must be a cancer in the *Leb-ensweise*, the way of life itself."[24] Cavell writes with this passage in mind, "Given my sense of two directions in the idea of a form of life, von Wright's appeal here to 'a cancer in the way of life' makes me uneasy. 'Way of Life' again to me sounds too exclusively social, horizontal, to be allied so directly with human language as such, the life form of talkers."[25] There may be a number of reasons why Cavell is made uneasy by von Wright's choice of words here; they strike me, however, as altogether true to Wittgenstein. At any rate, I am quite sure that part of that sense of uneasiness stems both from Cavell's belief that exaggerating the importance of practices and customs in Wittgenstein's later thought has led many to regard him as a conservative and from his belief that if practices and customs do play too large a role in Wittgenstein's later work, then it would be correct to regard him as one. As to the first concern, Cavell writes,

> Wittgenstein's formulation about having to accept [forms of life as] the given plays its part, I feel sure, in conveying a political or social sense of the *Investiga-tions* as conservative. This was the earliest of the political or social descriptions, or accusations, I recall entered against the *Investigations*. Writers as different as Bertrand Russell and Ernest Gellner greeted the book's appeal to the ordinary or everyday as the expression of a so to speak petit bourgeois fear of change, whether of individual inventiveness or of social revolution.[26]

That Cavell regards his own emphasis on the naturalist elements in the *Investi-gations* as a counter to an untoward conservatism that, were it not for these ele-ments, would be correctly attributable to Wittgenstein, is also clear: "I have suggested that the biological interpretation of form of life is not merely another available interpretation to that of the ethnological, but contests its sense of politi-cal or social conservatism."[27] Indeed, one even senses a suspicion that overem-phasizing the significance of practices in one's reading of Wittgenstein on, for example, skepticism about other minds opens up for him quite pernicious forms of oppression.

> Because if what we "accept" as human beings "turn out to be" automata or aliens, then can't we take it that automata or aliens marry and own private property and shake hands and possess language? You may reply that once it turns out who these things are we (who?) will no longer fully say that they (or no longer let them?) marry, own, shake, speak. Perhaps not, but then this shows that from the

fact of their exhibiting or "participating in" social forms it does not follow that they are human.[28]

I will not address this here except to say that I find Cavell's interpretative concerns unwarranted.[29] There is no good reason to think that an interpretation that stresses the importance of social practice and an "ethnological" sense of form of life issues from some kind of conservatism (assuming without argument for the moment that that is *obviously* a bad thing).[30] In fact, here is a place where Cavell's having restricted himself to *Philosophical Investigations* may have adversely affected his interpretation of Wittgenstein's thought. I take it, for example, that it is *practices* that are in the forefront of Wittgenstein's mind in most, if not all, of *On Certainty*. The image of the riverbed (§96–§99) that he calls forth there certainly suggests that the "ethnological" plays more than a merely "horizontal" role in his later thinking about our relation to each other and understanding of the world.[31] And Wittgenstein's employment of this image serves to make another point, one that does not strike me as conservative, namely, that a background of underlying practices can shift and can be critically engaged.

6.5

It is true, of course, that in many places Wittgenstein writes as though it were our *language itself* that bewitches us and leads us into philosophical confusion. We read in the *Investigations*,

> Philosophy is a battle against the bewitchment of our intelligence by means of language.

> A picture held us captive. And we could not get outside it, for it lay in our language and language seemed to repeat it to us inexorably.

> A main source of our failure to understand is that we do not command a clear view of the use of our words.—Our grammar is lacking in this sort of perspicuity.

> We remain unconscious of the prodigious diversity of all the every-day language-games because the clothing of our language makes everything alike.[32]

These kinds of remarks no doubt lend weight to the idea that Wittgenstein believed that metaphysical confusion is part and parcel of our life with language, and they can make it seem as though Wittgenstein is giving a diagnosis of the origins of philosophical perplexity that is close in spirit to Kant's assertion in the preface of the *Critique of Pure Reason* that "Human reason has this peculiar fate that in one species of its knowledge it is burdened by questions which, as prescribed by the very nature of reason itself, it is not able to ignore, but which, as transcending all its powers, it is also not able to answer."[33]

Nevertheless, it is also the case that Wittgenstein believes that in philosophy we often exhibit a strong resistance to a careful consideration of the particular uses to which we put language. This is precisely why he goads his reader to look at these particular uses, even when he runs the risk of sounding imperious in doing so:

> Consider for example the proceedings that we call "games." I mean board-games, card-games, ball-games, Olympic games, and so on. What is common to them all?—Don't say: "There *must* be something common, or they would not be called 'games'"—but *look and see* whether there is anything common to all.—For if you look at them you will not see something that is common to *all*, but similarities, relationships, and a whole series of them at that. To repeat: don't think, but look![34]

But what is it "that opposes such an examination of details in philosophy" (*Philosophical Investigations*, §52)? *Why* the "urge to misunderstand" (§109), and why are we convinced before we look that there *must* be something in common to all games, since otherwise we would not have one word, "game," that covered all the different cases? One natural answer is suggested by the remarks from Wittgenstein that I just quoted: the clothing of our language makes everything look alike, makes it seem as though nothing philosophically valuable will be found by looking into individual circumstances in which we use the word "game." But this answer only raises another question: why does Wittgenstein think we are so content with appearances here? Does he really believe that it is only the surface homogeneity of our language that leads to metaphysical confusion? Or this, along with our natural indolence that makes looking at particulars feel like too much trouble? Or our natural craving for generality that can make this examination feel impossible or seem unphilosophical or unscientific?[35]

According to von Wright, Wittgenstein located the wellsprings of metaphysical problems not in the nature of our life with language but in the complicated web of ways of acting, thinking, and speaking that make up our cultural inheritance. "Wittgenstein thus thought that the problems with which he was struggling were somehow connected with the '*Lebensweise*' or the way people live, that is, with features of the culture or civilization to which he and his pupils belonged."[36] "The problems of philosophy have their roots in a distortion or malfunctioning of the language-games which in its turn signalizes that something is wrong with the ways in which men live. On the intellectual level this malfunctioning consists in certain unhealthy habits of thought ('*Denkgewohnheiten*') permeating the intellectual culture of a period."[37] It may be that there is no conclusive way to settle this issue. But there are passages, like these two from 1946 and 1947 respectively, that not only seem to bear out von Wright's view that Wittgenstein thought that the problems of Western metaphysics were connected to Western culture but that go beyond this idea, by suggesting he believed it both possible and desirable for there to be a substantial cultural shift that would allow those problems to evaporate:

> 1. Grasping the difficulty *in its depth* is what is hard. For if you interpret it in a shallow way the difficulty just remains. It has to be pulled out by the root; and that means, you have to start thinking about these things in a new way. The change is as decisive e.g. as that from the alchemical to the chemical way of thinking.—The new way of thinking is what is so hard to establish.
>
> Once it is established the old problems disappear; indeed it becomes hard to recapture them. For they are embedded in the way we express ourselves; and if we clothe ourselves in a new form of expression, the old problems are discarded along with the old garment.[38]
>
> 2. It is by no means clear to me that I wish for a continuation of my work by others more than a change in the way of life which would make all these questions superfluous. (For this reason I could never found a school.)[39]

Some discretion is clearly called for in deciding how much weight to lend to such remarks; they do not wear their rhetorical or philosophical intent on their sleeves, so to speak. Yet there seems little reason to understand Wittgenstein to be giving a "mythological description" in his connecting philosophical problems with how people think and live.[40] He does not seem so much to be displaying what he is (or we are) "inclined"[41] or "tempted"[42] to say, so much as he seems to be simply recording what he thinks. It would thus make little sense for him to express himself as he does if he did not think his words denoted a genuine possibility. So while such remarks are too few to decide conclusively such an important question as the one I am discussing here, I find it very difficult to reconcile what Wittgenstein says here and elsewhere with the kind of interpretation given by Cavell or McDowell.[43]

It is certainly true that in the long march from Plato to his own day, there were figures in the history of Western philosophy whom Wittgenstein admired.[44] Drury recorded this comment in his notes for 1930: "Man's need for metaphysics. I think

I can see very well what Schopenhauer got out of his philosophy. Don't think I despise metaphysics. I regard some of the great philosophical systems of the past as among the noblest productions of the human mind. For some people it would require an heroic effort to give up this sort of writing."[45] There were many things that Wittgenstein could admire in a philosopher; certainly, writing ability ranked very high with him. But the most important traits were seriousness and honesty. If he felt these were lacking, nothing else could compensate for them.[46] I believe a hallmark of the honesty of these philosophers for Wittgenstein was their recognition of limitation not only of their own powers of understanding and expression but also, I think, the presence in their thinking of a "clearly acknowledged terminus" where explanations stop, something he saw notably absent in the "scientific world view" (and which I feel certain he would have found even more conspicuously absent in the widespread naturalistic metaphysics of today). But Wittgenstein's occasionally avowed sympathy with some of the impulses to metaphysics does not mitigate his overall hostility to theory in philosophy. So, while it seems imaginable that he only hoped for a release from the pernicious influence of the scientific metaphysics of his own day, something he regarded as a kind of magic that had lost all of its charm, given that this represented an extreme expression of the pretension to theory in philosophy, it is difficult for me to imagine his thinking that any resting place could be found in, say, Berkeley or Leibniz, in whose thought the perverse role of theory that began with Plato already exerts a decisive influence. I am certainly not suggesting that Wittgenstein hoped for a release from the problems of human life, problems connected to our finitude and mortality. On this I agree with Cavell entirely. I am not even suggesting that Wittgenstein entertained the fantasy of an escape from problems of the intellect. What I am suggesting is that his philosophy does not rule out, and that he may himself have envisioned, the possibility and desirability of a radical break with the inheritance of Western metaphysics, a family line of problems of which modern naturalism and skepticism are two members.

6.6

These tentative conclusions concerning Wittgenstein's attitude toward metaphysics can be viewed from what we might call short- and long-term perspectives. In the short-term perspective, the idea that the problems of Western metaphysics are fundamentally tied to dominant practices of Western culture, while not exactly a philosophical thesis, is an idea to which a philosopher can be led, provided the right sort of *Leitfaden* guides his or her philosophical inquiry. McDowell says that he credits "Wittgenstein with the aspiration of seeing through the apparent need for ordinary philosophy," and an important part of the Wittgensteinian diagnosis of the philosophical confusion he wants us to see through involves his bringing to the fore the role of *Bildung* in our acquiring the second nature that he thinks bridges the apparently unbridgeable logical gap between mind and world. But what I think is McDowell's correct insight on this point also has implications for the question I am discussing here. *Bildung* is a concept that concerns how we are raised and, consequently, how we live. That we *come to* an appreciation of *Bildung*, to our forms of life, as part of the dissolution of philosophical confusion implies that this confusion was connected to our having lacked such an appreciation. This then begs the question of whether this lack of appreciation may have been part and parcel of that specific upbringing. Now it may be true that even the philosopher who comes to regard the problems of metaphysics largely as a symptom of his form of life will not necessarily be free from all forms of philosophical perplexity in the future; the problems and their roots do indeed run deep in us. Nor is there any guarantee that he will immediately be able to find or produce the reminders that allow him to see through the apparent need to philosophize in each case. The way he lives and uses words may continue to lead him away from seeing the way he lives and uses words. But his momentary perplexity need not break out into full-blown philosophical panic. Experience can teach him not only to become more skilful at knowing where and how to look for relief from particular cases of metaphysical confusion; it can also teach him to regard its occurrences with skepticism and to begin to envisage the possibility and desirability of more radical stances toward its sources.

In a long-term perspective, it is difficult to know what sort of role Wittgenstein believed there was for the philosopher to play in the establishment of a new way of life and a new way of thinking. Von Wright's view is that Wittgenstein's assessment of this matter was extremely negative.

> It is vain to think that by fighting the symptoms one can cure the illness. Curing it would mean changing the language-games, reforming language—and therewith the ways of thoughts and the way of life of the community. Wittgenstein certainly did not think this possible through the efforts of one individual. He is most emphatic about that. All the philosopher can do is to expose the disorder in the language-game, describe it, and thereby rid his mind of the torments produced by the unrecognized illness. But this intellectual cure—"*Friede in den Gedanken*" ("thoughts that are at peace") which, he says (*Culture and Value*, 50), is the main aim of philosophy—will have no important consequences of a social nature, either for habits of thinking or for ways of living.[47]

If, indeed, this was the whole of Wittgenstein's view, then I think it expresses a somewhat unwarranted pessimism. What philosophers say and write does exert *some* influence on the shape of our intellectual culture, and our intellectual culture, in turn, does exert *some* influence on how people live. If, just to take one example, philosophers abandoned metaphysics *cum* scientific naturalism, they might at the very least stop *contributing* to problems associated with that view, problems, for example, connected to certain reductive views of persons still prevalent in fields that affect the lives of many people. But there are also reasons to believe that Wittgenstein saw some more concrete positive role for the philosopher to play in the establishment of a new form of life. Consider this remark: "Science: enrichment and impoverishment. The *one* method elbows all others aside. Compared with this they all seem paltry, preliminary stages at best. You must climb down to the sources to see them all side by side, the disregarded and the preferred."[48] Wittgenstein speaks here of neglected and preferred methods. In a remark I quoted in chapter 3 (97–98) he talks about giving each kind of assertion its due. At one point in his remarks on Frazer, Wittgenstein comments that "an entire mythology is stored in our language."[49] He is struck, for example, by the extent to which we are still able to understand the peoples whose magical practices Frazer writes about. He says that much too little fuss is made over the fact that words such as "soul," "spirit," and "shade" are still counted as part of our vocabulary.[50] His point is that it is only because we and Frazer still have such expressions in our language that we can form a coherent idea of the meaning of these peoples' rituals in the first place. Yet we tend to ignore the significance of the presence of such expressions in our language, though we might be hard pressed to account for our making sense of them. Likewise, I take Wittgenstein's use of the image of an ancient city in the *Investigations* to be partly in service of an attempt to change the philosopher's way of regarding the neglected and untidy inner city for the orderly suburbs of scientific theory: "Our language can be seen as an ancient city: a maze of little streets and squares, of old and new houses, and of houses with additions from various periods; and this surrounded by a multitude of new boroughs with straight regular streets and uniform houses."[51] My point here is that Wittgenstein wants to draw our attention to the fact that there are ways of talking still with us and to which in former times members of our culture had a much less casual relationship than we do at present. More importantly, perhaps, to the extent that they retain an interest for us, there may also remain a possibility of retrieving aspects of the way of life to which these ways of talking belong. This is not to say that he thinks that such work of retrieval merely amounts to a wholesale substitution of the old way of talking for the new. Someone who tried such a thing would be largely unintelligible to his peers, for this would amount to the anachronistic attempt to force the old forms of speaking into our present channels of thought, channels in which they simply might not make any sense. (Such insensitivity to the relation between the words we speak and the lives we lead is one of the most character-istic traits of metaphysics itself.) I take something like these considerations to lie behind this remark.

> You can as it were restore an old style in a new language; perform it afresh so to speak in a manner that suits our times. In so doing you really only reproduce. I have done this in my building work.
>
> What I mean is *not* however giving an old style a new trim. You don't take the old forms and fix them up to suit today's taste. No, you are really speaking, maybe unconsciously, the old language, but speaking it in a manner that belongs to the newer world, though on that account necessarily one that is to its taste.[52]

What is more, Wittgenstein acknowledges that the kind of project I am attribut-ing to him here places him less in the traditional role of the philosopher than in that of the poet: "If I do not want to teach a more *correct* way of thinking, but rather a movement of thought [*eine Gedankenbewegung*], then my aim is a 'trans-valuation of values' [*Umwertung von Werten*] and I think of Nietzsche, also in so far as in my opinion, the philosopher should be a poet."[53]

Nevertheless, as these passages attest, von Wright is correct in maintaining that Wittgenstein certainly did not believe that a philosopher *alone* could bring about a fundamental change in the ways in which people live.

> The philosopher says "Look at things *like this*!"—but first, that is not to say that people will look at things like this, second, he may be altogether too late with his admonition, and it's possible too that such an admonition can achieve abso-lutely nothing and that the impulse towards such a change in the way things are perceived must come from another direction. For instance it is quite unclear whether Bacon started anything moving, except the surface of his readers' minds.
>
> Nothing seems to me more unlikely than that a scientist or mathematician, who reads me, should be seriously influenced thereby in the way he works. (In that respect my warnings are like the posters on the ticket offices at English rail-way stations "Is your journey really necessary?" As if anyone reading that would say to himself, "On second thoughts *no*.") Quite different artillery is needed here from anything I am in a position to muster. Most likely I could still achieve an effect in that, above all, a *whole lot* of garbage is written in response to my

stimulus and that *perhaps* this provides the stimulus for something good. I ought always to hope only for the most indirect influence.[54]

The sickness of a time is cured by an alteration in the mode of life of human beings, and it was possible for the sickness of philosophical problems to get cured only through a changed mode of thought and of life, not through a medicine invented by an individual.

Think of the use of the motor-car producing or encouraging certain sicknesses, and mankind being plagued by such sickness until, from some cause or other, as the result of some development or other, it abandons the habit of driving.[55]

Whether Wittgenstein had any definite vision of how a new way of life and thought might establish itself in the West, there seems little doubt that a hope for a fundamental change in our current way of life informed both his philosophical work and his spiritual life.[56]

I once said, and perhaps rightly: The earlier culture will become a heap of rubble and finally a heap of ashes, but spirits will hover over the ashes.[57]

In big-city civilization the spirit can only confine itself to a corner. In so doing it is not so much atavistic and superfluous, but rather hovers over the ashes of the culture as an eternal witness—as God's avenger as it were.

As though it awaited its reincarnation (in a new culture).[58]

NOTES

INTRODUCTION

1. Janik and Toulmin, *Wittgenstein's Vienna*, 22.

2. This is from an early draft of recollections of conversations with Wittgenstein that Drury worked on for many years but never completed to his satisfaction. The last draft appears as "Conversations with Wittgenstein," in Rhees, *Personal Recollections*, 112–189. This quotation is taken from Rhees's introduction (xi).

3. I should add that these points apply not least to Wittgenstein himself. I take it that very few of the confusions or temptations of thought that are dealt with in his work were ones that he never succumbed to himself.

4. Wittgenstein, *Culture and Value*, 45.

5. Ibid., 85.

6. Waismann, *Wittgenstein and the Vienna Circle*, 68.

7. See ibid., 115–116. McGuinness in the footnotes suggests (115, n. 80) that Wittgenstein's remarks here on value are probably directed to Schlick's *Problems of Ethics*, especially §9, "Ethics as Factual Science."

8. Cavell, *The Claim of Reason*, 40.

9. Von Wright, "Wittgenstein in Relation to His Times," in his *Wittgenstein*, 204–205.

10. This is especially the case when it comes to apparently anti-Semitic remarks in Wittgenstein's diaries. While I would not attempt to explain the remarks away, I would suggest that understood in context they need not be read as though they were the "rantings of a fascist anti-Semite," as Monk describes them. In fact, just here I think Monk fails to come to grips with an aspect of Wittgenstein's thought in a way that is all too typical. While, for example, he mentions in passing Wittgenstein's tendency to equate Jew and Englishman in certain contexts, and while he also notes that Weininger made similar comparisons, he fails to investigate what historical-cultural significance, if any, this might have had for Wittgenstein. Instead, Monk interprets such remarks as psychological and idiosyncratic, deriving *only* from Wittgenstein's struggles with his own Jewishness and with his, for Monk, inexplicable fascination with Weininger. See Monk, *Ludwig Wittgenstein: The Duty of Genius*, 312–316. I

think that Janik and Toulmin do a better job in this regard at explaining the relevance of the Viennese cultural setting for an understanding of Wittgenstein. While they don't discuss the anti-Semitic journal entries per se, much of their book directly pertains to this issue.

11.   Kanterian, *Wittgenstein*.

12.   I think that some internal challenges to mainstream analytic ethics do represent a recognition of the importance of these problems. This certainly fits much of Cavell's work, as it does that of Cora Diamond and perhaps even that of John McDowell, all three of whom I rely on here in different ways. See also Lovibond, *Realism and Imagination in Ethics*; and Wiggins, "Truth, Invention, and the Meaning of Life."

13.   Toulmin writes, "If there was an intellectual gulf between us and him, it was not because his philosophical methods, style of exposition and subject matter were (as we supposed) unique and unparalleled. It was a sign, rather, of a culture clash." Janik and Toulmin, *Wittgenstein's Vienna*, 22.

14.   For a concise and illuminating discussion of the way these issues are woven together, see Alice Crary's introduction to Crary and Read, *The New Wittgenstein*, 1–18.

15.   While clearly different in scope and methodology, there are some relevant similarities between my project here and Stephen Mulhall's recent book on the remarks on private language. There are, of course, his obvious sympathies with resolute readings of the *Tractatus* and therapeutic approaches to the *Investigations* (as well as the implication of continuity between the two works that this suggests). More relevant still, Mulhall's reference on the last page of his book (143) to "our sense of an unbridgeable gulf" between soul and body should not be taken as only or even primarily implicating philosophers. His own exploration of the connections between the remarks on private language and themes in Kafka's *Metamorphosis* shows a willingness to explore how something cultural and historical is at stake in the kind of discussion of the subject and subjectivity that takes place in Wittgenstein's text. See Mulhall, *Wittgenstein's Private Language*.

16.   Taylor, "*Lichtung* and *Lebensform*," in his *Philosophical Arguments*, 75–76.

17.   This paragraph was originally composed less with the aim of staking out the originality of my reading the *Tractatus* in light of themes found in *Being and Time* and more with the hope of forestalling a knee-jerk skepticism toward the very idea of bringing these works into close contact. My sense of philosophical isolation (and to some degree of originality), however, was partially punctured by an anonymous reviewer who made me aware of the relevance of Eli Friedlander's very interesting book *Signs of Sense: Reading Wittgenstein's Tractatus*. He writes in the introduction: "Parts of the book will sound closer to analytic elaborations of notions like logic, signs, and symbols. Other parts, elaborating concepts such as world, the subject, the ethical, and the mystical will have a distinctly different tone. Since I have learned much on how to read these topics of the *Tractatus* from reading Heidegger, I find it fruitful to make Wittgenstein's pronouncements resonate with what one might think of as Heideggerian formulations" (xix–xx). Besides revealing an embarrassing gap in my reading, this presented me with the question of how to respond to a somewhat perplexing discovery: while some of my formulations expressing some fairly unorthodox thoughts on the resonance between the early work of these two thinkers come strikingly close to some of Friedlander's formulations on the same topic, there are nevertheless some important differences in our understanding of each thinker taken separately. This seems

especially true of the *Tractatus*. For example, although evidently very different from more traditional, metaphysical readings of the book, Friedlander's views on how elucidations and nonsense are supposed to work in the *Tractatus* stand at most in a complicated relation to those of Diamond and Conant. It is complicated to such an extent, I think, that it would be somewhat stretched to read him as offering a "resolute" reading. Perhaps an even more significant difference in the present context concerns how one reads the *Tractatus* in relation to its times. Friedlander claims that "Wittgenstein himself, early and late, does not explicitly bring into play the historical or cultural context of his writings. This in itself constitutes a feature of his writing that has to be interpreted" (xviii). A bit further on he adds: "This . . . means that I will avoid at most junctures references to various influences, the intellectual context, and other works of Wittgenstein's. I have mostly restricted myself to considering only the text of the *Tractatus*. At times, I make exceptions to that rule and refer to the *Notebooks* and the 'Lecture on Ethics'" (xviii). While I do not think that Friedlander's first claim here is simply false, my whole treatment of the *Tractatus* (indeed my entire book) is premised on the idea that more can and should be made of the presence of the historical and cultural context in and around Wittgenstein's writings than he seems to assume. In particular, my discussion of wonder in the *Tractatus*, as it is connected both to the ethical aim of the book and to its failure to achieve that aim, is closely tied to my understanding of the role in the book of modern science, more specifically, the role of the remarks on mechanics, the law of causality, explanation, and the laws of nature. Interestingly, on the other hand, Friedlander's book is in tune with the transhistorical aspirations of *Being and Time*, whereas my more "historical" reading of the *Tractatus* is to some extent out of sync with Heidegger's project of fundamental ontology. But again, as I indicate at several junctures of my discussion, this is not an ambition of Heidegger's book that sits altogether well with its execution (see esp. chap. 2, notes 20, 73, 89). (Friedlander also assumes his reader is fairly familiar with the early Heidegger's ideas, whereas my sketch of his thought in section 3 of chapter 2 rests on the opposite assumption.) In sum, while it is certainly plausible that there would have been some differences in the text had it first been composed with Friedlander's book in mind, as far as I can tell this would not have substantially changed its main themes or arguments. Consequently, rather than making a substantial engagement with his text central to my discussion, I have chosen to weave in occasional comments in footnotes where I think there are interesting points of contact.

18. Cf. chap. 4, note 43.

19. I am intentionally avoiding here the editorial question of exactly what a philosophical work of Wittgenstein is.

20. These issues are incisively treated in several of the essays in Cavell, *Must We Mean What We Say?* See especially the essay "A Matter of Meaning It."

21. In particular, I have Stanley Cavell in mind as someone who might give such a response. As will be evident, my thinking about Wittgenstein's later work intersects Cavell's in several ways and places, both in its agreements and disagreements. In his essay "Declining Decline: Wittgenstein as a Philosopher of Culture," Cavell devotes significant attention to the ways in which he sees the style and form of the *Investigations* cohering with and being part of the expression of its philosophy of culture as well as of its overall philosophical message. There is also a considerable downplaying of the significance of remarks where Wittgenstein addresses himself explicitly to cultural matters for our evaluation of the cultural significance

of his thought, and there is an emphasis on, in this case, the text of *Philosophical Investigations* itself. To see some differences and similarities with my own approach here, it is worth comparing Cavell's idea of the text of the *Philosophical Investigations* presenting us directly with a philosophy of culture with what Jacques Bouveresse says in his essay "'The Darkness of this Time': Wittgenstein and the Modern World." Bouveresse makes a sharp distinction between Wittgenstein the cultural thinker and Wittgenstein the philosopher who produces clean, objective results. So, finding no cultural remarks per se in, for example, the *Investigations*, he proceeds as though Wittgenstein's cultural outlook is essentially absent from the text. While it is true that Bouveresse does not explicitly reject Cavell's idea that a philosophy of culture might somehow be presented in the text of the *Investigations*, his practice in effect urges us to do just that. To this end, except for a brief discussion of the original context of the motto, Bouveresse remains entirely outside Wittgenstein's philosophical texts for his discussion of his cultural thought. For all their apparent differences, however, a point of intersection between Cavell and Bouveresse seems to me to be that there is little or no exploration of the possibility that Wittgenstein's philosophical texts and those texts where cultural topics are more explicitly taken up may shed light on each other. But I am not convinced that an adequate story about the cultural significance of Wittgenstein's philosophy can be found directly or conclusively in the *Investigations* or in any other writings. I am much more inclined to think that this understanding has to be teased out and that what one purports to discover in any given text is best supported by using material from other sources. This is the method I use here. While I agree with Cavell that remarks such as those found in *Culture and Value* don't "constitute Wittgenstein's claim to be a philosopher of culture," I do think that these and other remarks can go a long way toward helping us understand just what kind of a philosopher of culture he was. I also believe that properly interpreted in relation to his "philosophical remarks," they can be seen as containing philosophy themselves, especially as many of the remarks are long enough and coherent enough to stand on their own. Furthermore, some of these remarks are repeated in Wittgenstein's manuscripts and typescripts, sometimes over the span of several years, and display variant formulations by Wittgenstein, showing that he returned to them out of dissatisfaction with their original wording. All of this suggests to me that it would be mistaken to see these remarks as mere asides interspersed amongst properly philosophical remarks. See Stanley Cavell, "Declining Decline: Wittgenstein as a Philosopher of Culture," in his *This New yet Unapproachable America*, 52–75. See also Jacques Bouveresse, "'The Darkness of This Time': Wittgenstein and the Modern World."

22. It is difficult to tell whether this passage is an actual part of the sketch for a foreword or a comment on the sketch. At any rate, it is clear that it is connected to that sketch. See Wittgenstein, *Culture and Value*, 10, 11.

23. See the preface to Wittgenstein, *Philosophical Remarks*.

24. Ibid.

25. The same considerations hold, of course, for my use of recorded conversations and lecture notes. However, Norman Malcolm's report that Wittgenstein "said that he always regarded his lectures as a form of publication" should go a long way toward easing anxieties over the mere use of the latter. Malcolm, *Ludwig Wittgenstein*, 48.

26. Wittgenstein, *Culture and Value*, x.

I. INTERPRETING THE *TRACTATUS*

1. Wittgenstein, *Prototractatus*, 16. Throughout what follows, I generally stick to the translation of *Sinn* as "point" (sometimes substituting "goal" or "aim"). *Sinn* could also be translated as "sense" or "meaning," however, and each of these alternatives might give what Wittgenstein writes here a different inflection. In any case, I do not think this has any real consequences for my arguments.

2. Ibid.

3. Wittgenstein, *Tractatus Logico-philosophicus*, 3. Unless otherwise stated, I use the Pears and McGuinness translation. My amendment of the Pears and McGuinness translation of "*wovon man nicht reden kann, darüber muss man schweigen*" is a more colloquial rendering of Ogden's "Whereof one cannot speak, thereof one must be silent." Pears and McGuinness's translation reads "what we cannot talk about we must pass over in silence."

4. Ibid.

5. Ibid., 3–4.

6. Pears and McGuinness translate the German *überwinden* as "to transcend." I have amended this to the somewhat more prosaic "overcome," which is closer to the Ogden translation's "surmount." "Transcend" perhaps carries with it a transcendental flavor that is not necessarily warranted by the German.

7. I have omitted §4.1211, §4.1213, and §4.123 for reasons of space. I do not believe this adversely affects my discussion. See also the discussion of formal concepts from §4.126 to §4.1274.

8. Wittgenstein, *Tractatus Logico-philosophicus*, xxi.

9. The latter seems to have been Russell's own feeling on the matter. Gilbert Ryle epitomizes the attitude behind the "straightforward" interpretation, an attitude that insists simply on contradicting Wittgenstein, by reading much of the "nonsense" of the *Tractatus* as a set of philosophical theses. Ryle, in "Ludwig Wittgenstein," writes, "Now it is true that philosophical clarity is achieved in the acts of appreciating arguments rather than in propounding theorems. But is it true that all philosophical talk is nonsensical talk? Wittgenstein himself said very effective things, and talking effectively is not talking non-sensically." Besides Russell, those who have in one way or another taken this approach include Ramsey in his 1923 review of the *Tractatus* (reprinted in his *Foundations of Mathematics*, 270–286); Carnap, *The Logical Syntax of Language*, 282ff; and Max Black, *A Companion to Wittgenstein's Tractatus*, 378ff. More recently, see Peter Carruthers, *The Metaphysics of the Tractatus*.

10. In a letter to Schlick dated August 8, 1932, Wittgenstein leaves little doubt about his attitude to Carnap's approach: "I cannot imagine that Carnap should have so completely misunderstood the last sentences of the book and hence the fundamental conception of the entire book." See Nedo and Ranchetti, *Ludwig Wittgenstein: Sein Leben in Bildern und Texten*, 255.

11. One may in fact attempt to introduce more than one distinction. P. M. S. Hacker, for example, makes a distinction between "overt" and "covert" nonsense. Overt nonsense is nonsense that can be immediately recognized as such. Gibberish is an example of overt nonsense. We may require philosophical analysis, on the other hand, to recognize something as a bit of

covert nonsense. As far as Hacker's work is concerned, my discussion here touches on his attempt to introduce a distinction into covert nonsense only. See Hacker, *Insight and Illusion*, 18.

12.   Anscombe, *An Introduction to Wittgenstein's Tractatus*, 162. Peter Sullivan has criticized Cora Diamond for ascribing to Anscombe this idea that Wittgenstein wanted to convey inexpressible truths by means of nonsense. See Sullivan, "Ineffability and Nonsense," 200–202.

13.   Anscombe, *An Introduction to Wittgenstein's Tractatus*, 162.

14.   Hacker, *Insight and Illusion*, 54. D. F. Pears does not address the question of the role of nonsense in the book, but he does ascribe to Wittgenstein an ineffabilist view similar to the one described by Anscombe and Hacker: "When Wittgenstein made his selection from his copious exploratory notes and put the *Tractatus* together, his leading idea was that we can see further than we can say. We can see all the way to the edge of language, but the most distant things that we can see cannot be expressed in sentences because they are the preconditions of saying anything." See Pears, *The False Prison*, 146–147.

15.   Hacker, *Insight and Illusion*, 18.

16.   Diamond and Conant think that while it might be correct to attribute such a conception of logical syntax to Carnap, it is a mistake to attribute it to Wittgenstein. More recently, Hacker has argued that resolute interpreters have misrepresented Wittgenstein, Carnap, and Hacker himself. Although Hacker directs most of his criticisms at Conant specifically, he no doubt believes that many of them apply in spirit to Diamond and others as well. See Hacker, "Wittgenstein, Carnap, and the New American Wittgensteinians."

17.   Hacker, *Insight and Illusion*, 19.

18.   Ibid., 26. Here is a somewhat more recent statement by Hacker of the same basic view: "There are . . . many positive claims about the nature of logic made in the wake of [Wittgenstein's] criticisms of Frege and Russell. . . . These claims, and many more too, are backed with solid argument. . . . But none of these important claims is a bipolar proposition with a sense. All of them involve the use of formal concepts, and by the lights of the *Tractatus* they are illegitimate in as much as they try to say something that can only be shown." Hacker, "Was He Trying to Whistle It?" 369.

19.   The original German reads as follows: "*Es gibt allerdings Unaussprechliches. Dies zeigt sich, es ist das Mystische.*" There is an important question, which I will mention here but not address in any detail, concerning whether Pears and McGuinness's translation of this passage has itself inclined some interpreters to give the kind of interpretation of the *Tractatus* that I am outlining. There is certainly nothing in the original German text that forces on us a reading that implies that the "Mystical" is composed of a plurality of distinct things that cannot be put into words but make themselves manifest. The passage can *at least* equally well be translated as: "There is indeed the inexpressible. This shows itself, it is the Mystical." I make note of this because the alternative translation I have given here is more consistent with approaches to the text (e.g., Diamond's) that I depend on for my own discussion, ones according to which Wittgenstein need not be read as trying to gesture at inexpressible truths at all. Michael Kremer discusses this issue in "The Purpose of *Tractarian* Nonsense," esp. 60–62.

20.   Wittgenstein, *Tractatus Logico-philosophicus*, §5.621.

21. This is not to suggest, however, that Schopenhauer is the only thinker whose influence commentators purport to find in these passages.
22. Anscombe, *An Introduction to Wittgenstein's Tractatus*, 12.
23. Hacker, *Insight and Illusion*, 2.
24. Ibid, 81. Although Hacker's discussion of Wittgenstein and Schopenhauer focuses on the remarks on solipsism in the *Tractatus*, these are routinely connected by other authors to the remarks on value, which my discussion here focuses on. That Hacker would endorse making this connection seems to be implied in his reference to Wittgenstein's "notion of the mystical" having been molded by Schopenhauer. Wittgenstein's references to "the mystical" occur among the passages on ethics that I am discussing, not in those touching on solipsism. See also Gardner, "Schopenhauer and Wittgenstein," in his *Schopenhauer*, 275–282; Griffiths, "Wittgenstein and the Four-Fold Root of the Principle of Sufficient Reason," 1–20. Rudolph Haller and Allan Janik have each argued that the influence of Otto Weininger may be at least as important as Schopenhauer for understanding these parts of the *Tractatus*. Wittgenstein did, of course, read Weininger with great enthusiasm. But Weininger himself was in many ways an enthusiastic Schopenhauerian. In any case, for my purposes here, very little rides on whether Wittgenstein is directly treating Schopenhauerian themes, those themes as filtered through Weininger, or some of each. See Haller, "What Do Wittgenstein and Weininger Have in Common?" in his *Questions on Wittgenstein*, 90–99. See also Janik, "Wittgenstein and Weininger," in his *Essays on Wittgenstein and Weininger*, 64–95.
25. Schopenhauer, *The World as Will and Representation*. See especially the appendix, "Criticism of the Kantian Philosophy" (1:501–528). See also Schopenhauer, *The Four-fold Root of the Principle of Sufficient Reason*, 164, 168, 172, 176–177. Whether or not Schopenhauer has interpreted Kant correctly on this matter is less relevant here than the fact that he does interpret him this way.
26. Schopenhauer, *The World as Will and Representation*, 1:477–480; Schopenhauer, *The Four-fold Root of the Principle of Sufficient Reason*, 145–164.
27. Schopenhauer, *The Four-fold Root of the Principle of Sufficient Reason*, 164–180.
28. Schopenhauer, *The World as Will and Representation*, 1:204–205.
29. Ibid., 1:389–392.
30. Ibid., book 3, *passim*, esp. 178–207.
31. See Anscombe, *An Introduction to Wittgenstein's Tractatus*, 11; See also G. H. von Wright's biographical sketch in Malcolm, *Ludwig Wittgenstein, a Memoir*, 5.
32. Wittgenstein, *Notebooks*, 72–73. I have retained the editors' parenthetical notes, which indicate the place in the *Tractatus* where the corresponding remark is to be found.
33. Ibid., 85. These last lines, where Wittgenstein refers to the spirit of the snake and lion, seem especially to bear Weininger's stamp. See Janik, "Wittgenstein and Weininger," n. 8.
34. Phillips Griffiths, in "Wittgenstein and the Four-fold Root of the Principle of Sufficient Reason," argues that such remarks should be read as places where Wittgenstein is reminding himself of orthodox Schopenhauerian doctrine and thus entering into a dialogue with Schopenhauer.
35. Wittgenstein, *Notebooks*, 85.

36. Ibid., 83.

37. Wittgenstein, *Tractatus Logico-philosophicus*, §6.45.

38. Wittgenstein, "Lecture on Ethics," 41.

39. Anscombe, *An Introduction to Wittgenstein's Tractatus*, 171–172. Anscombe also notes that many of the passages on the Will in the *Notebooks* do, however, appear much closer to Schopenhauer. This is not the place to go through detailed interpretive contortions in order to demonstrate that, differences on topics such as the Will and the a priori notwithstanding, to these passages a coherent reading can be given in which Wittgenstein's remarks are seen as consistent with and even derivable from Schopenhauer's ontology and ethics. See Goodman, "Schopenhauer and Wittgenstein on Ethics," 437–447; Young, "Wittgenstein, Kant, Schopenhauer, and Critical Philosophy," 73–105. Goodman and Young have each done a rather nice job of working out the apparent logic of these Schopenhauerian passages in the *Tractatus* and *Notebooks*. Nevertheless, I think that there are some serious difficulties with their interpretative approaches when it comes to Wittgenstein's book. One problem, something that they share with many other commentators, concerns their handling of the *Notebooks*. There is no question that it is useful to read the *Notebooks* for a better understanding of the *Tractatus*. It is a dubious practice, however, to deal with them on the same textual level and to reconstruct whole arguments by extracting passages out of both.

40. Janik and Toulmin, *Wittgenstein's Vienna*, 195. See also Hacker, *Insight and Illusion*, chap. 4.

41. Quoted in Engel, "Schopenhauer's Impact on Wittgenstein," n. 88.

42. It is certainly not the case that Schopenhauer is unable or unready to call a bit of language meaningless or nonsensical. On the contrary, one merely has to read his polemics against Fichte, Schelling, and Hegel to see that this is not so. Cf. Schopenhauer, *The Four-fold Root of the Principle of Sufficient Reason*, 59–61. He even employs these categories as more formal terms of art. See Schopenhauer, *Essays and Aphorisms*, 59, 67. The point is rather that he does not hold his depictions of mystical experience to the same standards.

43. Hacker, *Insight and Illusion*, 99–100. There is more than one way to understand Schopenhauer's influence on Wittgenstein in the *Tractatus*. Though Schopenhauer plays a significant role in his interpretation, Pears does not attribute an idealist outlook to Wittgenstein, as Hacker does. On the contrary, he reads the *Tractatus* as an argument for a very strong version of realism. He maintains that Wittgenstein rejects Schopenhauer's metaphysics altogether while retaining its spirit. For Pears, the ineffable truths of the *Tractatus* do not concern things-in-themselves at all but rather have to do with the structure of the phenomenal world. See Pears, *The False Prison*, 5–7.

44. Hacker, *Insight and Illusion*, 107.

45. Janik and Toulmin, *Wittgenstein's Vienna*, 198.

46. Ibid., 195. Janik and Toulmin summarize the *Tractatus* as a "certain type of language mysticism" (197).

47. I have already cited Pears and Janik and Toulmin in this regard. Other are: Maslow, *A Study in Wittgenstein's Tractatus*; Edwards, *Ethics Without Philosophy*; Hintikka and Hintikka, *Investigating Wittgenstein*; and Geach, "Saying and Showing in Frege and Wittgenstein."

48. See Cora Diamond, "Frege and Nonsense," "Throwing Away the Ladder: How to Read the *Tractatus*," "What Nonsense Might Be," "Ethics, Imagination, and the Method of Wittgenstein's

Tractatus," "Criss-cross Philosophy," and "Logical Syntax in Wittgenstein's *Tractatus*." See also Conant, "Must We Show What We Cannot Say?" "Throwing Away the Top of the Ladder," "Kierkegaard, Wittgenstein, and Nonsense," "Putting Two and Two Together," "Two Conceptions of *Die Überwindung der Metaphysik*," "The Method of the *Tractatus*," and (with Cora Diamond) "On Reading the *Tractatus* Resolutely."

49. Conant, "The Method of the *Tractatus*," 398–405. Though I do not go into this issue here, it is interesting to note that while Hacker thinks that Wittgenstein's purported ineffabilist view is ultimately incoherent, his own way of explicating the *Tractatus* seems to lead him to a vigorous defense of the cogency, plausibility, and coherence of the views he finds in the book.

50. Diamond, "Ethics, Imagination, and the Method of Wittgenstein's *Tractatus*," 153.

51. See note 16. Hacker has argued that his critics have misrepresented him, Wittgenstein, and Carnap. See Hacker, "Wittgenstein, Carnap, and the New American Wittgensteinians." Although Hacker directs most of his arguments at Conant specifically, he no doubt believes that many of them apply to Diamond and others as well.

52. Diamond, "Throwing Away the Ladder," 200. Michael Kremer has argued that even tautologies and equations can be regarded as having a meaning when they have a use in connection with sentences that say something, when, for example, they serve as shorthand guides for future inferences between significant propositions. See Michael Kremer, "Mathematics and Meaning in the *Tractatus*."

53. Wittgenstein, *Tractatus Logico-philosophicus*, §6.53. See also §5.473–5.4733.

54. Diamond, "Ethics," 149.

55. Wittgenstein, *Tractatus Logico-philosophicus*, 3.

56. Diamond, "Ethics, Imagination, and the Method of Wittgenstein's *Tractatus*," 150.

57. Conant, "Throwing Away the Top of the Ladder," 346. See also Conant, "Method," 424.

58. Conant, "Putting Two and Two Together," 296.

59. Kremer, "The Purpose of Tractarian Nonsense," 42. Diamond writes in a similar vein: "To throw the ladder away is, among other things, to throw away in the end the attempt to take seriously the language of 'features of reality.' To read Wittgenstein himself as not chickening out is to say that it is not, not really, his view that there are features of reality that cannot be put into words but show themselves. What is his view is that that way of talking may be useful or even for a time essential, but it is in the end to be let go of and honestly taken to be real nonsense, plain nonsense, which we are not in the end to think of as corresponding to an ineffable truth. "Throwing Away the Ladder," 181. Neither the passage from Kremer just quoted nor this one from Diamond—nor the one above where Conant speaks of exploding the philosopher's illusion from within—should be read as a summary of *the* resolute reading or of any particular resolute readings, if only because as of now there is no completed resolute reading or readings of which it might be a summary. Conant and Diamond argue that a resolute reading of the *Tractatus* actually has very few core commitments. Taken together, these commitments amount primarily to a view about how the book ought *not* to be read, namely, "according to which the truths of the theory supposedly advanced in the body of the book prescribing what can and cannot make sense are themselves supposed to be necessarily ineffable." They stress that this kind of minimal commitment allows for multiple and competing resolute readings (as in fact there are). Thus, "resolute reading" should be understood as indicating a starting point for reading the book, not for any single

interpretation. Even if Conant and Diamond think that this starting point is clearly supe-
rior to more standard approaches, they emphasize that any fully worked-out resolute reading has the obligation to provide the details of *how* various passages in the book fall apart
when the reader tries to work through them, how, that is, that we end up with what Kremer
calls here "strings of signs with only structural similarities to sensible argumentation." See
Conant and Diamond, "On Reading the *Tractatus* Resolutely," 46–48.

60. Diamond, "Ethics, Imagination, and the Method of Wittgenstein's *Tractatus*," 157–158.

61. Ibid., 159.

62. Ibid.

63. Ibid.

64. Ibid. Conant, in "The Method of the *Tractatus*," writes, along the same lines: "Thus what
happens to us as readers of the *Tractatus*—assuming the work succeeds in its aim—is that we
are drawn into an illusion of occupying a certain sort of a perspective. From this perspective,
we take ourselves to be able to survey the possibilities that undergird how we must represent
things as being, fixing what is 'logically' necessary and what is merely contingent. From this
perspective, we contemplate the logical structure of thought as it is and imagine that we are
also able to contemplate the possibility of its being otherwise. We take ourselves to be occupying a perspective from which we can view the logical structure of language 'from sideways
on'" (422).

65. This comparison is based on Henry Allison's interpretation of the two "mathematical"
Antinomies. See his *Kant's Transcendental Idealism*, 35–38. I am not suggesting that the
Antinomies are written with the same self-understanding as the *Tractatus*. I am merely mak-
ing use of an interesting conceptual connection between their methods.

66. Diamond, "Ethics, Imagination, and the Method of Wittgenstein's *Tractatus*," 160.

67. Ibid., 161. As I understand it, the *Tractatus* as a whole is not itself intended as an example of
ethical nonsense, although it may contain instances of it, particularly in the §6.4s. That is,
I take it that there can be a distinction between the overall ethical aim of the book itself, a
book written for people of a particular philosophical bent, and the intentions behind self-
aware utterances of ethical nonsense such as the kind Wittgenstein describes in the "Lecture
on Ethics." As I will argue in the next chapter, one way of describing the ethical aim of the
Tractatus is that its elucidatory sentences put the reader in touch with his impulse to speak
ethical nonsense by clarifying his relationship to language. Presumably, this kind of elucidatory function need not be at work in most self-conscious utterances of ethical nonsense,
although ethical nonsense may have a vital role to play when, like the *Tractatus*, a book is
written with such an ethical point.

68. Ibid., 162.

69. Ibid., 161.

70. Ayer, *Language, Truth, and Logic*, 31. While Ayer's views on ethics were not contemporane-
ous with those of the early Wittgenstein, using his book as a contrast to Wittgenstein has
the advantage that Ayer's presentation of ethics is both clear and quite well known. Without
denying the differences among their positions, few of the positivists are more associated
with the "positivist position on ethics" than is Ayer. Since his book contributed significantly
to the misinterpretation of the *Tractatus* in the English-speaking world, there is, perhaps,

also something appropriate with using him as a foil to mark out the early Wittgenstein's views on ethics more clearly.

71. Ibid., 102.

72. Ibid., 108.

73. Ibid., 112.

74. Diamond, "Ethics, Imagination, and the Method of Wittgenstein's *Tractatus*," 161.

75. Ibid., 76.

76. Wittgenstein, "Lecture on Ethics," 44.

77. Ibid.

78. Diamond, "Ethics, Imagination, and the Method of Wittgenstein's *Tractatus*," 164.

79. Ibid., 168.

80. So long, that is, as we recognize that for Wittgenstein, unlike Kant, there is nothing like Reason to appeal to as a source for practical knowledge.

81. My use of "better" here is not merely intended as a polite gesture of philosophical modesty but as an acknowledgement that, while on the whole I find their work convincing enough to let it guide my discussion, there are challenges facing Diamond's and Conant's reading of the book. Some of these challenges concern so-called external evidence, that is, things Wittgenstein said or wrote that are relevant to interpreting the *Tractatus* yet that are not part of the book itself. For example, I find troubling what is said at *Philosophical Investigations* §46 about objects in the *Tractatus*. What Wittgenstein writes in "Some Remarks on Logical Form" (in Wittgenstein, *Philosophical Occasions*, 29–35) also seems difficult to reconcile with resolute approaches to the *Tractatus*, although there note that Wittgenstein strongly disavowed this paper almost immediately after it was written and apparently did so repeatedly later. At any rate, lest it seem that I assume that Diamond's and Conant's interpretation of the *Tractatus* can simply be insulated from the very possibility of being disconfirmed by external evidence, imagine one of Wittgenstein's close philosophical or personal confidants having recorded Wittgenstein making the following remark in conversation: "When I wrote the *Tractatus*, I thought that I could use nonsense to convey ineffable truths about the nature of thought, language, and reality. In particular, I believed it possible to lead a reader to see the necessary features of thought, language, and reality by the ways certain pseudosentences in the book violated the laws of logical syntax, specifically by the ways in which expressions belonging to certain syntactical categories were improperly combined in these pseudosentences. I later came to regard these ideas on based on false theories of logic and meaning." I would regard such a passage, or any passage relevantly resembling it, as providing excellent reasons for thinking that Diamond's and Conant's interpretations are untenable. Of course, in reality, evaluating the overall evidence for any textual interpretation is usually a much more piecemeal matter, involving putting together a total picture from many small bits of evidence. But it is, nevertheless, very significant to my mind that, in the extant external evidence regarding the *Tractatus*, there is nothing even remotely approaching the gold standard provided by my imagined example above that weighs against Diamond's and Conant's views, widespread prejudices to the contrary notwithstanding. Kremer addresses some of the external evidence toward the end of "The Purpose of Tractarian Nonsense" and in "The Cardinal Problem of Philosophy." The latter piece deals in particular with a 1919

letter from Wittgenstein to Russell that has been taken by some as obviously weighing against resolute readings. See Wittgenstein, *Cambridge Letters*, 68.

2. THE ETHICAL PURPOSE OF THE *TRACTATUS*

1. Diamond, "Throwing Away the Ladder," 179. In the second introduction to *The Realistic Spirit*, Diamond writes, "If we read the *Tractatus* as containing metaphysical claims about reality, if we take the metaphysics that we think we find in it to be joined with the idea that metaphysical claims cannot be put into genuine propositions, we shall miss entirely the character of Wittgenstein's later philosophy" (20). In both this passage and the one quoted above, I think Diamond overstates the connection between resolute readings of the *Tractatus* and therapeutic readings of Wittgenstein's later work. This is to say that it does not seem inconceivable to me that a reader could hold a standard reading of the *Tractatus* and a genuinely therapeutic reading of the *Investigations* yet still get much out of the later book, even by Diamond's own lights. The minimal requirement for combining these two possibilities would be the belief that *sometime* after finishing the *Tractatus* Wittgenstein came to see philosophy as a fundamentally therapeutic activity, even if it took him several years to work out what that idea came to when carried through thoroughly. Naturally, this would mean that one would understand Wittgenstein's later criticisms of his earlier work differently, depending on whether one held a standard or resolute reading of the *Tractatus*. One's understanding of *that part* of his later thought would depend crucially on how one read the earlier work. But Wittgenstein engages much more philosophy in his later writings than merely his former self. And so it seems to me unwarranted to insist that a resolute reading of the *Tractatus* is practically a requirement for a therapeutic understanding of his later work. All this being said, on the whole I do believe that resolute approaches to the *Tractatus* and therapeutic approaches to the later work do fit well together, do strengthen each other, and that the resolute-therapeutic lineage does make the most sense of much of the material I deal with here.

2. Diamond, "Throwing Away the Ladder," 200.

3. Wittgenstein, *Tractatus Logico-philosophicus*, §6.53. This means that even the sentences of the *Tractatus* are not *essentially* nonsensical. On the resolute reading, there is no such thing as a sentence's being essentially nonsensical. Nonsense results from our not giving a meaning to certain signs in our sentences. If we want to say that there is a "problem" with the sentences of the *Tractatus*, then we would have to say that those sentences are written in such a way so as to tempt us to think that we have given each of their constituent signs a meaning when in fact we have not done so. I have been helped here by discussion with Michael Kremer. Cf. *Tractatus Logico-philosophicus*, §5.473, §5.4733.

4. Wittgenstein, *Tractatus Logico-philosophicus*, §6.53.

5. Kremer, "The Purpose of Tractarian Nonsense," 45.

6. Ibid., 47.

7. I also agree with Kremer when he writes: "The view that I will develop is, I think, suggested by scattered remarks in Diamond and Conant's many writings on the *Tractatus*. Still, I think

it is fair to say that neither of them has attempted a unified account of the purpose of Wittgenstein's use of nonsense." Ibid., 46.

8. What follows is by no means intended as a full account of intentionality.

9. Waismann, *Wittgenstein and the Vienna Circle*, 68.

10. Wittgenstein, "Lecture on Ethics," 44.

11. Conant writes, "the premise underlying the procedure of the *Tractatus* (and this is connected to why the point of the work is an ethical one) is that our most profound confusions of soul show themselves in—and can be revealed to us through an attention to—our confusions concerning what we mean (and, in particular, what we fail to mean) by our words." Conant, "Method," 421.

12. My use of Heidegger in this chapter draws substantially on Hubert Dreyfus's *Being-in-the-World*. See also Richard Polt, *Heidegger: An Introduction*; and Stephen Mulhall, *Heidegger and* Being and Time. My discussion here follows Dreyfus especially closely in the way it presents Heidegger's exposition of resolute authenticity in *Being and Time* as containing a part that stresses Dasein's formal constancy vis-à-vis the average, everyday practices of the "they" and a part that includes a fuller exposition of authenticity in terms of anticipatory resoluteness and authentic historicality (see section 2.11, below). In a later paper, Dreyfus claims that the presentation of everydayness and authenticity in his commentary was marred by a failure to recognize Heidegger's two-staged uncovering of authenticity in division 2 of *Being and Time*. The first stage is characterized by Heidegger as an acknowledgment of guilt, where the German word *Schuld* brings out the sense of Dasein's indebtedness to the "they" for its average everyday understanding of things. Resoluteness at this stage captures what I've just called Dasein's formal constancy vis-à-vis the everyday, anyone practices of the "they." As we'll see below, this kind of resoluteness also makes it possible for Dasein to adapt creatively the practices of the "they" to the specifics of new situations. Dreyfus, citing the work of Theodore Kisiel, claims Heidegger develops this idea based on Aristotle's description of the man of practical wisdom (*phronimos*). These features of formal constancy are reflected to some extent in what Dreyfus says in his commentary concerning authentic Dasein's openness to the Situation. His point in the later paper is rather that his earlier discussion did not appreciate the full significance of Heidegger's description of guilt as this phenomenon gets interpreted in the light of insights already found in Aristotle's ethics. The second stage of authenticity, anticipatory resoluteness, involves Dasein's facing the full anxiety of death, which opens it up to getting a whole new understanding of itself and its world. Dreyfus argues that this stage of Heidegger's account develops out of his understanding of authentic temporality as that gets worked out in relation to the Pauline doctrine of the moment of conversion (*Augenblick*) in Luther and later in Kierkegaard. My argument in this chapter that it is helpful for understanding the ethical aim of the *Tractatus* to regard it as close in spirit and conception to formal authenticity in *Being and Time* does not explore the relevance of anything like Heideggerian *phronesis* for our understanding of early Wittgenstein's view of our relation to language. It does, however, seem to be an upshot of resolute readings of the *Tractatus* that coming to understand the ethical aim of the book would necessarily involve recognizing the different intentions behind coming out with either routine or creative uses of language (say, in science), on the one hand (both of these falling on the side of the public and ultimately

senseful uses of language), and the intention behind the impulse to speak ethical nonsense, on the other. See Hubert Dreyfus, "Could Anything Be More Intelligible Than Everyday Intelligibility?" See also Kisiel, *The Genesis of Heidegger's* Being and Time.

13. The project thus described refers only to what Heidegger envisioned for part 1 of *Being and Time*. Part 2 was supposed to involve a stepwise, systematic "destruction of the history of ontology" that would begin with Kant, move back through Descartes, and ultimately arrive at Aristotle. Much of Heidegger's writing after *Being and Time* can to a certain extent be understood as in fact carrying out this destruction, but no longer in the original overall context of the project of fundamental ontology. See the introduction to *Being and Time*.

14. See Heidegger, *Being and Time*, 32–33, 70. It may be helpful to think of this complementary pair of concepts as an ontological analogue to the transcendental/empirical distinction in Kant.

15. Ibid., 231. Though clumsier than "ground mood," I believe that "fundamental attunement" is actually closer to what Heidegger means by "*Grundstimmung.*"

16. Ibid., 230.

17. Ibid., 232.

18. Ibid., 25, 32.

19. Ibid., 167. Heidegger thinks that most of the time situations and equipment only show up for us as intelligible or usable because they are articulated for us as average. That is, a way to understand the background skills is to see them as providing general ways of dealing with various situations: one drives a car thus and so, one uses a hammer thus and so, one greets a friend thus and so, etc. For this reason, Dreyfus has suggested that a more interesting translation for *Das Man* would be "The One." See Dreyfus, *Being-In-The-World*, xi.

20. Even so, there is tension between Heidegger's frequent reminders to his readers that he is engaged in a project of fundamental ontology and his dark description of the "they." For example, when (167) Heidegger claims that "leveling down" (*Einebnung*) is a way of being of the "they" that constitutes its "publicness" (*Offentlichkeit*), he clearly seems to be inviting his reader to connect his discussion with Kierkegaard's culturally specific critique of modern nihilism, *The Present Age*. There, we read, "The public is, in fact, the real Leveling-Master rather than the actual leveler, for whenever leveling is only approximately accomplished it is done by something, but the public is a monstrous nothing" (60). Here we can see one of the (clearly many) important differences between the *Tractatus* and *Being and Time*. Whereas I will show in sections 2.4 through 2.6 that while the *Tractatus* is quite consciously directed at what Wittgenstein regards as the idolatry of science in the modern West, the role that cultural critique plays in *Being and Time* is ambiguous at best. See also notes 73 and 89, below.

21. Heidegger, *Being and Time*, 167. Italics in the original.

22. Heidegger's term for equipment that shows up for us in this way is the "ready-to-hand" (*zuhanden*). For a well-developed account of this picture of human agency, see Merleau-Ponty, *The Phenomenology of Perception*. For an account of its results for the field of artificial intelligence, see Dreyfus and Dreyfus, *Mind Over Machine*.

23. Traditional philosophers and cognitive scientists have learned to respond to this kind of case by claiming that since thinking is necessary for intelligent behavior, there must be something equivalent to "unconscious thought" occurring here.

24. Heidegger, *Basic Problems of Phenomenology*, 290. Quoted in Guignon and Pereboom, *Existentialism*, 197.

25. Guignon and Pereboom, *Existentialism*, 180.

26. Heidegger, *Being and Time*, 220.

27. Authentic Dasein encounters these same entities and roles, but its stance toward them is different. Read ahead for more on this.

28. Heidegger's term for what I here call social roles is "for-the-sake-of-which" (*das Worumwillen*). Dreyfus, in *Being-in-the-World*, points out some problems with interpreting "for-the-sake-of-which" as "social role" (95), but his worries are overly fine for my purposes here. He does allow "social role" as a first approximation of "for-the-sake-of-which." See Heidegger, *Being and Time*, 116–117.

29. Heidegger, *Being and Time*, 153–154, 163–164.

30. Ibid., 231.

31. Ibid., 232.

32. Ibid., 231.

33. Ibid., 222, 233.

34. Ibid., 235.

35. Ibid., 343.

36. Ibid., 345. This is made even clearer elsewhere: "[Resoluteness's] relation to being is one of letting-be. The idea that all willing should be grounded in letting-be offends the understanding." Heidegger, *Introduction to Metaphysics*, 17. "The resoluteness intended in *Being and Time* is not the deliberate action of a subject, but the opening up of [Dasein], out of its captivity in that which is, to the openness of being." "The Origin of the Work of Art," in *Poetry, Language, Thought*, 67.

37. Heidegger, *Being and Time*, 345.

38. Ibid., 346. Macquarrie and Robinson translate Heidegger's use of the ordinary German word *Lage* as "situation" and his use of *Situation* in German as "Situation" with a capital *S* in English. Dreyfus translates the German *Situation* as "Unique Situation" in order to emphasize this difference. See *Being-in-the-World*, 320. See also note 12, above.

39. Cooper, *Heidegger*, 47.

40. Heidegger, *Being and Time*, 346.

41. Ibid., 344. Heidegger earlier writes, "*Authentic* existence is not something which floats above falling everydayness; existentially, it is only a modified way in which such everydayness is seized upon" (224). These passages should suggest that if the popular conception of authenticity has any basis at all, it is not to be found in Heidegger.

42. Ibid., 346.

43. Ibid., 344.

44. Ibid., 358.

45. My discussion here builds on a suggestion made by Diamond, where she points out the importance of historical and cultural context for understanding the ethical point of the *Tractatus*. She writes, "My suggestion is that we do not read the *Tractatus* well unless we see how its temper is opposed to the spirit of the times, and how it understands that spirit as expressed in connected ways in the idea of natural laws as explanatory of phenomena, in

philosophy, and in relation to what Wittgenstein thinks of as ethics." See Diamond, "Ethics, Imagination, and the Method of the *Tractatus*," 171.

46. Wittgenstein, *Philosophical Investigations*, preface. For two quite different (yet I believe complementary) understandings of the nature of this critique, see Cavell, "Declining Decline," and Taylor, "*Lichtung* and *Lebensform*," in his *Philosophical Arguments*.

47. If, moreover, one thinks, as I do, that Wittgenstein's attitude to his work throughout his life was characterized by essentially a constant *moral* seriousness, then one would be justified in suspecting that the cultural critique embodied in his later work will, like the *Tractatus*, have been written with an "ethical point." I take this issue up in chapters 4 and 5.

48. Of course, Wittgenstein had no complaint with causal explanations or scientific thinking per se. Rather, his complaints in this vein are almost always lodged against a confused kind of mechanistic thinking that he saw as pervasive in philosophy, in Russell's *Analysis of Mind*, for example (cf. Wittgenstein, *Philosophical Remarks*, §21–26, pp. 64–65). These are the misuses of causal thinking that are relevant for my discussion here. I do not address the possibility of whether there might be other kinds of causal explanation in philosophy to which Wittgenstein did not object. On this, see Klagge, "Wittgenstein on Non-Mediative Causality."

49. Wittgenstein, *Wittgenstein's Nachlass*, 219 81 (January 1933), my translation. The original German reads "Das ist das Verhängnisvolle an der wissenschaftlichen Denkweise (die heute die ganze Welt besitzt), [daß sie jede Beunruhigung mit einer Erklärung beantworten will. / daß sie jede Beunruhigung für eine Frage hält und sich wundert, sie nicht beantworten zu können.]" The material inside the brackets indicates that Wittgenstein never settled on a final formulation for this passage. I have chosen to translate the first formulation. The reference given above reflects the standard numbering system devised by G. H. von Wright for Wittgenstein's *Nachlass*, which was adopted by the *Wittgensteinarkivet* at the University of Bergen, Norway, for putting together the *Bergen Electronic Edition*. The first pair of numbers, in this case "219 81," indicates typescript 219, page 81. In all future references to the *Nachlass*, when the first member of this pair of numbers falls between 100 and 199, this indicates a manuscript. When this number falls between 200 and 299, this indicates a typescript. When possible, this pair of numbers is followed by the complete date of composition. See von Wright, "The Wittgenstein Papers," in his *Wittgenstein*, 35–62. See also the "2002 Addendum to von Wright's 'The Wittgenstein Papers'" in Wittgenstein, *Ludwig Wittgenstein: Public and Private Occasions*.

50. Wittgenstein, *Culture and Value*, 37.

51. Given, moreover, how in certain contexts causal explanations can function (both logically and psychologically) as justifications, my discussion here remains in close conceptual contact with Kremer's discussion of the *Tractatus*' ethical purpose (see pages 76–78). I should make it clear that I do not pretend to give a comprehensive treatment here of all of the possibly relevant issues or texts that are pertinent for understanding the relation between the *Tractatus*, causality, culture, and ethics. In particular, I do not discuss the function of the remarks that deal with the freedom of the will (§5.1362), the logical independence of the world and the will (§6.373–§6.374), and the will as the subject of ethical attributes §6.423–§6.43. Diamond has a superb discussion of the relation between the will and ethics in the *Tractatus* in "Ethics, Imagination, and the Method of the *Tractatus*."

52. In chapter 4, I explore the idea that one of the ways in which *Philosophical Investigations* can be seen as making progress over the *Tractatus* as a piece of therapeutic philosophy is intertwined with the way in which it forms a critique of a culture committed to a meta-physical conception of progress. My criticisms in chapter 3 of the *Tractatus* might also be thought of as pointing ahead to how the later work makes progress in its attempt at cultural critique.

53. Wittgenstein, *Wittgenstein's Nachlass*, 183 21 (my translation). MS 183 is also known as the "Koder diaries." The text of the original diaries along with an English translation appears in Wittgenstein, *Public and Private Occasions*, 8–251. The above passage appears there on 29.

54. Wittgenstein, *Notebooks*, 128–129.

55. Ibid., 108–119. The same is true for the 1913 *Notes on Logic*, found in the same volume (93–107).

56. Ibid., 41.

57. By far the majority of the remarks making up the §6.3s were composed between December 1914 and May 1915.

58. Cf. Wittgenstein, *Tractatus Logico-philosophicus*, §6.341–6.342, §6.35. There does not seem to have been much significant change in the wording of the §6.3s between the *Prototractatus* and the *Tractatus*. Nor have their relative or absolute positions changed much either. It is interesting to read these remarks against the background of Hertz's discussion of a nota-tion (or "images" as he says) for a system of mechanics in the introduction to the *Principles of Mechanics*. Hertz first gives two requirements that any system must fulfill: that the sys-tem not "contradict the laws of our thought," that is, that it be "logically permissible—or briefly . . . permissible," and that the essential relations of the system not contradict the essential relations, that is, that the system of images be "correct." A third characteristic that a system of images ought to have according to Hertz is that it be "appropriate." This he describes as follows: "Of two images of the same object that is the more appropriate which pictures more of the essential relations of the object, —the one which we may call the more distinct. Of two images of equal distinctness the more appropriate is the one which con-tains, in addition to the essential characteristics, the smaller number of superfluous or empty relations, —the simpler of the two." Hertz, *The Principles of Mechanics*, 2.

59. In the passage quoted above, Wittgenstein writes of "*eine Betrachtung der Welt.*" Here he writes "*die Anschauung der Welt.*"

60. Wittgenstein, "Lecture on Ethics," 41. To avoid misunderstanding here (even at the risk of seeming pedantic), I will note that the two questions Wittgenstein mentions as glosses on his feeling of wonder should not be taken in a cosmological sense. I take him to be mak-ing this very same point in the following remark from 1950: "If the believer in God looks around & asks 'Where does everything I see come from?' 'Where does all that come from?', what he hankers after is *not* a (causal) explanation; and the point of his question is that it is the expression of this hankering. He is expressing, then, a stance towards all explanations." Wittgenstein, *Culture and Value*, 96–97 (MS 173 92r: 1950). That the experience of wonder he describes in the "Lecture on Ethics" is not to be equated with the kind of amazement we feel when we observe something incredible is made clear by his example of a man's growing a lion's head. This is merely a case of our having yet to subsume a seemingly freakish event under a causal law. Wittgenstein mentions two other experiences, what he calls the "experience

of feeling *absolutely* safe" (41) or, later in the lecture, "safe in the hands of God" (42) and the feeling of guilt or "that God disapproves of our conduct" (42).

61.   Wittgenstein, "Lecture on Ethics," 42–43, my emphasis. There is a question whether Wittgenstein should be taken here and in the *Tractatus* as arguing for conventionalism concerning causality and the laws of mechanics. I believe what he says is best understood as part of a deflationary attack on a metaphysical conception of necessity that says that the world must be viewed in causal-scientific terms.

62.   For a related discussion emphasizing the importance of these different senses of "world" in the *Tractatus*, see Friedlander, *Signs of Sense*, 163–164.

63.   Wittgenstein, "Lecture on Ethics," 42. Wittgenstein articulates these themes in a remarkably similar way in this remark recorded in a manuscript dating from 1947: "In the way in which asking a question, insisting on an answer, or not asking it, expresses a different attitude, a different way of living, *so* too, in this sense, an utterance like 'It is God's will' or 'We are not masters of our fate.' What this sentence does, or at least something similar, a commandment too could do. Including one that you give to yourself. And conversely a commandment, e.g. 'Do not grumble!' can be uttered like the affirmation of a truth." Wittgenstein, *Culture and Value*, 69–70 (MS 134 143: 13–14.4.1947).

64.   Wittgenstein, "Lecture on Ethics," 42–43. Cf. Diamond, "Ethics, Imagination, and the Method of the *Tractatus*," 168.

65.   It's worth pointing out that the placement of these remarks toward the very end of the §6.3s makes it natural to read them both as summing up the prior discussion of causality and mechanics and as forming part of a bridge into the discussion of ethics in the §6.4s.

66.   One could also take these passages as pressing the reader to make sense with the sign "everything" (*alles*).

67.   Waismann, *Wittgenstein and the Vienna Circle*, 230.

68.   Some of Wittgenstein's criticisms of Frege and Russell concern the analogously ambiguous role played by logical truths in their respective systems. Consider too in this vein a passage found at Wittgenstein, *Wittgenstein's Nachlass*, MS 108 198–199, one of the manuscripts for *Philosophische Bemerkungen*. It is dated June 29, 1930. It also appears at TS 236 6, but the date of transcription is not known. "It is very remarkable that in the explanations for a book on the differential calculus, one finds set-theoretic expressions and symbols that completely disappear in the calculus. This reminds one of the first declarations in physics textbooks where there is talk of the law of causality and the like, which are never mentioned again once we get to the point." In other words, the law of causality is presented as though it were some kind of foundational and substantive truth, but it finds no real application in the actual subject matter of physics. See also Waismann, *Wittgenstein and the Vienna Circle*, 164.

69.   Wittgenstein, *Tractatus Logico-philosophicus*, §5.136.

70.   Ibid., §4.0312. Paul Ernst's description of "magical conceptions" in his postscript to the Grimm fairy tales made a profound impact on Wittgenstein, as is evident in this remark from 1931: "Should my book ever be published, its foreword must contain an acknowledgement to the foreword of Paul Ernst to his edition of Grimm's Fairy Tales, which I should have acknowledged already in the [*Tractatus*] as the source of the expression 'misunderstanding the logic of language.'" Wittgenstein, *Wittgenstein's Nachlass*, MS 110 184 (June 20, 1931). Quoted in Nyíri, "Wittgenstein's Later Work in Relation to Conservatism," 51–52.

Nyiri points out that the "foreword" to which Wittgenstein refers is actually a postscript to the third volume of Ernst's edition of the *Grimmische Kinder- und Hausmärchen*. In this context, compare *Philosophical Investigations*, §192: "You have no model of this superlative fact, but you are seduced into using a super-expression. (It might be called a philosophical superlative.)"

71. Wittgenstein, *Culture and Value*, 7–8 (MS 109 200). In the first edition of *Culture and Value* (1980), Winch translated *heben* as "intensify." He changed this to "enhance" in the second edition (1998). I have replaced these with "remove," which, although a secondary meaning of *heben*, is what I believe fits better in the context of Wittgenstein's remark. For the reference to Renan, see Renan: *History of the People of Israel*, vol. 1, chapter 3.

72. The charges that Wittgenstein makes here against Renan are, in effect, the same as those he levels elsewhere against the anthropologist Sir James Frazer. See "Remarks on Frazer's Golden Bough," reprinted in Wittgenstein, *Philosophical Occasions*, 115–155.

73. In claiming as I do here that the *Tractatus* is engaged in a kind of cultural critique that is internal to its attaining its ethical point, I am also bringing attention to an evident difference between the book's conception and that behind *Being and Time*. This is because Heidegger conceived of his book as a cross-cultural project of fundamental ontology, part of which is an examination and critique of the purportedly cross-cultural problem of inauthenticity. Nevertheless, as I indicate elsewhere (see notes 20 and 89), there is a degree of ambiguity running through *Being and Time* on this point, and the philosophical and cultural status of natural science is one of the many issues that the ambiguity concerns. Heidegger's existential account of science is, after all, both an attempt to put science in a proper philosophical context and an attempt to dissuade us from seeing scientific modes of intelligibility as basic. But this is surely an error that only people belonging to scientific cultures would be tempted to commit. So there is a perfectly genuine sense in which *Being and Time* targets those sharing a particular cultural heritage. Still, given his explicitly stated project of fundamental ontology, Heidegger seems committed to the idea that regardless of whichever particular inauthentic interpretations happen to be most tempting to *Western* Dasein, some or other leveled interpretations will always be on hand to tempt *any* Dasein into inauthenticity, regardless of the culture to which he or she belongs. Whether or not Wittgenstein held a similar view when he wrote the *Tractatus* is, I think, very unclear.

74. I should make clear here that I am not taking *Tractatus Logico-philosophicus* §6.53, §6.54, or §7 to function as elucidatory nonsense. On this, see Diamond, "Ethics, Imagination, and the Method of the *Tractatus*," and Conant, "The Method of the *Tractatus*."

75. Wittgenstein, "Lecture on Ethics," 44.

76. Waismann, *Wittgenstein and the Vienna Circle*, 68–69.

77. Ibid., 117. The conversation is dated December 17, 1930.

78. Ibid.

79. I have this phrase from Dreyfus, *Being-in-the-World*, 335.

80. As we will see presently, wonder and authenticity are connected by Heidegger as well.

81. Let me emphasize that I am *not* addressing every aspect of the question of whether Wittgenstein is attempting to put his reader in touch with "exactly the same phenomena" as the ones Heidegger calls "anxiety" and "authenticity." For example, internal to Heidegger's account of each of these phenomena are his existential interpretations of death and guilt, and my

discussion does not deal with the question of whether these two themes are present in the *Tractatus* in a recognizably Heideggerian form. Friedlander has done so in the case of death, however, and what he says has very interesting connections to my discussion of the subject on pages 67–68. He writes: "I have claimed earlier that the notion of world is tied essentially to the way in which a subject is made manifest by appropriating meaning. Possibilities are essentially dependent on my taking language upon myself: they are always fraught with the possibility that nothing may happen any more. The possible is to be understood not as an objective space external to the subject, but as something which always contains within its horizon the possibility that nothing is possible, that of my death. In this case, the possibility of having possibilities, of having a world, is internally related to the possibility of losing a world. Friedlander, "Signs of Sense," 136.

82. Wittgenstein, "Lecture on Ethics," 41.

83. Ibid., 43–44.

84. Ibid.

85. A remark by Friedlander about *Tractatus Logico-philosophicus* §7.0 seems to cast this point primarily in terms of remaining silent in the face of the impulse to speak nonsense: "For human beings, silence manifests itself in the form of a demand. This is not the Kantian imperative arising from the division between nature and reason, but rather, it is the sign that the source of the significance of speech manifests itself only through the drive to nonsense. The imperative in language cannot be heard apart from the temptation to nonsense, to noise. This is precisely why being silent is possible only as an imperative. The imperative to listen in silence is the demand to do away with the noisy elements of nonsense that surround us, but the imperative form precisely means that silence is ever to be achieved through overcoming the temptation to noise. We cannot listen to pure silence." Friedlander, *Signs of Sense*, 150. I think this is right, but it is not the whole story. Part of the point of my discussion on pages 58–59, where I refer to Wittgenstein's claim that he can imagine a religion in which there is no talking, is that depending on the context either silence or the production of ethical nonsense can manifest clarity about significance. In a footnote to the above passage (n. 4, p. 150), Friedlander connects this issue to conscience: "Listening has always been a favorite philosophical figure for the appearance of the ethical imperative, the voice of conscience." My point could be rephrased by saying that speaking and the call of conscience need not exclude one another. See also note 107, below.

86. I take it that both Wittgenstein and Heidegger saw their work of clarification as aimed primarily at philosophical audiences. Certainly Wittgenstein saw the possibility of embodying a kind of clarity about language that made philosophical clarification superfluous in certain cases. For example, I think his (idiosyncratic) rendering of a passage in Augustine's *Confessions* (see page 64) makes it evident that he would not have thought that understanding the *Tractatus*, which he says in the preface deals with the problems of philosophy, was necessary for someone who was simply willing to experience and express religious wonder without feeling the need to offer a philosophical justification for doing so. Similar considerations apply to *Being and Time*. Heidegger does not think that a philosophical understanding of Dasein's fundamental structure is a prerequisite for authenticity. On the other hand, I think it is untenable to argue that Heidegger believed that his existential phenomenology can succeed without the philosopher seeing for himself the substantial connections between

the structures of Dasein that Heidegger is trying to uncover and the ways in which those structures inform the philosopher's own self-understanding and his own lived experience. I think that what is most true to say is that there is a certain ambiguity running through the book concerning the relation between philosophical understanding and authenticity.

87. By taking up the issue of the emotional tenor of these terms, I should not be understood as expressing an interest in addressing what I consider to be an irrelevant question, viz., whether "wonder" and "anxiety" "pick out" the same feelings. On the contrary, I mean to bring out more clearly how the use of these expressions by Heidegger and Wittgenstein indicates structural similarities in their thought that are mutually illuminating. Nevertheless, it perhaps bears repeating that in *Being and Time* Heidegger describes anxiety as a ground mood that uncovers for Dasein its basic structure as Care (thrown, fallen, projection in the anonymous interpretations of the "they"). On a resolute reading, however, the *Tractatus* is supposed to leave us with only ordinary sentences, and so it is not supposed to result in anything like a description of the fundamental nature of language. (I will discuss how the *Tractatus* fails to live up to this ambition in the next chapter.)

88. Heidegger, "What Is Metaphysics?" 108.

89. Dreyfus argues that it is in fact unclear how in the context of the project of fundamental ontology Heidegger can accommodate the idea that Dasein ordinarily flees anxiety. According to Dreyfus, Heidegger's importation from Kierkegaard of a Western, specifically Christian-*psychological* understanding of fleeing into his story about authenticity simply will not work, given the overall cross-cultural, *ontological* framework within which he is (supposed to be) working. Dreyfus's point seems to be that even if it makes a great deal of ontic, psychological sense to those raised in a Christian culture, no conceptual analysis of the aloneness and groundlessness of anxiety will show why, as a matter of *ontology*, anxiety is something one would ordinarily flee from, especially when holding on to it makes possible the unshakable joy of resolute authenticity. In other words, it's hard to make sense of the view that an analysis of the structures that allow Dasein to have an intelligible world should reveal Dasein to be a kind of being that can't stand being the kind of being it is. See Dreyfus, *Being-in-the-World*, 333–336. See also notes 20 and 73. If we think about this question in relation to the aims of the *Tractatus*, it's interesting to see why a parallel problem connected to what could be called "our tendency to flee the groundlessness of giving expression to our wonder" need not arise, at least given the self-understanding from which the book is written. This is because the strategy of the *Tractatus* takes for granted a kind of psychological perspective on its modern reader that, if Dreyfus is right, will not fit into the self-understanding of Heidegger's project of fundamental ontology. As will become clear in the next chapter, however, this part of the *Tractatus'* strategy loses its appearance of innocence once seen against the background of the book's own concealed foundationalism.

90. Heidegger, *Being and Time*, 161. This is the only time in this text that I have made use of Stambaugh's translation.

91. Ibid., 318. The sense of the German text is somewhat shaped by the fact that the German word for curiosity, *Neugier*, literally means "greed for the new."

92. Heidegger, "What Is Metaphysics?" 104–112. In making my point here, I am compressing a number of passages found toward the end of the lecture. But what I say does follow clearly from the logic of those passages. In a new introduction to "What Is Metaphysics?" written

in 1948, Heidegger warns against a cosmological understanding of the question with which he concludes the lecture. See Heidegger, "The Way Back Into the Ground of Metaphysics," 277–279. By the late 1930s, after he had abandoned the project of fundamental ontology, Heidegger turned his attention directly to wonder itself without regarding it as grounded in anxiety. Wonder is one of the central themes in a 1937–1938 lecture course (published as *Basic Questions in Philosophy*). The main topic of these lectures is the early Greek understanding of truth as uncovering or unconcealment (*aletheia*) and its transformation to an understanding of truth as correspondence (*homoiosis*). Corresponding to this change, Heidegger claims, is a degeneration from wonder to curiosity. I have benefited here from a paper by Stone, "Curiosity as the Thief of Wonder."

93.   In fact, these "bipolar" descriptions are not uncommon: "A solemn state of mind is never crude or simple—it seems to contain a certain measure of its own opposite in solution. A solemn joy preserves a sort of bitter in its sweetness: a solemn sorrow is one to which we intimately consent." James, *The Varieties of Religious Experience*, 51.

94.   Perhaps for a certain kind of reader of Heidegger, my calling attention to the fact that wonder plays a significant role in both Wittgenstein's and Heidegger's thinking will be enough to confirm a suspicion that I am on the wrong track. I am thinking mainly about a suspicion that goes like this: In *Basic Questions*, Heidegger not only distinguishes wonder (*Erstaunen*) from curiosity (*Neugier*) but also distinguishes carefully between wonder and what on the surface seem to be three closely related stances toward the world: amazement (*Sichwundern*), admiration (*Bewundern*), and astonishment (*Bestaunen*). These three stances turn out, however, to have nothing in common with wonder and much in common with curiosity. It might then seem as though Heidegger and Wittgenstein must be speaking past each other when they speak of wonder, since in the passage I cite on pages 56–57 where he criticizes Ernst Renan, Wittgenstein basically uses *sichwundern, staunen, erstaunen*, and *anstaunen* interchangeably. Similar worries might be voiced about the connection that Wittgenstein makes in the same passage between wonder and fear (*Furcht*). This concern arises because in *Being and Time* Heidegger distinguishes sharply between fear and anxiety, where the ontic emotion of fear is a kind of inauthentic interpretation of the ontological structure of anxiety; authentic Dasein is fearless. See especially *Being and Time*, sections 30 and 40. And so, it might be thought, Wittgenstein's reference to fear in the Renan passage must not have any relevant connection to anxiety or wonder as these are understood by Heidegger. In response, it's worth repeating first that what Wittgenstein says in the "Lecture on Ethics" about the case of a man growing a lion's head (see page 53 and note 60) and about his temptation "to say that the right expression in language for the miracle of the existence of the world, though it is not any proposition *in* language, is the existence of language itself" (see page 61) make it unreasonable to interpret what he says about wonder in anything like a causal or cosmological sense. More importantly, to insist that the mere occurrences of the expressions *sichwundern* or *Furcht* in the Renan passage are enough to undermine the connections I am trying to make amounts to nothing more than a kind of textual fetishism that only gets in the way of genuine philosophical understanding. Wittgenstein is not operating in the same philosophical tradition as Heidegger, and so his choice of words can hardly be expected to conform to Heidegger's in every respect. Understood in context, the mere appearance of certain expressions in the Renan passage shouldn't provoke any particular

knee-jerk interpretative response on the part of the Heideggerian purist. What I am arguing for should stand or fall on whether these and other expressions are being *used* by Wittgenstein in ways that make interesting philosophical contact with Heidegger's thought.

95. Waismann, *Wittgenstein and the Vienna Circle*, 68–69. This is Wittgenstein's paraphrase of *Confess*. 1.4: "et vae tacentibus de te, quoniam loquaces muti sunt" ("Yet woe betide those who are silent about you! For even those who are most gifted with speech cannot find words to describe you"). See Augustine, *Confessions*, 23. In an undated conversation, Drury recalls Wittgenstein paraphrasing the same passage as "And woe to those who say nothing concerning thee just because the chatterboxes talk a lot of nonsense." See Rhees, *Personal Recollections*, 104.

96. Wittgenstein, *Culture and Value*, 64. In a remark from 1931, he says that it is essential to clarification that it be carried out with courage. See ibid., 16.

97. Wittgenstein, *Cambridge Letters*, 14. The date of the letter is June 22. Wittgenstein's student and friend Maurice Drury recalls the following exchange, which he dates from 1930:

> Drury: I find Lotze very heavy going, very dull.
> Wittgenstein: Probably a man who shouldn't have been allowed to write philosophy. A book you should read is William James's *Varieties of Religious Experience*; that was a book that helped me a lot at one time.
> Drury: Oh yes, I have read that. I always enjoy reading anything of William James. He is such a human person.
> Wittgenstein: That is what makes him a good philosopher; he was a real human being.

Rhees, *Personal Recollections*, 121. Although I don't endorse his reading of the *Tractatus* itself, the second chapter of Goodman's *Wittgenstein and William James* has a very useful discussion of Wittgenstein's relation to James's *Varieties of Religious Experience*.

98. James, *Varieties of Religious Experience*, 224–225. A few pages later, James quotes with approval this summary of these experiences from the psychologist James Leuba: "When the sense of estrangement . . . fencing man about in a narrowly limited ego, breaks down, the individual finds himself 'at one with all creation.' He lives in the universal life: he and man, he and nature, he and God, are one. That state of confidence, trust, union with all things, following upon the achievement of moral unity, is the *Faith-state*" (227).

99. Certainly among these would have been St. Paul, Luther, and Tolstoy (as quoted in James and independently). Whether Wittgenstein had read Augustine or Kierkegaard before he completed the *Tractatus* is less certain. In a 1953 letter to Ludwig Ficker, Wittgenstein's friend Ludwig Hänsel writes that he and Wittgenstein read Augustine together during the year they were prisoners of war in Monte Cassino. See Hänsel, *Ludwig Wittgenstein*, 251. After he saw Wittgenstein again for the first time since the war, Russell wrote to Ottoline Morrel from The Hague on December 20, 1919: "I had felt in his book a flavour of mysticism, but was astonished when I found that he has become a complete mystic. He reads people like Kierkegaard and Angelus Silesius, and he seriously contemplates becoming a monk. It all started from William James's *Varieties of Religious Experience*, and grew (not unnaturally) during the winter he spent alone in Norway before the war, when he was nearly mad." Wittgenstein, *Cambridge Letters*, 140. McGuinness claims that Wittgenstein would

have likely been familiar with Kierkegaard before his captivity through the translations into German in *Der Brenner* by T. Haecker. See McGuinness, *Young Ludwig*, 205. At any rate, Wittgenstein had certainly read both Augustine and Kierkegaard by the time he gave the "Lecture on Ethics."

100. As to the universal efficacy of these experiences, James writes, "I do indeed believe that if the Subject have no liability to such subconscious activity, or if his conscious fields have a hard rind of a margin that resists incursions from beyond it, his conversion must be gradual if it occur, and must resemble any simple growth into new habits." James, *Varieties of Religious Experience*, 223.

101. It should be pointed out, however, that in contrast to James's and Wittgenstein's attitudes of respectful neutrality, the early Heidegger interpreted the tendency to ascribe anxiety's call of conscience to something outside the self, to a higher power, for example, as an objectifying inauthentic interpretation of the "they." See Heidegger, *Being and Time*, 323.

102. Wittgenstein, *Tractatus Logico-philosophicus*, §5.541, §5.542, and §5.5421, which I take to be directed at the account of propositional attitudes in Russell's multiple-relation theory of judgment, suggest just how far Wittgenstein intends to carry this "impersonal" view of language. In a related vein, Diamond has pointed out how Wittgenstein's view of quantifiers in the *Tractatus* can be seen as amounting to a criticism of the view of proper names Russell argues for in, for example, "Knowledge by Acquaintance and Knowledge by Description," in *Mysticism and Logic*, 202–224. Diamond notes how these criticisms can be seen as an early private-language argument. See Diamond, "Does Bismarck Have a Beetle in His Box?" 262–292.

103. That the reader is meant to connect these themes with ethics is shown, for instance, by their return at §6.43, where Wittgenstein writes, "If the good or bad exercise of the will does alter the world, it can alter only the limits of the world, not the facts—not what can be expressed by means of language. In short the effect must be that it becomes an altogether different world. It must, so to speak, wax and wane as a whole. The world of the happy man is a different one from that the unhappy man." Compare this with the following from James: "When we come to study the phenomenon of conversion or religious regeneration, we shall see that a not infrequent consequence of the change in the subject is a transfiguration of the face of nature in his eyes. A new heaven seems to shine upon a new earth. In melancholiacs there is usually a similar change, only it is in the reverse direction. The world now looks remote, strange, sinister, uncanny. Its color is gone, its breath is cold, there is no speculation in the eyes it glares with." James, *Varieties of Religious Experience*, 141–142.

104. Waismann, *Wittgenstein and the Vienna Circle*, 117.

105. Waismann (ibid., 92–93) records the following on January 5, 1930, under the heading "Lecture on Ethics":

In ethics our expressions have a double meaning: a psychological one of which you can speak and a non-psychological one: "good tennis-player," "good." We are constantly using the different expressions to indicate the same thing.

Astonishment at the fact of the world. Every attempt to express it leads to nonsense.

Man has an inclination to run against the limits of language. This running against them signalizes ethics. Everything I describe is within the world. An ethical proposition never occurs in the complete description of the world, not even when I am describing a murderer. What is ethical is not a state of affairs.

106. I take Friedlander to be touching on a closely related theme in the following passage: "The subject is associated with the assuming of possibilities. It is not to be identified with some object in the world, but always with the possibilities of existence revealed in language. This does not mean that to be a subject is only to be an authentic subject who has assumed the limits of language, but rather, that to be a subject is essentially to assume one's utmost possibilities or to avoid them; the subject is essentially happy or unhappy." Friedlander, *Signs of Sense*, 127.

107. Heidegger takes up relevant themes in *Being and Time* in his discussion of anxiety, "mineness," and the "call of conscience." I quote here without elaboration three relevant passages. "Dasein is an entity which, in its very Being, comports itself understandingly towards that Being. In saying this, we are calling attention to the formal concept of existence. Dasein exists. Furthermore, Dasein is an entity which in each case I myself am. Mineness belongs to any existent Dasein, and belongs to it as the condition which makes authenticity and inauthenticity possible" (78). "In anxiety there lies the possibility of a disclosure which is quite distinctive; for anxiety individualizes. This individualization brings Dasein back from its falling, and makes manifest to it that authenticity and inauthenticity are possibilities of its Being. These basic possibilities of Dasein (and Dasein is in each case mine) show themselves in anxiety as they are in themselves—undisguised by entities within-the-world, to which, proximally and for the most part, Dasein clings" (235). "Uncanniness is the basic kind of Being-in-the-world, even though in an everyday way it has been covered up. Out of the depths of this kind of Being, Dasein itself, as conscience, calls. The 'it calls me' [*es ruft mich*] is a distinctive kind of discourse for Dasein. The call whose mood has been attuned by anxiety is what makes it possible first and foremost for Dasein to project itself upon its ownmost *potentiality-for-Being*. The call of conscience, existentially understood, makes known for the first time what we have hitherto merely contended: that uncanniness pursues Dasein and is a threat to the lostness in which it has forgotten itself" (322). Of course, the early Wittgenstein would have regarded as nonsense talk of anxiety as a special revealing mood that attunes Dasein to the call of conscience. The early Heidegger would have likely responded by saying that Wittgenstein's grounds for calling talk of anxiety and conscience nonsense betrays an impoverished understanding of language. Both are half right.

108. I sense that Friedlander is getting at something close to this when he writes, "Such a book demands a relation to language that is more fundamental than is our being guided by established meanings. It must work its way toward the possibility of an event that itself exceeds the means of expression. This is the event of the *Tractatus*." Friedlander, *Signs of Sense*, 144.

109. Friedlander (ibid., 148) asks in this vein, "But why should it be difficult to accept language? Why the tendency to cover up language with noise? It is the simultaneous recognition of the groundlessness of meaning and of the dependence of the very being of the subject on the assumption of meaning that generates anxiety, and the concomitant tendency to conceal that anxiety by seeking to ground meaning systematically in metaphysics."

110. These "anyone" propositions, I should add, would include ordinary indexical statements such as "I am bored." See note 102 above. See also note 22 in chapter 3.

III. Wittgenstein, *Tractatus Logico-philosophicus*, 5. Emphasis is in the original.

II2. Heidegger, *Being and Time*, 257. The third thesis is "that Aristotle, the father of logic, not only has assigned truth to judgment as its primordial locus but has set going the definition of 'truth' as 'agreement.'"

II3. Ibid., 343. It bears repeating that there is an inherent tension in drawing the kind of connection between the early Wittgenstein and the early Heidegger that I am attempting here. Heidegger almost certainly does not think of the sentences that make up this passage to be "ordinary" in the sense I have used that term in the context of articulating a resolute reading of the *Tractatus*. On a resolute reading, Wittgenstein would consider these sentences to be (possibly elucidatory) nonsense.

II4. Ibid., 78.

II5. Here, perhaps, is an "isomorphism" between language and world that some commentators find in the *Tractatus'* "picture theory" of the proposition. I should stress that I am *not* saying here that Heidegger thinks an authentic relation to language lets us see that the world only gets disclosed through ordinary sentences. This recognition is part of what I am claiming for "Tractarian" authenticity.

II6. Kremer, in "The Purpose of Tractarian Nonsense," 25–27, addresses this issue as well, substantially along the same lines that I do here. My way of connecting truth and ethics in the *Tractatus* via *Being and Time'*s discussion of truth at paragraph 44 seems to me strikingly close to Friedlander's (*Signs of Sense*, 126–127) way of connecting ethics in the *Tractatus* with Heidegger's description of significance and worldhood at paragraph 18. He writes: "Whereas the sensicality of a proposition is always a matter of fact, significance makes a world of difference. It is not one part of the world that has of itself absolute value in itself or is the ground for significance as such. It is, rather, the world as a whole that is illumined with significance, that waxes and wanes for us. That kind of significance, associated with having a world, is never partial, which is why it seems at times so remote, so inaccessible." One might say, then, that the primary ethical dimension has to do with inhabiting language, with acknowledging its conditions, with opening the space for action. "The fundamental ethical act is the act of assuming significance, the manifestation of the subject through the sphere of significance, its possibilities and its demands. The correlate of that act, in respect of the subject, is the world rather than a particular fact in the world" (Friedlander, *Signs of Sense*, 133). What I see as the nearness of our thought here is perhaps not so surprising given Heidegger's own connection of truth with worldhood: "Being-true as Being uncovering, is . . . ontologically possible only on the basis of Being-in-the-world. This latter phenomenon, which we have known as a basic state of Dasein, is the foundation for the primordial phenomenon of truth" (Heidegger, *Being and Time*, 261).

II7. I take Diamond to be hitting on closely related themes when she writes: "When logic or ethics is said by Wittgenstein to be transcendental, this does not mean that it is concerned with the activities of some transcendental subject. What 'transcendental' means in the *Tractatus* is that the 'sign' for whatever is called transcendental is the general form of a proposition, not some particular proposition or set of propositions that says something in particular. The only thing that could be said to do any meaning here—in logic or in ethics—is a sign that *says* nothing, but which contains (in a sense) every combination of signs to which we do give sense, every combination of signs that does say something, and no one of which

expresses a logical state of affairs or an ethical one. There—in the general form of a proposition—you can see that logic and ethics are not spheres in which we express ourselves by
means of signs." Diamond, "Ethics, Imagination, and the Method of the *Tractatus*," 168.

118. The strands in Heidegger's and Wittgenstein's thought that I am discussing here are help-
fully brought together in "Wittgenstein, Heidegger, and Humility," a paper by David
Cooper. He comments: "I suggest that the mystery, the proper object of wonder, is the same
for both men. It resides ... in that meeting of language (or thought) and world—that fitting
together of two inseparable components—whose 'joint product' is our world, the world as
experienced and described. When Wittgenstein and Heidegger wonder that anything exists
at all, this is not amazement at some cosmic event, the 'big bang' or whatever: but wonder
that we and the world are so fitted for one another that anything can, as it were, be a *something*, an identifiable thing present for us in thought and speech" (113). My quoting this passage in the context of my discussion of the *Tractatus* is somewhat misleading, since it is clear
in his paper that Cooper intends a comparison between only the later Wittgenstein and
Heidegger, while I think it expresses well what I want to say about the early Wittgenstein
too. Although there is much in his understanding of the *Tractatus* that I do not endorse, I
found Cooper's discussion very insightful nonetheless. In a paper from 1966 ("The Mysticism of the *Tractatus*"), Brian McGuinness interestingly suggests that holistic themes in
the *Tractatus* be read as Wittgenstein's response to views that Russell expresses in the essay
"Mysticism and Logic" about the relations between science, mysticism, and metaphysics.

119. And here I mean to align already the early Wittgenstein with a tradition where something
like Herder's concept of *Besonnenheit* shapes the terms of philosophical criticism. On this,
see part 3 of Charles Taylor, *Philosophical Papers: Volume 1, Human Agency and Language*.
Friedlander writes: "The original experience of the very possibility of a significant world is
characterized in Wittgenstein's 'Lecture on Ethics' in terms of the sense of wonder at the
very existence of the world, or alternatively, at the very existence of language.... The source
of significance, the transcendence involved in significance as such, can be related to the concept of a miracle. But this is not a miracle that occurs at one time in a particular place in the
world. There is no burning bush. Rather, the only sense that can be given to this miracu-
lousness is related to the existence of significance altogether. The existence of a meaningful
world, or, what comes to the same, the existence of language as such, is to be considered a
miracle. It is in this sense that the *Tractatus* can be regarded as dealing with creation itself.
For when it comes to this dimension, one does not feel the happiness associated with the
recognition of what things are, with the showing of significance, but rather one's experience
concerns the very existence of a significant world rather than nothing." Friedlander, *Signs of
Sense*, 140.

120. Waismann, *Wittgenstein and the Vienna Circle*, 68. I have amended the translation slightly.
The German reads: "Ich kann mir wohl denken was Heidegger mit Sein und Angst meint.
Der Mensch hat den Trieb, gegen die Grenzen der Sprache anzurennen. Denken Sie z.B.
an das Erstaunen, dass etwas existiert. Das Erstaunen kann nicht in Form einer Frage aus-
gedrückt werden, und es gibt auch gar keine Antwort. Alles, was wir sagen mögen, kann
a priori nur Unsinn sein. Trotzdem rennen wir gegen die Grenze der Sprache an. Dieses
Anrennen hat auch Kierkegaard gesehen und es sogar ganz ähnlich (als Anrennen gegen
das Paradoxon) bezeichnet. Dieses Anrennen gegen die Grenze der Sprache ist die *Ethik*."

Other parts of this same excerpt from Waismann's notes are quoted on pages 58 (cf. note 76) and 64 (cf. note 95). The reference seems to be to Kierkegaard, *Philosophical Fragments*, 37. In 1965, *The Philosophical Review* 74 (January) published Wittgenstein's "Lecture on Ethics," which he delivered shortly after returning to Cambridge in 1929. As an addendum to this, *The Philosophical Review* included a few lines from the notes recorded by Friedrich Waismann in conversation with Wittgenstein a few weeks after the lecture. Strangely, the editors expunged Waismann's own heading for the passage, "Apropos of Heidegger," as well as the first line, where Wittgenstein refers to Heidegger.

121. My discussion here has benefited from a paper by Keicher, "Untersuchungen zu Wittgenstein's 'Diktat für Schlick.'" See also Murray, "A Note on Wittgenstein and Heidegger."

122. Waismann, *Wittgenstein and the Vienna Circle*, n. 25, 68. The footnote text is taken from Heidegger, *Being and Time*, 230–231, and reads as follows: "*That in the face of which one has anxiety is Being-in-the-world as such.* What is the difference phenomenally between that in the face of which anxiety is anxious and that in the face of which fear is afraid? That in the face of which one has anxiety is not an entity within-the-world . . . *the world as such is that in the face of which one has anxiety.*"

123. Heidegger *Being and Time*, n. iv, 492. Heidegger's reference is to Kierkegaard's *Der Begriff der Angst* [*The Concept of Anxiety*], 1844, *Gesammelte Werke* (Diedrichs), vol. 5. Heidegger also refers here to Augustine and Luther as prefiguring Kierkegaard's analysis. On this question, see Rentsch, *Heidegger und Wittgenstein*, 211.

124. In particular, Carnap tries to demonstrate how Heidegger's sentence "*Das Nichts selbst nichtet*" ("The Nothing itself nihilates") violates the laws of logical syntax. See Rudolf Carnap, "The Elimination of Metaphysics Through Logical Analysis of Language." Carnap and Heidegger had met in the spring of 1929 in Davos, Switzerland, where Carnap not only heard Heidegger debate Ernst Cassirer but also held informal discussions with him. See Friedman, *A Parting of the Ways*.

125. I say "block of text" rather than "passage," because Carnap has literally strung together sentences that are spread over several pages of Heidegger's lecture. I have not used Arthur Pap's translation here (cf. Ayer, *Logical Positivism*, 69) but rather assembled the corresponding translations from Heidegger's lecture found in Krell's *Martin Heidegger: Basic Writings*, 97–105. The other block of text printed in Carnap's paper, broken up by his interjection, runs as follows:

> With regard to the nothing question and answer alike are inherently absurd. — — The commonly cited ground rule of all thinking, the proposition that contradiction is to be avoided, universal "logic" itself, lays low this question. *Basic Writings*, 99.
>
> [Carnap's interjection:] So much the worse for logic! We must overthrow its reign:
>
> If the power of the intellect in the field of inquiry into the nothing and into Being is thus shattered, then the destiny of the reign of "logic" in philosophy is thereby decided. The idea of "logic" itself disintegrates in the turbulence of a more original questioning. *Basic Writings*, 107.

126. The *Diktat für Schlick*, item 302 in Wittgenstein, *Wittgenstein's Nachlass*, stems from the period 1931–1933. See Conant's "Two Conceptions of *Die Überwindung der Metaphysik*" for

an excellent discussion of Wittgenstein's remarks on Carnap's paper and of how that paper has shaped both early and later receptions of the *Tractatus.*

127. And, to repeat, neither of them is speaking to the cosmological question.

128. Of course, it cannot be ruled out a priori that Wittgenstein knew of Heidegger's brief mention of wonder in *Being and Time.* But for Wittgenstein to have traced the connections between this brief mention back to authenticity and anxiety would have required a much more detailed knowledge of the way that those concepts hang together in Heidegger's book than I believe it plausible to ascribe to him.

129. In fact, this is why I believe Wittgenstein mentions Kierkegaard after Heidegger in the conversation. Of course, it's not unthinkable that Wittgenstein may have been stimulated by Heidegger's lecture to consult *Being and Time.* Since Kierkegaard is mentioned in the book but not in the lecture, this could partly account for Wittgenstein's reference to him immediately after the reference to Heidegger and anxiety. But I don't think it is necessary to invoke this remote possibility; Wittgenstein could have simply seen the philosophical connections between what he had read of each man's work.

130. I am not suggesting that Heidegger would have recognized Wittgenstein's reaction in the conversation with Waismann nor the idea of Tractarian "authenticity" that I have been operating with here. Heidegger's account of authenticity concerns all of the practices of the "they" and all of Dasein's involvements, whereas the authenticity that I am arguing is a goal of the *Tractatus* seems to concern only our relation to language. Moreover, it is fair to say that the early Heidegger has a much richer conception of language than does the early Wittgenstein, since even the "anyone" linguistic practices of the "they" include a wide variety of uses, whereas the locus of engagement between Wittgenstein and his reader is restricted to a narrow construal of language, what for Heidegger would have amounted to an understanding fundamentally in terms of assertion (*apophansis*). See *Being and Time*, paragraphs 33 and 34). Without denying this important difference, it's worth noting, first, that talking itself is an activity and, second, that language permeates so many of our other activities that it is arguable that the kind of alteration in one's relation to it that I am arguing Wittgenstein sought to bring about would result in a change in the way one engaged in many of those activities as well.

131. Heidegger, *Being and Time*, 435.

132. Ibid., 329.

133. Cooper, *Heidegger*, 49.

134. Heidegger, *Being and Time*, 435.

135. Ibid., 437. See page 46 for a brief explanation of the terms "existentiell" and "existential."

136. Ibid., 437. Dreyfus suggests Martin Luther King Jr. as an example of someone who explicitly repeated an aspect of the Christian heritage when he took it upon himself to be the advocate for the poor and oppressed. One might also see King as having chosen Jesus for his hero, or perhaps Jesus and Gandhi as his heroes. In the future, people may in turn choose King for their hero.

137. See especially Conant's "Must We Show What We Cannot Say?", "Kierkegaard, Wittgenstein, and Nonsense," and "Putting Two and Two Together."

138. I am not claiming that the discussion of this section concerns the only important difference between the *Tractatus* and the understanding of authenticity at work in *Being and Time*

(cf. note 130, above). Rather, the difference between those two works that I have focused on here is important for understanding my criticisms of Kremer and Conant in the next section, in particular because I see it as essentially the same difference that they overlook in their discussions comparing the *Tractatus* to the works of Paul, Augustine, and Kierkegaard. A question that I cannot take up here is whether Heidegger's talk of authentic Dasein's historicality, in particular its choosing its hero, is *actually coherent*. The question does not arise for all such talk, not, for example, for Paul's talk about Christ in his epistles, but rather because there is a question about the overall coherence of the context in which Heidegger's talk of the heritage and hero takes place; that is, there is a question about the coherence of Heidegger's project of fundamental ontology itself.

139. Kremer, "The Purpose of Tractarian Nonsense," 47. *New International Version* (Barker, 1985) cited by book, chapter, and verse.

140. Kremer, "The Purpose of Tractarian Nonsense," 47–48. Cf. Romans 7.

141. Kremer, "The Purpose of Tractarian Nonsense," 49. Cf. Augustine, *City of God*, 852.

142. Kremer, "The Purpose of Tractarian Nonsense," 52.

143. Ibid., 51.

144. Ibid., 56.

145. Conant, "Must We Show What We Cannot Say?" "Throwing Away the Top of the Ladder," "Kierkegaard, Wittgenstein, and Nonsense," "Putting Two and Two Together," "Two Conceptions of *Die Überwindung der Metaphysik*," "The Method of the *Tractatus*," and (with Cora Diamond) "On Reading the *Tractatus* Resolutely."

146. Conant, "Putting Two and Two Together," 249.

147. From *Concluding Unscientific Postscript to Philosophical Fragments*, translated by Walter Lowrie (Princeton, N.J.: Princeton University Press, 1941). Reprinted in Guignon and Pereboom, *Existentialism: Basic Writings*, 83.

148. Conant, "Must We Show What We Cannot Say?" 261.

149. Conant, "Putting Two and Two Together," 283.

150. Conant, "Must We Show What We Cannot Say?" 262.

151. Conant, "Kierkegaard, Wittgenstein, and Nonsense," 205.

152. Ibid.

153. Ibid., 206.

154. Ibid. Elsewhere, he writes, "the attack in Kierkegaard is on a form of reflection which subserves a strategy of evasion—a form of reflection that offers the promise of enlightening us as to the nature of the ethical or religious life but in fact prevents us from ever arriving at the performance of a decisive action and hence from properly embarking on such a life." Conant, "Putting Two and Two Together," 311, n. 35.

155. Conant, "Must We Show What We Cannot Say?" 254. Conant also writes: "Kierkegaard sometimes describes his pseudonymous writings as works of ethics. What these authors have in mind here seems to be accurately captured in the claim that they thought of their works as ethical deeds. . . . The vigilance they call upon us to exercise in our use of language (and hence the vigilance with which they ask us to live our lives) can be justifiably termed an ethical demand. . . . The ethical purpose that guides them lies in nothing more, and nothing less than their hopes of changing one or another of their readers." Conant, "Putting Two and Two Together," n. 25, p. 278. Conant does not tell the reader where Kierkegaard says this

nor to which pseudonymous works Kierkegaard is referring. Thus it is difficult to render a judgment about the significance of Kierkegaard's utterance. This is unfortunate, since it is possible to take this utterance as making a very different point from the one Conant takes it to be making. If one understands Kierkegaard as I do, then one might think he was *limiting* the significance of some portion of his pseudonymous authorship by pointing out that since it consists of works of ethics, it does not give expression to the highest sphere, namely, the religious. At any rate, what Conant says correctly implies that in whatever sense Wittgenstein meant the *Tractatus* to be ethical, it certainly is not in the same sense as that in which the idea of *the ethical* is to be found in *Fear and Trembling*. There the idea of the ethical concerns universal ethical principles, and this is clearly not what Wittgenstein is referring to in his letter to Ficker or in the "Lecture on Ethics."

156. In order to keep the focus of the main text on the interpretation of Wittgenstein, I will sketch my differences with Conant over Kierkegaard as best I can in this long footnote. These differences mainly concern the significance of Kierkegaard's pseudonymous authorship, specifically, what to make of Religiousness B. Based on his understanding of Climacus's revocation at the end of the book, Conant would have us throw Religiousness B away with the rest of the *Concluding Unscientific Postscript*. He describes the authorial strategy of the *Postscript* as one in which "a host of apparently fully objective distinctions (such as, for example, that between Religiousness A and Religiousness B)" are drawn by Climacus, Kierkegaard's pseudonym (Conant, "Putting Two and Two Together," 263). He then adds, "the crucial question that Climacus gradually urges the reader up the work's dialectical ladder toward is the following: if the paradox [Religiousness B] is only objectively identifiable in virtue of the fact that it represents the utmost pitch of incomprehensibility, how are we to distinguish it from other extreme forms of incomprehensibility?" (261). Conant's answer is that we cannot objectively identify Religiousness B and that this is one of the things that the humorist Climacus was leading us to see. Conant thus believes that Kierkegaard employs plain nonsense in the *Postscript* in much the same way, and for many of the same reasons, as Wittgenstein does in the *Tractatus*: "That one *can* indeed genuinely imagine that one grasps a distinction where none has been drawn—that a projection of false necessities, beneath or beyond the conditions upon which our mastery of language rests, can prove mysteriously irresistible and gratifying—*this* is what these two books are, above all, about." ("Must We Show What We Cannot Say?" 254). Though I believe that what he writes here is true of the *Tractatus*, I believe that it is misleading when it comes to Kierkegaard. In fact, the problem may arise in part because Conant's almost exclusive focus on the *Postscript* prevents him from seeing that work in the broader context of Kierkegaard's writing.

To elaborate a bit further, Conant understands Kierkegaard's use of nonsense in the *Postscript* as having two main goals. First, to show the philosopher who assumes that understanding Christianity consists in acquiring abstruse knowledge that he is not a Christian (Conant, "Putting Two and Two Together," 275). "The attraction to the use of such concepts is often tied, he thinks, to the user's wish to sustain for himself the illusion of being a Christian. Kierkegaard's sense of the difficulty of his project is tied to a suspicion that his reader may have deeply entrenched motives—motives which he conceals from himself—for not wishing to clarify for himself what it is that he means when he employs such concepts" (ibid., 277). The second, related, goal consists of unraveling conceptual confusions of the philosopher from within, confusions that result from the philosopher's fleeing from the ordinary in his life, fleeing, that is, what Conant, echoing Stanley Cavell, calls knowledge "which one cannot help but already have." And in bursting the bubble of the philosopher's illusions that stem from this fleeing, Kierkegaard returns the philosopher to himself, to the everyday or ordinary in his life. Though he clearly acknowledges that Kierkegaard distinguishes between religious and ethical categories, the following passage makes it evident that Conant reads Kierkegaard as accomplishing this task by following in the footsteps of Socrates: "Most of what the ancients called 'philosophy' falls under the category of the ethical for Kierkegaard. Socrates is his paradigm of the ethical teacher (see for example, Chapter 1 of *Philosophical Fragments*). The ethical teacher's aim is to serve as a midwife who enables us to give birth to our true self. This he does not by imparting a doctrine but by serving as an occasion through which the repression of knowledge—*which one cannot help but already have*—is undone" (ibid., 314, n. 38, my emphasis). Since, on Conant's view, the original fleeing from oneself is not itself motivated by intellectual difficulties, he would not regard his claim that Kierkegaard means to clear up conceptual confusions as ascribing to him an overly intellectualist goal. But Conant does think that clearing up conceptual confusion, especially his philosophical reader's confusion about Christianity, is all that Kierkegaard himself thought could be accomplished through his writings.

Though it is of course correct that one must be aware of the literary strategy of the *Postscript*, in *The Sickness Unto Death*, Religiousness B is not described from the standpoint of a disinterested humorist (like Climacus) but from that of a committed Christian, Anti-Climacus. Precisely because Climacus himself is a philosopher, we ought to be suspicious about taking his logicizing away Religiousness B as Kierkegaard's intended resting place for his reader and so be wary of putting as much weight on the *Postscript* as Conant does for our overall interpretation of Kierkegaard. (Here too I should acknowledge the influence of Hubert Dreyfus on my views. This comes in part from the appendix to *Being-in-the-World*, which he co-wrote with Jane Rubin, but mostly through what I have taken away from many discussions with him over many years. I make no claim, however, that what I say here precisely represents either of their views.)

It is true that Conant himself states that his discussion is essentially limited to the pseudonymous works authored by Johannes Climacus: "This is perhaps the place to remark that I do not take what I say in this essay about the structure of the pseudonymous authorship to apply to the works authored by Anti-Climacus. They do not belong to the corpus of what Kierkegaard calls 'the aesthetic works.' His comments in *The Point of View* about the method of indirect communication as employed by the other pseudonyms—as a strategy of deceiving the reader into truth—are not meant to apply to Anti-Climacus. The reasons for employing the device of pseudonymity in this case lie elsewhere. Kierkegaard is not prepared to say of himself, as Anti-Climacus will say of himself, that he is 'an extraordinary Christian such as there has never been.' Hence the name Anti-Climacus: he is the antithesis—the polar opposite—of Climacus, the pseudonym who repeatedly says of himself that he is not a Christian" (Conant, "Putting Two and Two Together," 327, n. 97). Nevertheless, I do not think Conant acknowledges the degree to which this admission bears on his interpretation. First, there are references to the spheres of existence, which Conant would have us throw away as part of the ladder of the *Postscript*, in nonpseudonymous works such as *The Present Age* and the *Edifying Discourses*, suggesting that Kierkegaard did not merely take these to be literary devices. Moreover, in the 1851 piece "My Activity as a Writer," in *The Point of View for My Work as an Author*, Kierkegaard indicates that *The Sickness Unto Death* represents the right attitude toward Christianity. He writes of Anti-Climacus, "All the earlier pseudonyms are lower than the 'edifying author' [Kierkegaard, in this context]; the new pseudonym represents a higher pseudonymity" (Kierkegaard, *Point of View*, 142). In a supplement to this piece, he tells us that although he "knows what Christianity is, my imperfection as a Christian I fully recognize" (153). And when he adds, "I am infinitely concerned that the requirements of the ideal [Christianity] may at least be heard," it seems clear from the context that it is Anti-Climacus who "ventures to say everything" concerning that ideal that Kierkegaard admits to falling short of (153). Yet this nonpseudonymous work is a precursor to the longer, posthumously published *The Point of View for My Work as an Author*, which is claimed by Conant himself as one of the few reliable sources we have for how to read the pseudonymous authorship. It may be true that Kierkegaard is not prepared to say of himself that he is a Christian, but it is arguable that what he does say in *The Point of View* strongly suggests that he wanted *someone* to speak from this (perhaps logically confused non-) standpoint. As a Christian, Anti-Climacus *cannot* entertain the possibility that the disinterested humorist Climacus can, that the paradox of the god-man's existence is not *actually* necessary. For someone like Anti-Climacus, who has actually taken on the risk and commitment of Christianity, *both* the passion of faith *and* its object, that Jesus was the savior, are necessary.

Once the Religiousness B of *Sickness Unto Death* is identified as Christianity, one gets a very different reading on where Kierkegaard intends to leave his reader. Instead of leaving him with the ordinary knowledge that he has had all along, Kierkegaard wants to lead his reader to the realization that his true condition is despair and that this despair can only be eradicated by Christianity. It is therefore problematic to suggest, as Conant does, that Kierkegaard is interested in guiding his reader to the insight that the ordinary in life is adequate for satisfying his needs. Rather, the reader is to see that in despair he is powerless to meet his own needs, and so he must relate himself to something outside of himself, ideally Jesus. While I take it to be one of his correct insights that becoming a Christian for Kierkegaard is definitely not a matter of acquiring new knowledge, Conant neglects the possibility that Kierkegaard believed there is a way (exemplified by Anti-Climacus) to embody the passion of faith in the paradox of the god-man that would make it irrelevant that Climacus (or we) cannot understand it. Consequently, Conant puts too much emphasis on problems raised by Kierkegaard's philosophical humorist. The notion that the self is incomplete without faith in God and a relation to a savior (or at least some other object outside the self) seems to me more in line with the nature of the religious dimension of Kierkegaard's thought than Conant's interpretation will have it.

157. For example, Augustine writes in 4.1 of the *Confessions*, "Without you I am my own guide to the brink of perdition. And even when all is well with me, what am I but a creature suckled on your milk and feeding on yourself, the food that never perishes? And what is any man, if he is only man?" At 5.3, paraphrasing *Psalms* and *1 Corinthians* he writes, "Your wisdom is inscrutable, but your only-begotten Son was given us to be our wisdom, our justification, and our sanctification."

158. Kremer, "The Purpose of Tractarian Nonsense," 58.

159. Ibid.

160. Ibid.

161. Ibid., 61.

162. Ibid., 49.

163. The demands that Wittgenstein places on his readers may well require certain virtues, but this is very different from *showing* his reader how to live or from indicating what the showing and learning of virtues comes to in human life. The philosophy of the *Tractatus* does try to lay the groundwork for the possibility of what I have been characterizing as a kind of authenticity, an important part of which is the example given by the wonder expressed by the clear-sighted speaker of ethical nonsense. This is a position which Wittgenstein seems to take himself to be exemplifying in the "Lecture on Ethics." But as I will show in the next chapter, Wittgenstein's own tacit metaphysical assumptions about language during his Tractarian period preclude him from imparting an understanding that helps his reader to appropriate this possibility in any serviceable way.

164. I am not at all claiming here that the *Tractatus* actually *forbids* such a relation, only that it does not take itself to point the way to one. At one time, I thought that the *Tractatus* could be read as a response to the problem of contemporary nihilism. Mainly because of the issues discussed in this paragraph (the appreciation of which I owe to criticisms by Hubert Dreyfus), I no longer believe this is correct. What I still think is the case, however, is that Wittgenstein believed that modernity's obsession with justification obscured the meaning of our impulse to come out with ethical nonsense and that to the extent that he understood himself as attempting to clarify the nature of this impulse in his reader, he also saw himself as battling a historical trend.

165. My criticisms in this section of Kremer (and, by implication, Conant) are focused on a significant disanalogy that he overlooks between the *Tractatus* and the writings of Paul and Augustine. I am also arguing that it tracks an important difference between the *Tractatus* and *Being and Time*, given the latter's self-understanding. I am not arguing, however, for the coherence of Heidegger's project of fundamental ontology and so for the coherence of his idea that authentic Dasein can choose its hero, per se.

3. A RESOLUTE FAILURE

1. It is not uncommon, moreover, for commentators on the early Heidegger to have recourse to later Wittgensteinian ideas or terminology, especially when they are attempting to explain Heidegger to a broader philosophical audience. Dreyfus sometimes adopts this strategy in *Being-in-the-World*. See also Guignon, *Heidegger and the Problem of Knowledge*; and Cooper, *Existentialism: A Reconstruction*.

2. See Rorty, "Heidegger, Wittgenstein, and the Reification of Language."

3. I would also dispute Rorty's reading of Heidegger's philosophical development but can only say a few words about this here. Toward the end of "The Way Back Into the Ground of Metaphysics," Heidegger describes the project of *Being and Time* as in some sense still in

the grip of traditional ontology: "From the point of view of metaphysics, to be sure, the title 'fundamental ontology' says something that is correct; but precisely for that reason it is misleading, for what matters is success in the transition from metaphysics to recalling the truth of Being. As long as this thinking calls itself 'fundamental ontology' it blocks and obscures its own way with this title. For what the title 'fundamental ontology' suggests is, of course, that the attempt to recall the truth of Being—and not, like all ontology, the truth of beings—is itself (seeing that it is called 'fundamental ontology') still a kind of ontology. In fact, the attempt to recall the truth of Being sets out on the way back into the ground of metaphysics, and with its first step it immediately leaves the realm of all ontology. On the other hand, every philosophy which revolves around an indirect or direct conception of 'transcendence' remains of necessity essentially an ontology, whether it achieves a new foundation of ontology or whether it assures us that it repudiates ontology as a conceptual freezing of experience" (276–277). I understand what Heidegger says here to be not only an important reflection on his own early work but in essence as expressing a perspective that Wittgenstein himself could later have taken when reflecting on the shortcomings of the *Tractatus*. With both philosophers, the later work reflects a greater awareness of the situatedness of philosophical activity, a deeper appreciation for the difficulties of relating to the philosophical tradition, and thus the necessary radicalization of contextualist elements already present, but incompletely developed, in their early work. See Guignon, *Heidegger and the Problem of Knowledge*, esp. 117–127, 208–248; and Blattner, "Remarks on Iain Thomson's *Heidegger on Ontotheology*."

4.   See pages 33–36.

5.   This view is forcefully given by Malcolm, in *Nothing Is Hidden*.

6.   Conant, "Putting Two and Two Together," 297. Among remarks on philosophical method that he recorded in 1931, Wittgenstein himself writes, "All reflections can be carried out in a much more homespun manner than I used to do." See "Philosophy," in Wittgenstein, *Philosophical Occasions*, 180.

7.   Conant, "Putting Two and Two Together," 302.

8.   Wittgenstein, *Tractatus Logico-philosophicus*, 3.

9.   Wittgenstein, *Philosophical Investigations*, §66.

10. Wittgenstein, *Tractatus Logico-philosophicus*, 5. If we put together what I go on to say here with what I said in the previous chapter about how "truth" might be understood in this passage, then we get the thought that the *Tractatus* means to leave us with an understanding of the seamlessness of mind and world but that instead its elucidations narrate a story of our attunements in monotone.

11. There may in fact be several elucidatory stages in the book where we come to see or suspect that something we took for argumentation was in fact pseudoargumentation. But only at §6.54 does Wittgenstein "come clean," as it were.

12. Conant, "Putting Two and Two Together," 303. Diamond writes in a similar vein, "It . . . marks a great change in Wittgenstein's views that he got rid of the idea that you can replace philosophical thinking by carrying out a kind of complete analysis of sentences in which the essential features of sentence sense as such are totally visible." Diamond, "Throwing Away the Ladder," 184.

13. See also Wittgenstein, *Philosophical Investigations*, §593: "A main cause of philosophical disease—a one-sided diet: one nourishes one's thinking with only one kind of example."

14. Wittgenstein writes in the preface, "Here I am conscious of having fallen a long way short of what is possible. Simply because my powers are too slight for the accomplishment of the task.—May others come and do it better." I take this as an admission that perhaps another writer could have employed the method of elucidatory nonsense more skillfully to lead the reader to the same insight concerning the nature of language that Wittgenstein himself tries to impart in the *Tractatus*. I do not take him to be questioning either that method or that goal.

15. Cf. Waismann, *Wittgenstein and the Vienna Circle*, 182–184.

16. See Conant, "The Method of the *Tractatus*," 412–414.

17. See Diamond, "What Does a Concept Script Do?"

18. See Wittgenstein, *Tractatus Logico-philosophicus*, §3.325.

19. See ibid., §4.112.

20. See ibid., §3.333, where Russell's paradox is "disposed of" in short order.

21. Cf. Kremer, "The Purpose of Tractarian Nonsense," 42.

22. Diamond and Conant give an extensive list of what they call the "metaphysical commitments . . . underlying the conception advanced in the *Tractatus* of how the activity of clarification must proceed." See "On Reading the *Tractatus* Resolutely," 82–83. Many of these commitments are the very theses attributed to Wittgenstein on more standard readings of the *Tractatus*. I should make clear that I do not assume that Diamond, Conant, or other resolute readers would accept what I say here, especially about the role of science and mechanics in the *Tractatus*. Having said that, it is not clear to me whether at §6.53 we are supposed to understand the propositions of natural science to be actually *identical* with the system of propositions we construct in mechanics or whether we are merely left to assume that the latter enjoy a privileged status among the former. In any case, the implications of the comparison made at §6.341 between mechanics and a geometrical mesh, where the point seems to be that just as we could choose different meshes of different size and shape to describe a surface so too we could choose a different system for constructing the propositions we use to describe the world, should not be taken to indicate the possibility of any robust logical difference among possible forms of description. Given the *Tractatus*'s underlying metaphysics of language, we are constrained to imagine *all* descriptions of the world as unified or at least unifiable in a single logical space, whether or not we want to imagine that space as being given by mechanics in the broadest sense. The requirement of a single logical space also provides the basis for a guess that I will venture here concerning part of the history of *Tractatus* §6.343. In the final version of the text, the remark runs as follows: "Mechanics is an attempt to construct all the *true* propositions that we need for the description of the world according to a single plan." (I have altered the word order of the translation here so as to be more in line with the German. This brings out better the contrast between the early and later version of this remark. The later version, by the way, appears in the *Prototractatus* at §6.341.) Wittgenstein recorded an early formulation of this remark in his wartime notebooks on December 6, 1914 (see Wittgenstein, *Notebooks*, 36). The earlier formulation goes this way: "Mechanics is *one* attempt to construct all the propositions that we need for the description of the world according to a *single* plan (Hertz's invisible masses)." My hunch is that

Wittgenstein came to notice that this way of putting things could easily be interpreted as suggesting the possibility of a multiplicity of schema on the basis of which logically diverse sets of propositions that describe the world truly could be constructed. This is an interpretation that the later formulation excludes.

23. Kuusela, *The Struggle Against Dogmatism*, 65.

24. Diamond, "Criss-cross Philosophy," 207.

25. Here is how Diamond describes Wittgenstein's view at this time: "A sentence is a sort of sign such that *which* sign it is of that general sort is tied to its maintaining truth-valuedness throughout any variation in truth values of some range of sentences." Diamond, "Throwing Away the Ladder," 190.

26. Cf. Wittgenstein, *Tractatus Logico-philosophicus*, §§3326–3328, §4241, §6211.

27. This claim must be qualified somewhat, because the *Tractatus* indicates uses for other types of sentences, such as tautologies, equations, and sentences expressing the "logical apparatus"

28. Wittgenstein, *Remarks on the Philosophy of Psychology*, §38 (TS 229 197). Quoted in Brenner, *Wittgenstein's Philosophical Investigations*, 10.

29. M. O. C. Drury recorded Wittgenstein remarking once in conversation how the *Tractatus* might be read in light of such considerations: "[C. D.] Broad was quite right when he said of the *Tractatus* that it was highly syncopated. Every sentence in the *Tractatus* should be seen as the heading of a chapter, needing further exposition. My present style is quite different; I am trying to avoid that error." Rhees, *Personal Recollections*, 159.

30. Wittgenstein, *Blue and Brown Books*, 17–18.

31. Wittgenstein, *Culture and Value*, 69–70, MS 134 145 (April 14, 1947).

32. I am grateful to Craig Fox for this point. I find it tempting to describe the impoverished vision of language we find in the *Tractatus*, a vision that cannot accommodate full-blown uses of language that are not statements of anyone's scientific facts, as an expression of the "oblivion of Being" in Wittgenstein's early thought.

CONCLUSION TO PART I

1. Wittgenstein, *Wittgenstein's Nachlass*, 183 16–17 (my translation). See also Wittgenstein, *Public and Private Occasions*, 24. I will have more to say about Wittgenstein's relation to Spengler in chapter 5.

2. This issue is directly connected to two remarks by Wittgenstein recorded by Friedrich Waismann concerning the preconception of what necessarily belongs to a calculus: "What I want to object to in this context is the view that we can define what a calculus is" and "What I should like to object to in this context is the view that we can prove that a system of rules is a calculus." Waismann, *Wittgenstein and the Vienna Circle*, 202, 206. Wittgenstein's suspicion of metaphysical uses of "complete" can also be seen at *Philosophical Investigations* §2. I take it that one of the points of this remark is to challenge the very notion that we have a philosophically serviceable grasp of such a concept. See also Wittgenstein, *Blue and Brown Books*, 19.

3. The recollection on the law of causality is followed by a remark in which Wittgenstein notes that in one sense he is a "very modern person" because of the wonderful relaxation

he finds in going to the cinema (in particular to see an American movie) and how the dreamlike quality of film naturally lends itself to Freudian thought. He then returns to the issue of systems of thought, claiming that discoveries in science, and actions more generally, gain whatever particular significance they have by their belonging to an overall system of meanings.

4. In the conversations with Waismann, he compares these to the rules of a game and to the configurations of a game. Waismann, *Wittgenstein and the Vienna Circle*, 103, 119.

5. In a closely related indication of Wittgenstein's distance to the *Tractatus* at this time, Drury has Wittgenstein making this observation in 1930: "There is no one central problem in philosophy, but countless different problems. Each has to be dealt with on its own. Philosophy is like trying to open a safe with a combination lock. Each little adjustment of the dials seems to achieve nothing, only when everything is in place does the door open." Rhees, *Personal Recollections*, 126.

6. Lovibond, *Realism and Imagination in Ethics*, 90–91.

7. Ibid., 25.

8. Ibid.

9. Of course, in light of my support for the idea that the *Tractatus* had no metaphysical aspirations, we should think of such requirements as operative in the book but unacknowledged and unrecognized by Wittgenstein.

10. Diamond, "Wittgenstein, Mathematics, and Ethics," 229.

11. Ibid.

12. Elsewhere, Diamond remarks on the relation of Wittgenstein's later work to moral realism in a way that to some extent anticipates the interpretative use I make here of the continuity of his cultural outlook: "If we understand the temper of the *Tractatus*, we are not likely to read Wittgenstein's later work as enabling us to be more in tune with the times. The reading of that later work as enabling us to put ethics back into the world is at best a partial truth." Diamond, "Ethics, Imagination, and the Method of the *Tractatus*," 171.

4. THE CONCEPT OF PROGRESS IN WITTGENSTEIN'S THOUGHT

1. The line comes from act 4, scene 10 of Nestroy's play. The English translation given here is taken from David Stern (see note 4 for reference).

2. I should make clear that I do not assume that any of the interpreters of Wittgenstein whose work has been most influential for my thinking about the philosophical relation between the *Tractatus* and the *Philosophical Investigations* would endorse the methods or conclusions of my discussion.

3. This last sentence refers to the possibility that some readers may think that my reading tries to accommodate both an "immanent" approach with a "genetic" or "contextualist" approach, where it is assumed that these terms signal approaches to texts that must be mutually exclusive.

4. Haller and Puhl, *Proceedings of the Twenty-fourth International Wittgenstein-Symposium*, 425–445.

5. I will not address here issues concerning the translation of the motto. Stern discusses these questions at some length.

6. Cf. Wittgenstein, *Philosophische Untersuchungen*.

7. Stern "Nestroy, Augustine, and the Opening of the *Philosophical Investigations*," 427.

8. Ibid., 428.

9. Ibid.

10. Ibid. See Glock, "*Philosophical Investigations*: Principles of Interpretation," 153.

11. Stern, "Nestroy, Augustine, and the Opening of the *Philosophical Investigations*," 428.

12. Ibid., 429. See Genette, *Paratexts*, 407–409.

13. Here, I would only add to Stern's analysis by noting that it is not only the purely immanent reader who is a fiction. The same is true of the purely genetic reader. In the context of Wittgenstein scholarship, a genetic approach is usually understood as emphasizing the idea that one cannot understand a text such as the *Investigations* without taking into account the complicated textual history of the passages that comprise the book. Yet the process of tracing a text to its various sources and contexts cannot go on indefinitely. Eventually it must end with sources and contexts that we simply must do our best to understand without necessarily tracing these to further sources and contexts. In short, a sharp distinction between immanent and genetic approaches is a fiction any way you look at it.

14. See Wittgenstein, *Letters to C. K. Ogden*, 47, 55. Emphasis in the original. On the subject of the motto to the *Tractatus*, it seems as though even less has been written on it than has been written on the motto to the *Investigations*. In noting certain ironic features of the *Tractatus*, Brian McGuinness writes, "Look too at the motto: anything that we really know, that is not mere rumbling and roaring that we have heard, can be said in a couple of words ['Alles, was man weiss, nicht bloss rauschen und brausen gehört hat, läßt sich in drei Worten sagen']. Isn't this a challenge to the book itself? The more so perhaps if one looks at the origin of the quotation—Kürnberger uses it to introduce a maxim (that modern art is graphic, ancient plastic) to which he immediately proceeds to produce a counterexample." I would simply add to this that the motto may also function as a challenge to the reader to be careful about how to receive what she is about to read. See Brian McGuinness, "Wittgenstein: Philosophy and Literature," 332. The motto for the *Tractatus* is taken from Ferdinand Kürnberger, "Über das Denkmalsetzen in der Opposition," reprinted in *Literarische Herzenssachen* (Wien, 1887). Cited by McGuinness, "Wittgenstein: Philosophy and Literature," 333, n. 13.

15. See Stern, "Nestroy, Augustine, and the Opening of the *Philosophical Investigations*," 427–428.

16. It is clear that Wittgenstein's placing of such a passage at the beginning of his book can reasonably be taken as pointing the reader in several directions at once, and I do not pretend to give some sort of exhaustive list or discussion of the ways in which the motto may be functioning. Stern suggests in particular that the motto can also be read as indicating uncertainty or modesty on Wittgenstein's part regarding the achievement of the *Philosophical Investigations*, both taken in itself and as it relates to the *Tractatus*; that the motto is an initial exercise in making sense of a sentence out of context, something that alerts the reader to ambiguity and context generally and to this particular sentence's ambiguities specifically; that the motto warns us not to take what follows at face value, that we should be especially

wary of the way in which we take the *Investigations* to be progress; and finally that the motto can be read as introducing us to the use of voices other than Wittgenstein's own.

17. Baker and Hacker, *An Analytical Commentary on Wittgenstein's* Philosophical Investigations, 1:4.

18. Ibid.

19. See, for example, Baker and Hacker, *Wittgenstein: Rules, Grammar and Necessity*; Bloor, *Wittgenstein, Rules, and Institutions*; Fogelin, *Wittgenstein*; Kenny, *Wittgenstein*; Kripke, *Wittgenstein on Rules and Private Language*; Malcolm, *Nothing Is Hidden*; Hilmy, *The Later Wittgenstein*; von Savigny, *Wittgenstein's "Philosophische Untersuchungen"*; Williams, *Wittgenstein, Mind, and Meaning*.

20. This involves adopting a "resolute" reading of the *Tractatus* and a "therapeutic" or "quietist" reading of the *Investigations*.

21. I am thinking primarily of John McDowell, Cora Diamond, and Warren Goldfarb, but there are others, too.

22. See Kripke, *Wittgenstein on Rules and Private Language*.

23. Goldfarb, "Kripke on Wittgenstein on Rules," 488.

24. McDowell, "Meaning and Intentionality in Wittgenstein's Later Philosophy," 51.

25. Taylor, "*Lichtung* and *Lebensform*," in his *Philosophical Arguments*, 63.

26. Ibid.

27. As should be evident from chapter 2, I regard this point as holding not only for *Philosophical Investigations* but for Wittgenstein's work in general. My discussion here relies on what I take to be the cultural significance of the remarks on rule-following, even though these were composed somewhat later than many of the "cultural remarks" that I cite in support of my interpretation. As I have already maintained in the introduction, however, Wittgenstein's sense of the philosophical significance of cultural matters was roughly constant from the time he wrote the *Tractatus* until the end of his life. Why his later work is so much more successful at giving expression to this sense than are his early or middle writings is, I think, largely a function of his having overcome precisely his early philosophical prejudices, which I discuss in chapter 3.

28. Cavell "Declining Decline," 59. I should make very clear that I neither assume that Cavell would recognize the perspective I claim to find nor that he would endorse my ways of finding it. See the introduction and chapter 6, where I take up some of my methodological and substantive disagreements with Cavell.

29. McDowell, "Non-Cognitivism and Rule-Following," 145–146.

30. McDowell, "Wittgenstein on Following a Rule," 351–352.

31. McDowell, "Non-Cognitivism and Rule-Following," 150–151.

32. The discussion of second nature and *Bildung* can be found in lecture 4. The view that these meet the requirements of rationality McDowell calls "naturalized platonism." See McDowell, *Mind and World*.

33. Goldfarb, "Kripke on Wittgenstein on Rules," 487. Wittgenstein writes at *Philosophical Investigations*, §192: "You have no model of this superlative fact, but you are seduced into using a super-expression. (It might be called a philosophical superlative.)" In fact, §84 anticipates this point: "I said that the application of a word is not everywhere bounded

by rules. But what does a game look like that is everywhere bounded by rules? Whose rules never let a doubt creep in, but stop up all the cracks where it might?—Can't we imagine a rule determining the application of a rule, and a doubt which *it* removes—and so on?"

34. McDowell, "Non-Cognitivism and Rule-Following," 146.

35. Charles Taylor, "To Follow a Rule," 178. At *On Certainty*, §139 Wittgenstein writes, "Not only rules, but also examples are needed for establishing a practice. Our rules leave loopholes open, and the practice has to speak for itself."

36. McDowell, "Meaning and Intentionality," 50–51. Cf. Wittgenstein, *Philosophical Investigations*, p. 226, §109, §128.

37. Cora Diamond, "Rules: Looking in the Right Place," 15. Diamond's warning here is no less applicable to some of McDowell's earlier work on rule-following. Here is a passage from the 1984 paper "Wittgenstein on Following a Rule": "How can a performance both be nothing but a 'blind' reaction to a situation, not an attempt to act on an interpretation (avoiding Scylla): and be a case of going by a rule (avoiding Charybdis)? The answer is: by belonging to a custom (*PI* 198), practice (*PI* 202), or institution (*RFM* VI–31). Until more is said about how exactly the appeal to communal practice makes the middle course available, this is only a programme for a solution to Wittgenstein's problem. But even if we were at a loss as to how he might have thought the programme could be executed . . . this would be no ground for ignoring the clear textual evidence that the programme is Wittgenstein's own." McDowell, "Wittgenstein on Following a Rule," 342. In "Meaning and Intentionality," McDowell states clearly that the tone of his 1984 paper suggests far more sympathy on his part for a programmatic reading of Wittgenstein than is warranted. He no doubt has passages such as this one in mind.

38. Elsewhere, Wittgenstein writes,

To what extent can the function of language be described? If someone is not master of a language, I may bring him to a mastery of it by training. Someone who is master of it, I may remind of the kind of training, or I may describe it; for a particular purpose; thus already using a technique of the language.

To what extent can the function of a rule be described? Someone who is master of none, I can only train. But how can I explain the nature of a rule to myself?

The difficult thing here is not, to dig down to the ground; no, it is to recognize the ground that lies before us as the ground.

For the ground keeps on giving us the illusory image of a greater depth, and when we seek to reach this, we keep on finding ourselves on the old level.

Our disease is one of wanting to explain.

See Wittgenstein, *Remarks on the Foundations of Mathematics*, part 6, §31.

39. See Goldfarb, "Kripke on Wittgenstein on Rules," 485.

40. Diamond, "Rules: Looking in the Right Place," 27–28. Wittgenstein copies down approvingly this slogan from Goethe in a 1947 manuscript: "Man suche nichts hinter den Phänomenen; sie selbst sind die Lehre. (Goethe.)" *Wittgenstein's Nachlass*, 134 78 30 (March 1947).

41. McDowell, "Meaning and Intentionality," 47.

42. I should stress that the problem does not concern our mere capacity to take a disengaged, theoretical *stance* per se. The issue arises, rather, when a more "flexible" understanding of ourselves, an understanding in which the disengaged stance is seen as merely one way we may comport ourselves toward things, hardens into the disengaged view or picture, wherein the disengaged stance is taken to indicate how we are fundamentally. When, on the other hand, one realizes that the ability to take this stance toward the world is only one mode of our understanding, one can also become aware that the disengaged view of human beings exhibits a kind of cultural commitment. This is because when we become aware of the background understanding necessary for comporting ourselves toward the world in this way, we realize too that the main source of the forgetfulness, the source of the commitment to the interpretation of ourselves as disengaged subjects, is that very background understanding, not anything that pertains to our ability to take the stance itself. One way to see what the cultural commitment is that drives the disengaged view in philosophy is to take stock of why the disengaged stance is so highly prized in our culture. One obvious reason for this is that taking a disengaged stance toward the world increases our powers of prediction and control. On this, see Taylor, *Sources of the Self*, esp. chaps. 8–9. This power is not the only value associated with the disengaged view, however. As Taylor notes, it is also closely tied to our modern sense of ourselves as ethical and political agents, which probably accounts for a large part of our reluctance to abandon it: "Among the practices that have helped to create this modern sense are those that discipline our thought to disengagement from embodied agency and social embedding. Each of us is called upon to become a responsible, thinking mind, self-reliant in our judgments (this, at least, is the standard)." Taylor, "To Follow a Rule," 169.

43. In fact, sometimes Taylor himself seems on occasion succumb to this temptation. When, for example, he writes, "Intellectualism leaves us only with the choice between an understanding that consists of representations and no understanding at all. . . . Embodied understanding provides us with the third alternative we need to make sense of ourselves" ("To Follow a Rule," 173), he seems to be equating theoretical, representational thinking with intellectualism (another term for the disengaged view of rules as rails), thereby degrading the first while dignifying the second. The mistake here would be to construe embodied understanding as a kind of substratum that, while not itself shaped by meaning and understanding, *explains and provides a substantive answer* to philosophical questions about, say, our rule-following behavior. I think McDowell would rightly say that while representational, theoretical thinking certainly plays a part in our confusions about meaning and understanding, it is very much a secondary culprit. This is because while McDowell might agree that practical, embodied understanding is a necessary background for theoretical, representational thinking to take place, the latter, like the former, is situational and contextual in its nature, though less obviously so. Certainly our culture's bias toward a kind of less obviously context-dependent theoretical intelligence tends to blot out the importance of our more obviously situational embodied understanding that Taylor wants to emphasize, and thus it contributes to a view of meaning and understanding whereby context dependence falls out of view altogether. But once we see this as a myth, it is not something we should read back into theoretical understanding itself. These issues are in the forefront of recent debate between

McDowell and Hubert Dreyfus. See Dreyfus, "Overcoming the Myth of the Mental"; McDowell, "What Myth?"; Dreyfus, "The Return of the Myth of the Mental"; McDowell, "Response to Dreyfus"; Dreyfus, "Response to McDowell." See also John McDowell, "Can We Conceive Meaning, Understanding, etc. as States of Mind?" For an excellent paper that appeared slightly before this debate but presages many of its issues see McManus, "Rules, Regression, and the 'Background.'"

44. What I am saying here is not intended to imply that the rule-following remarks are only meant to draw our attention to the sociocultural dimension of practices to the exclusion of the natural dimension of our embodying them. I am merely focusing on the sociocultural dimension for the purposes of my discussion here. So I do not mean to pick a fight with Cavell at this point. That will come later.

45. Taylor, "*Lichtung* and *Lebensform*," in his *Philosophical Arguments*, 78.

46. I have in mind, for example, certain widespread conceptions of the nature of scientific rationality once (and perhaps still) prevalent in the philosophy of science and in popular histories of science. Two remarks by Wittgenstein are worth juxtaposing in this context. The first is from 1940, the second from 1947: "One of my most important methods is to imagine a historical development for our ideas different from what actually occurred. If we do that, the problem shows us a quite new side" (Wittgenstein, *Culture and Value*, 45) and "Perhaps one day a culture will arise out of this civilization. Then there will be a real history of the discoveries of the 18th, 19th, and 20th centuries, which will be of profound interest" (Wittgenstein, *Culture and Value*, 73). In this last passage and in several other passages quoted below, Wittgenstein invokes a Spenglerian distinction between culture and civilization. See the quotation by Spengler given on page 148, in chapter 5. The concept of progress plays a central role in Wittgenstein's criticisms of Frazer's writings on magic. I take this up briefly in chapter 5 in the context of my discussion of the influence of Spengler on Wittgenstein's thought.

47. Wittgenstein, *Culture and Value*, 9. Incidentally, this sketch was begun on November 6, 1930, the day after and in the same manuscript in which Wittgenstein recorded the remark criticizing Renan (see chapter 2, pages 56–57). The sketch was completed the next day, thus about seven weeks after Wittgenstein refers to the motto in the letter to Schlick referred to on page 110. The passage used by Rhees for the forward to *Philosophical Remarks* was written on November 8, 1930. My wording in the text above reflects my uncertainty as to whether that passage should be unproblematically taken to be the foreword to that book.

48. I shall quote at length here Stern's description of the motto's original context (the translations are his): "The lines that lead up to the motto in the play are spoken by Gottfried Herb, the hero, in a monologue that begins by deploring how little evil has been removed from the world, despite all our inventions, and then continues: 'And yet we live in an era of progress, don't we? I s'pose progress is like a newly discovered land; a flourishing colonial system on the coast, the interior still wilderness, steppe, prairie. Anyway, the thing about progress is that it looks much greater than it really is.' This line introduces a six-verse satirical song, complete with a full score, which drives home the point of Herb's observations about progress with lurid examples. Each verse divides into three parts: (1) how bad things used to be, (2) how much better they seem now, (3) why they're actually worse than ever. The refrain at the end of (2) is always: 'It's really *splendid*, How progress is so great!' and the last two lines of (3) are always 'So, progress examined more closely, Hasn't made the world much

happier.'" See Stern, "Nestroy, Augustine, and the Opening of the *Philosophical Investigations*," 430–431.

5. THE TRULY APOCALYPTIC VIEW

1. Bouwsma, *Wittgenstein: Conversations*, 66–68.

2. Toulmin, "Ludwig Wittgenstein," 59. Elsewhere, Toulmin writes: "The difference in priorities that divided Wittgenstein from so many of his fellow philosophers in Britain after 1945 is well captured in a remark by the Oxford analyst J. L. Austin. In the course of rebutting objections to the supposed triviality of his own laborious explanations of linguistic usage, Austin replied that he had never been convinced that the question, whether a philosophical question was an important question, was itself an important question." Janik and Toulmin, *Wittgenstein's Vienna*, 259.

3. Ray Monk has a nice gloss on Wittgenstein's typical silence regarding his "metaphilosophical" aims: "Explicit statements of what Wittgenstein is trying to accomplish in his philosophical work are rare, and it is perhaps not surprising that, as Drury put it, 'well-meaning commentators' have made it appear that Wittgenstein's writings 'were now easily assimilable into the very intellectual milieu they were largely a warning against.' But, after all, when we see somebody tidying a room, we do not usually hear them keeping up a commentary all the while explaining what they are doing and why they are doing it—they simply get on with the job. And it was, on the whole, with this strictly 'business-like' attitude that Wittgenstein pursued his own work." Monk, *Ludwig Wittgenstein: The Duty of Genius*, 304.

4. Wittgenstein, *Culture and Value*, 64. Wittgenstein writes at *On Certainty* §132, "Men have judged that a king can make rain; *we* say this contradicts all experience. Today they judge that aeroplanes and the radio etc. are means for the closer contact of peoples and the spread of culture." This reads to me as though Wittgenstein wants to add here, "And this contradicts all of my experience."

5. Wittgenstein, *Culture and Value*, 16. See also Rhees, *Personal Recollections*, 128, where Drury reports Wittgenstein having recommended to him to read Spengler around 1930.

6. Wittgenstein, *Wittgenstein's Nachlass*, 125 131. My translation. Of course, it's not clear from this remark alone what the influence is in the particular context. See also Wittgenstein's letter to von Wright (September 6, 1950) and von Wright's comment on the letter to the effect that he and Wittgenstein often discussed Spengler, in Wittgenstein, *Philosophical Occasions*, 477–478.

7. Haller, "Was Wittgenstein Influenced by Spengler," in his *Questions on Wittgenstein*, 78. Von Wright, *Wittgenstein*, 213, suggests that Wittgenstein may have adapted the idea of a family resemblance (*Familieaehnlichkeit*) from Spengler's idea of an *Ursymbol*, or archetype. It has been plausibly argued by S. Morris Engel, however, that Wittgenstein may well have first encountered the idea in Schopenhauer, who uses the term at least twice in *The World as Will and Representation*: "[Morphology] presents us with innumerable and infinitely varied forms that are nevertheless related by an unmistakable family likeness (*Familieaehnlichkeit*)" (97) and "Knowledge of the unity of the will as thing-in-itself, amid the endless diversity and multiplicity of the phenomena, alone affords us the true explanation of that wonderful,

unmistakable analogy of all nature's productions, of that family likeness (*Familieaehn-lichkeit*) which enables us to regard them as variations on the same ungiven theme" (154). Though there is no way of knowing for sure, the clear reference to morphology tempts me to think that Schopenhauer, in turn, may have had the notion of family resemblance from Goethe (whom Spengler acknowledges in the preface to *Decline of the West* as the source for many of the ideas in his work). Given Schopenhauer's admiration and personal acquaintance with Goethe, this seems to me to be entirely reasonable. See Engel, "Schopenhauer's Impact on Wittgenstein," 287. See note 9, below, for more on Goethe and Wittgenstein.

8. Haller, *Questions on Wittgenstein*, 79.

9. Wittgenstein, "Remarks on Frazer's *Golden Bough*," 133. I have changed the translation of *vermitteln* from "brings about" to "imparts." *Philosophical Investigations* §122 differs in the following ways: the order of the passages is reversed; what is here the second passage begins with "A main source of our failure to understand is that we do not command a clear view of the use of our words. —Our grammar is lacking in this sort of perspicuity"; "and inventing" is inserted after "finding" in what is here the second passage; and the parentheses contain only the question "Is this a *Weltanschauung*?" minus the reference to Spengler. The genesis of §122 also illustrates how Spengler's influence on Wittgenstein is woven together with that of Goethe. The early version of the remark quoted in the text is first found in MS 110 from 1931. Directly before the remark, Wittgenstein wrote "'Das ist keine Erfarhrung, das ist eine Idee.' (Schiller)," quoting Goethe's recollection of his well-known encounter with Schiller, where he tried unsuccessfully to describe to the latter his notion of an *Urpflanze*. This quotation is followed in Wittgenstein's manuscript by a sentence containing a quotation from Goethe's poem "The Metamorphosis of Plants" from 1797. The same sentence containing this quotation continues by taking up the theme of a perspicuous representation. This is then followed by the two passages quoted in the text that make up the protoversion of *Philosophical Investigations* §122. In TS 211, which von Wright dates to around 1932, where he collected many of the remarks on Frazer, Wittgenstein drops the mention of the discussion between Goethe and Schiller. Moreover, in the typescript the protoversion of §122 has been moved away from the quotation of Goethe's poem, with the two passages comprising the protoversion maintaining their order relative to each other. The reference to Spengler also remains. For reasons that are unclear to me, while most of the remarks on Frazer in *Philosophical Occasions* are taken from TS 211, the protoversion of *Philosophical Investigations* §122 that appears there retains its proximity to the quotation from Goethe's poem, that is, as the remark is placed in MS 110. It may in any case be neither possible nor necessary to disentangle the influence of Goethe and Spengler on Wittgenstein's thinking and to weigh their relative importance. If a justification for my focus on Spengler is needed, it can to some extent be that Wittgenstein acknowledges him, and not Goethe, when he mentions those who have influenced his thinking. But I would not want to rest too much on this, and the main reason is simply that it is Spengler who is more directly relevant to my concerns here. Two papers I have found especially informative concerning Wittgenstein's relation to Goethe are Schulte, "Chor und Gesetz"; and Rowe, "Goethe and Wittgenstein."

10. Wittgenstein, "Remarks on Frazer's *Golden Bough*," 133.

11. Ibid, 119.

12. In fact, we can see in these remarks important elements of continuity and discontinuity between the *Tractatus* and the early 1930s when these remarks were written, elements I alluded to briefly at the end of chapter 3. The element of continuity is that the causal *Betrachtungsform*, like the Law of Causality, is one way to arrange propositions. The discontinuity is that it is clear from these remarks that Wittgenstein now thinks it is only *one* way for making sense of things.

13. Wittgenstein, "Remarks on Frazer's *Golden Bough*," 131.

14. I am not saying here that those practices do not line up in *any* way with science or that there is *no* way in which science can be understood as progress over those practices, only that Frazer's work is part and parcel of a mythology of scientific rationality whereby the progress of theories follows a trajectory in principle discernible from a standpoint independent of the responses that characterize participants in scientific practice. My paraphrasing of McDowell (see chapter 4, p. 115) here is meant to underscore that the understanding of progress in work like Frazer's is liable to be vitiated by the same mythology of rationality that gives rise to the view of rules as rails.

15. Haller, *Questions on Wittgenstein*, 84.

16. Ibid.

17. Cf. Wittgenstein, *Philosophical Investigations*, §50.

18. Wittgenstein, *Culture and Value*, 30–31. As with *Philosophical Investigations* §122, Wittgenstein removed the references to Spengler in the final typescript. I have been unable to find the expression "*Betrachtungsform*" after thumbing through an abridged edition of *Der Untergang des Abendlandes* (München: Beck, 1959).

19. Although less significant for my purposes here, there is in fact a second point on which Haller's account is potentially misleading. Though Haller never actually argues that Wittgenstein thought that Spengler's method, or an adaptation of it, would, as Haller puts it, permit one to "foretell the direction to be taken by the development of history," he does allow this impression to stand. But this impression is false. There is no evidence to support the idea that Wittgenstein believed a Gestalt analysis of history could aid one in predicting what would characterize the next historical epoch, and remarks like the following, which span almost twenty years, strongly suggest just the opposite: "If we think of the world's future, we always mean the place it will get to if it keeps going as we see it going now and it doesn't occur to us that it is not going in a straight line but in a curve and that its direction is constantly changing" (Wittgenstein, *Culture and Value*, 5). "You can't *construct* clouds. And that's why the future you *dream* of never comes true. Before there was an aeroplane people dreamed about aeroplanes and what a world with them would look like. But, just as the reality was nothing like this, so we have no reason to believe that reality will develop in the way we dream. For our dreams are full of tinsel, like paper hats and costumes" (Wittgenstein, *Culture and Value*, 48). "It could only be by accident that someone's dreams about the future of philosophy, art, science, would come true. What he sees is a continuation of his own world in his dream, that is to say PERHAPS his wish (and perhaps not) but not reality" (Wittgenstein, *Culture and Value*, 64–65).

20. Wittgenstein, *Culture and Value*, 8. We also find the following entry in a different manuscript written about two months later, in January 1931: "If I say that my book is meant for

only a small circle of people (if it can be called a circle), I do not mean that I believe this circle to be the elite of mankind; but it does comprise those to whom I turn (not because they are better or worse than others but) because they form my cultural milieu, my fellow citizens as it were, in contrast to the rest who are *foreign* to me." Wittgenstein, *Culture and Value*, 12–13.

21. Haller, *Questions on Wittgenstein*, 76.

22. Spengler, *Decline of the West*, 31–32. Quoted in Klagge, "Wittgenstein in Exile," 312.

23. Rhees, *Personal Recollections*, 222–223. Rhees' recollection continues: "Walking home afterwards Wittgenstein remarked that when someone said he was optimistic *because* the law of historical development showed that things were bound to get better—this was nothing he could admire. 'On the other hand, if someone says: "By the look of them, things are getting worse, and I can find no evidence to suggest that they will improve. And yet in *spite* of this, I believe things will get better!" —I can admire that.' "

24. Along with nation and revolution, Charles Taylor calls progress one of modernity's dominant, interrelated "modes of narrativity." See Taylor, *Modern Social Imaginaries*, 175.

25. Wittgenstein, *Wittgenstein's Nachlass*, 134 153. My translation. See also Wittgenstein, *Zettel*, §458; and Wittgenstein, *Remarks on the Philosophy of Psychology*, §949.

26. Wittgenstein, *Culture and Value*, 21–22. Wittgenstein carried this remark over into one of his typescripts, 211 73. Interestingly, a reworked version of this remark appears two years later in yet another manuscript. See Wittgenstein, *Wittgenstein's Nachlass*, 115 56.

27. Without meaning to socialogize away Wittgenstein's concern with cultural decline, it is worth noting that the topic was somewhat of a preoccupation among intellectuals in the Vienna of Wittgenstein's youth. See Monk, *Ludwig Wittgenstein: Duty of Genius*, 20. Indeed, from Janik and Toulmin's description of *fin de siècle* Vienna, this preoccupation would appear to be entirely natural: "This was a society in which all established media, or means of expression—from the language of politics across the board to the principles of architectural design—had seemingly lost touch with their intended 'messages,' and had been robbed of all capacity to perform their proper functions." Janik and Toulmin, *Wittgenstein's Vienna*, 30.

28. Wittgenstein, *Wittgenstein's Nachlass*, 134 153–154. My translation and emphasis. This is a continuation of the remark about the essence of metaphysics quoted on page 133.

29. Ibid., 115 221. My translation. The remark is from August 25, 1936. In students' notes from a 1938 lecture course on aesthetics, we hear, "You can get a picture of what you may call a very high culture, e.g. German music in the last century and the century before, and what happens when this deteriorates." See Wittgenstein, *Lectures and Conversations*, 7.

30. *Lectures and Conversations*, 33. In notes for the same course we read:

I very often draw your attention to certain differences, e.g. in these classes I tried to show you that Infinity is not so mysterious as it looks. What I'm doing is also persuasion. If someone says: "There is not a difference," and I say: "There is a difference" I am persuading, I am saying "I don't want you to look at it like that." Suppose I wished to show you how very misleading the expressions of Cantor are. You ask: "What do you mean, it is misleading? Where does it lead you to?"

218 5. THE TRULY APOCALYPTIC VIEW

Jeans has written a book called *The Mysterious Universe* and I loathe it and call it misleading. . . . I might say the title *The Mysterious Universe* includes a kind of idol worship,
the idol being Science and the Scientist.

I am in a sense making propaganda for one style of thinking as opposed to another. I
am honestly disgusted with the other.

(27–28)

Rhees recounts a conversation where Wittgenstein claims that Marx's project was fundamentally persuasive. Nevertheless, as Rhees notes, Wittgenstein's assertion that Marx
" 'could describe the kind of society he would like to see; that is all' was not, as it had half
seemed to me, a disparagement or belittling of Marx. Not from Wittgenstein, anyway."
Rhees, *Personal Recollections*, 227.

31. Wittgenstein, *Culture and Value*, 91.

32. As this passage from 1931 indicates, however, there are in fact modes of expression that
Wittgenstein does find appropriate for speaking about the whole of a culture.

There are problems I never tackle, which do not lie in my path or belong to my world.
Problems of the intellectual world of the West which Beethoven (and perhaps Goethe
to a certain extent) tackled and wrestled with, but which no philosopher has ever confronted (perhaps Nietzsche passed close to them).

And perhaps they are lost to western philosophy, that is, there will be no one there
who experiences and so can describe the development of this culture as an epic. Or more
precisely it just is no longer an epic, or is one only for someone who observes it from
outside and perhaps Beethoven did this with prevision (as Spengler hints in one place).
It might be said that civilisation can only have its epic poets in advance. Just as one can
only foresee one's own death and describe it as something lying in the future, not report
it as it happens. So it might be said: If you want to see the epic of a whole culture written you will have to seek it in the works of its greatest figures and hence seek it at a time
when the end of this culture can only be *foreseen*, for later there is no one there any more
to describe it. So it is not to be wondered at that it should be written in the dark language of prevision and intelligible only to the very few.

(Wittgenstein, *Culture and Value*, 11–12)

33. Taylor, "*Lichtung* or *Lebensform*," in his *Philosophical Arguments*, 72, 76.

34. Ibid., 77. In the context of rebutting antirealist and behaviorist interpretations of Wittgenstein, McDowell has expressed views that are very close to Taylor's on this point: "We make
possible, moreover, a radically different conception of what it is to belong to a linguistic
community. 'Anti-realists' picture a community as a collection of individuals presenting
to one another exteriors that match in certain respects. They hope to humanize this bleak
picture by claiming that what meaning consists in lies on those exteriors as they conceive
them. . . . The picture of a linguistic community degenerates, then, under 'anti-realist'
assumptions, into a picture of a mere aggregate of individuals whom we have no convincing reason not to conceive as opaque to one another. . . . Shared membership in a linguistic
community is not just a matter of matching in aspects of an exterior that we present to
anyone whatever, but equips us to make our minds available to one another, by confronting

one another with a different exterior from that which we present to outsiders." McDowell, "Wittgenstein on Following a Rule," 350.

35. Wittgenstein, *Culture and Value*, 65. This passage also serves to reinforce my earlier point that he saw no incompatibility between that affective capacity and the intellectual demands made on us by rigorous scientific thought.

36. Malcolm, *Ludwig Wittgenstein, a Memoir*, 70–71. Two further things are worth mentioning in connection with what Malcolm says here. First, Malcolm tells us in a footnote that his belief about Wittgenstein and wonder had occurred to him *before* he had seen the text of Wittgenstein's "Lecture on Ethics," suggesting to me that the belief rested on things Wittgenstein said in conversation or when teaching. And second, just as I warn at various places in chapter 2 (see notes 60, 94, and 127), Malcolm too stresses that the sense of wonder he means to ascribe to Wittgenstein was strictly separate from cosmological questions about a first cause and that "any cosmological conception of a Deity, derived from the notions of cause or of infinity, would be repugnant to him."

37. Cavell, *The Claim of Reason*, 15. In an earlier essay, Cavell broaches this subject when defending the ordinary-language philosopher's procedure of investigating a philosophical problem by referring to what "we" say in specific situations without relying on empirical data. He writes, "If speaking for someone else seems to be a mysterious process, that may be because speaking to someone else does not seem mysterious enough." See "The Availability of Wittgenstein's Later Philosophy," in *Must We Mean What We Say?*, 68.

38. Cavell refers to what he calls a "modern wonder" which he describes "as a feeling of being sealed off from the world" (*The Claim of Reason*, 224). The business of individuating types of feelings may of course be a tricky one, but from Cavell's description I am inclined to say that the modern wonder he proposes as initiating the modern philosopher's (epistemological) investigation is pretty much the opposite of what I am claiming to be the feeling of wonder that informs Wittgenstein's work. That this may be no accident suggests, I think, that I may be closer to Cavell on this point than his choice of "surprise" might otherwise be taken to indicate.

39. Wittgenstein, *Philosophical Investigations*, §593. See also §23.

40. Cavell writes, "Wittgenstein, in sampling what we say, goes beyond the mere occurrence of the words, in ways that make him unlike other philosophers who proceed from ordinary language: unlike Austin, say" (*The Claim of Reason*, 20).

41. Wittgenstein, *Philosophical Investigations*, §19, §23, §241.

42. Cavell, *The Claim of Reason*, 94.

43. And there is no reason to think that this way of putting things entails antirealism regarding natural science. If essence is expressed by grammar (*Philosophical Investigations*, §371), and if grammar tells you what kind of object anything is (§373), then of course grammar tells you that pains, coins, and planets are essentially different in their degree of independence from our grammar. Of course, some philosophers will still prefer the incoherence of the mythology of rationality behind the view of rules as rails to this humanized picture. There is no pleasing some people.

44. Wittgenstein, *Philosophical Investigations*, preface.

45. While my formulations here make evident my indebtedness to Cavell and McDowell, I have some deep disagreements with each of them on this subject as well. I will take these up in the next chapter.

46. Apart from his *Tractatus* interpretation, Pears's brief discussion of this question seems to me to strike the right tone. See Pears, *The False Prison*, 17–18. There is an important issue lurking beneath these considerations, which, while I cannot discuss here, I feel I should mention. If one combines the idea that it is a mistake to search for reductive scientific or philosophical explanation of meaning and understanding with the idea that at some earlier time in the earth's evolution there were no creatures to be found whose lives were shaped by meaning and understanding, it seems to me that one is committed to accepting some idea of the emergence of mind and world.

47. And that there are such legitimate motivations I do not deny (cf. chapter 4, note 42). Whether among those motivations a coherent case can be made for something like a pure desire to know the natural world, I am agnostic.

48. Taylor, "*Lichtung* and *Lebensform*," in his *Philosophical Arguments*, 77–78.

49. Cavell, *The Claim of Reason*, 95.

50. Here I mean to be pointing out a concern that is not only central in shaping Wittgenstein's work but that I also regard as close in spirit to Kierkegaard's concern with leveling (*nivellering*), especially as that concern gets articulated in *The Present Age*, and to the later Heidegger's concern with nihilism.

51. Heidegger criticizes Spengler's pessimism in *What Is Called Thinking?* Heidegger's main objection in these lectures seems to be that Spengler focuses entirely on what Heidegger calls "destruction," where this term refers to such things as the destruction of nature and a decline in the arts. Heidegger contrasts destruction with "devastation," which is his term for the way he thinks our current set of practices is laying waste to our ability to be open to meaning at all and not merely accelerating the passing away of the natural world or the European culture of the last few centuries. See Heidegger, *What Is Called Thinking?*, 28–38. Despite the importance for Heidegger of the distinction between destruction and devastation, and despite the far greater philosophical importance he attaches to the latter notion, I believe that there is simply no question but that he shared Wittgenstein's concern for what he took to be the vast amount of *destruction* taking place in his lifetime. Moreover, while it would be far fetched to attribute Heidegger's exact views on the nature of devastation to Wittgenstein, I think that it is correct to see Wittgenstein and Heidegger as agreeing on a central point that the destruction/devastation distinction is supposed to mark: that the real problem is not to be found in the destruction of nature or culture, however regrettable this is, but in the way in which our distorted relation to our practices happens to bring such destruction about.

52. Wittgenstein, *Culture and Value*, 8–9. Von Wright (*Wittgenstein*, 213) writes of Wittgenstein employing the idea of a family resemblance to distinguish between cultures whose manifestations such as mathematics, architecture, and politics are related to each other as members of one family and those cultures in which such connections have dissolved. We find an excellent example of this idea in the following passage from 1931: "The music of every period corresponds to certain maxims of the good and the right from the same period. So we can recognize Keller's maxims in Brahms' music, etc. And therefore, any music that has been invented today or recently, one that is thus modern, must appear absurd, since if it corresponds to any one of the maxims that are *pronounced* today, it must be rubbish. This statement is not easy to understand, but it is true: No one is clever enough today to

articulate the good, and *all* formulas and maxims that are pronounced are nonsense. The truth would sound *quite* paradoxical to all people. And the composer who feels it within himself must stand with his feeling in opposition to everything that is pronounced now, and according to current standards must also appear absurd and idiotic. But not *pleasingly* absurd (since that is in fact what speaks to the current attitude) but rather as *utterly inexpressive (nichtssagend)*." *Wittgenstein's Nachlass*, 183 59, my translation, italics in the original. See also Wittgenstein, *Public and Private Occasions*, 67–68). Wittgenstein makes use of a slightly modified version of this example in a 1938 lecture course on aesthetics. See Wittgenstein, *Lectures and Conversations*, 32.

53. Wittgenstein, *Philosophical Remarks*, 7.

54. See the preface to Wittgenstein, *Philosophical Investigations*.

55. Rhees, *Personal Recollections*, 94. Cf. 173, where Drury sorts what seem to be notes from the same conversation, but minus this remark, under the year 1949. The same ambivalence comes out well in these two observations by Von Wright and Malcolm respectively. "It seems to me that there are two forms of seriousness of character. One is fixed in 'strong principles'; the other springs from a passionate heart. The former has to do with morality and the latter, I believe, is closer to religion. Wittgenstein was acutely and even painfully sensitive to considerations of duty, but the earnestness and severity of his personality were more of the second kind. Yet I do not know whether he can be said to have been 'religious' in any but a trivial sense of the word. Certainly he did not have a Christian faith. But neither was his view of life un-Christian, pagan, as was Goethe's" (Malcolm, *Ludwig Wittgenstein, a Memoir*, 19). "I do not wish to give the impression that Wittgenstein accepted any religious faith—he certainly did not—or that he was a religious person. But I think that there was in him, in some sense, the *possibility* of religion. I believe that he looked on religion as a 'form of life' (to use an expression from the *Investigations*) in which he did not participate, but with which he was sympathetic and which greatly interested him. Those who did participate he respected—although here as elsewhere he had contempt for insincerity" (Malcolm, *Ludwig Wittgenstein, a Memoir*, 72).

56. See Monk, *Ludwig Wittgenstein: Duty of Genius*, 158, 199–200. See also McGuinness, *Young Ludwig*, 274.

57. Drury recalls Wittgenstein telling him in 1929, "Oh don't depend on circumstances. Make sure that your religion is a matter between you and God only." Rhees, *Personal Recollections*, 117.

58. Engelmann, *Letters from Ludwig Wittgenstein*, 74–75.

59. We read (Wittgenstein, *Culture and Value*, 31) from 1937,

The solution of the problem you see in life is a way of living which makes what is problematic disappear.

The fact that life is problematic means that your life does not fit life's shape. So you must change your life, and once it fits the shape, what is problematic will disappear.

But don't we have the feeling that someone who doesn't see a problem there is blind to something important, indeed to what is most important of all?

Wouldn't I like to say he is living aimlessly—just blindly like a mole as it were; and if he could only see, he would see the problem?

Or shouldn't I say: someone who lives rightly does not experience the problem as *sorrow*, hence not after all as a problem, but rather as joy, that is so to speak as a bright halo round his life, not a murky background.

60.   "Anyone who is half-way decent will think himself utterly imperfect, but the religious person thinks himself *wretched*" (Wittgenstein, *Culture and Value*, 51 [c. 1944]); "The Christian religion is only for the one who needs infinite help, solely, that is, for the one who feels an infinite need. The whole Earth can suffer no greater need than *one* soul. The Christian faith—so I believe—is refuge in this *ultimate* need" (Wittgenstein, *Culture and Value*, 52 [c. 1944]).

61.   Klagge, "Exile," 318. Wittgenstein, of course, never rejected ritual in principle, nor even completely in his own case. He once told Drury, for example, that he was glad to have been made to attend mass while in the prison camp at Monte Cassino. Rhees, *Personal Recollections*, 179.

62.   Rhees, *Personal Recollections*, 129–130. Drury reports the conversation concluding with this: "Wittgenstein: 'But remember that Christianity is not a matter of saying a lot of prayers; in fact we are told not to do that. If you and I are to live religious lives, it mustn't be that we talk a lot about religion, but that our manner of life is different. It is my belief that only if you try to be helpful to other people will you in the end find your way to God.' Just as I was leaving he suddenly said, 'There is a sense in which you and I are both Christians.'"

63.   Reported by Drury from 1929. See Rhees, *Personal Recollections*, 117. See also ibid., 123; and Wittgenstein, *Culture and Value*, 34.

64.   Wittgenstein, *Culture and Value*, 37–38. I have omitted a short stretch of the manuscript text between the first and second paragraphs. See also ibid., 32 (MS 118 56r c: 4.9.1937). Given what Wittgenstein writes in *On Certainty* about the doctrines of virgin birth and transubstantiation, however, there also seems to be a place in his thought for the idea that the acceptance of particular concrete claims can be essential to religion, provided they are embedded logically deeply enough in the "riverbed" of a form of life. See Wittgenstein, *On Certainty*, 97, 239, 162. See also Wittgenstein, *Culture and Value*, 32–33. Perhaps a certain incredulity (at least about himself) that such embedding can come about through conversion instead of exclusively through early religious training is connected to this recollection by Malcolm: "I suspect that he regarded religious belief as based on qualities of character and will that he himself did not possess. Of Smythies and Anscombe, both of whom had become Roman Catholics, he once said to me: 'I could not possibly bring myself to believe all the things that they believe.' I think that in this remark he was not disparaging their belief. It was rather an observation about his own capacity." Malcolm, *Ludwig Wittgenstein, a Memoir*, 72.

65.   "The way you use the word 'God' does not show *whom* you mean, but what you mean." Wittgenstein, *Culture and Value*, 58. See also ibid., 97.

66.   Ibid., 73. See also 61, where Wittgenstein talks of *being seized by* a symbol system.

67.   I am neither implying here that there is nothing unique about Christianity (or about every religion, for that matter), nor am I implying that Wittgenstein did not feel that Christianity held out the possibility of meeting his needs in a way that other traditions did not. My discussion here is not intended to be either a comprehensive treatment of religion or of Wittgenstein's relation to it.

68. See, for example, Wittgenstein, *Culture and Value*, 38; and Monk, *Ludwig Wittgenstein: Duty of Genius*, 491, 534.

69. I am not, of course, claiming any direct influence from Aristotle, whom Wittgenstein hardly read.

70. Engelmann writes, "[Wittgenstein] 'saw life as a task,' and on that I agreed with him. Moreover, he looked upon all the features of life as it is, that is to say upon all facts, as an essential part of the conditions of that task; just as a person presented with a mathematical problem must not try to ease his task by modifying the problem. But—it may be asked—could it not be that for an individual of a suitable disposition such a modification of the data of the task may actually form *part of the task*, indeed may be felt in his conscience as vital to the task itself? Yet, the person who consistently believes that that reason for the discrepancy lies in himself alone must reject the belief that changes in external facts may be necessary and called for." Engelmann, *Letters from Ludwig Wittgenstein*, 79.

71. Wittgenstein, *Culture and Value*, 86.

72. Whatever interest Wittgenstein may have taken in the work of conservative thinkers such as Spengler, Weininger, and Ernst, it is far from clear that in the original context of *The Protogé* the motto to the *Investigations* expresses reactionary views, either those of the main character Gottfried Herb or those of Nestroy. Nestroy himself was no reactionary. Indeed, he was highly critical of the pre-1848 ruling powers. Furthermore, it was not likely to be just any conception of progress that an Austrian satirist of Nestroy's time and outlook could be expected to ridicule but rather a metaphysically charged one emanating from an increasingly domineering and self-confident Prussia. I am grateful for comments by Herbert Hrachovec and Walter Sokel on these issues.

73. Just to name a few: the already mentioned sketch for a forward to *Philosophical Remarks*; the printed forward to *Philosophical Remarks*; some of the "Remarks on Frazer's Golden Bough"; *Philosophical Investigations*, §471 and p. 226; *On Certainty*, §344; Rhees, *Personal Recollections*, 226; and Paul Engelmann's recounting of one of Wittgenstein's discussions with Russell in Innsbruck in Monk, *Ludwig Wittgenstein: Duty of Genius*, 211.

74. I have in mind, for example, Spengler, Weininger, Schopenhauer, Tolstoy, Dostoyevsky, and Ernst. One should also admit that he was repulsed by the ideas of some thinkers who could fairly be described as "progressive." Russell is perhaps the most significant example of the latter. See especially Rhees, *Personal Recollections*, 127. See also Wittgenstein, *Culture and Value*, 55–56.

75. In a letter to Malcolm from February 1948, Wittgenstein writes, "I am not reading much, thank God. I read in Grimm's fairy tales & in Bismarck's '*Gedanken & Erinnerungen*' which I admire greatly. I don't mean, of course, that my views are Bismarck's views." Malcolm, *Ludwig Wittgenstein, a Memoir*, 75.

76. Someone who has drawn this conclusion with great enthusiasm is J. C. Nyíri. What is interesting about Nyíri's writing on this subject is the way he explicitly connects his claim that Wittgenstein was a conservative with a reading of the *Investigations*. Nyíri finds in that work an account of meaning that he believes gives a theoretical underpinning to a particular brand of political conservatism, a cultural-relativistic conservatism for which he finds evidence in Wittgenstein's interest in thinkers including Spengler, Ernst, Dostoyevsky, etc. (Of course, one wonders which came first: finding the account of meaning in the text or finding the conservatism

in these remarks.) See Nyíri, "Wittgenstein's New Traditionalism," 1–3; and "Wittgenstein's Later Work in Relation to Conservatism," 44–68. In her paper "Wittgenstein's Philosophy in Relation to Political Thought" (*The New Wittgenstein*, 118–145), Alice Crary shows convincingly that Nyíri's interpretation of the *Investigations*, which forms the theoretical underpinning of his reading of Wittgenstein as a political conservative, is both unworkable and arbitrary as a reading of the text. Crary says that she is interested in the implications for political thought of Wittgenstein's philosophy (presumably there meaning the *Investigations*) and not in the nature or implications of his political inclinations. As a result, she does not say much about what Wittgenstein wrote and said elsewhere about culture and tradition that might have inclined Nyíri to find such a theory of meaning in the *Investigations* in the first place. I am unsure whether Crary is assuming in her paper that what counts as relevant for understanding Wittgenstein's philosophy should be restricted to the pages of his published work. That is obviously an assumption that I would want to reject. At any rate, I am arguing here that we can also resist the temptation to let this other material incline us in Nyíri's direction.

77. The next paragraph begins, "Needless to say, this peculiar approach exercised no political influence, completely confused the censors and was partly responsible for the decision to close down *Time* in 1863." This is from a review of a new translation of *Notes from Underground*. See Parks, "Description of a Struggle," 42–43.

78. Wittgenstein, *Culture and Value*, 8.

79. "What narrowness of spiritual life in Frazer! Hence: how impossible for him to comprehend a life different from the English life of his time. Frazer cannot imagine a priest who is not basically an English parson of our time, with all his stupidity and vapidness." See Wittgenstein, "Remarks on Frazer's Golden Bough," 125.

80. Nor should one assume that what I have referred to earlier as Wittgenstein's "pietism" in religion necessarily entails a quietism in politics. Rhees relates this story from around the same time in 1943 as when Wittgenstein attended the lecture on "Causal Laws in History" mentioned above:

> About this time Wittgenstein had taken Max Eastman's *Marxism: Is It Science?* from a shelf in my room and was turning the pages. He said Eastman seemed to think that if Marxism was to help revolution it must be made more scientific; which was a bad misunderstanding. "In fact, nothing is more conservative than science. Science lays down railway tracks. And for scientists it is important that their work should move along those tracks." Wittgenstein spoke at other times of "railway tracks" as the image behind the way some people thought and spoke of "scientific laws" or "natural necessity"; or, as in this case, "scientific method."
>
> Eastman said, for instance, (p. 215) "I still believed in that system of revolutionary engineering perfected by Lenin . . . (These chapters) show what I mean by substituting a scientific revolutionary attitude for the metaphysical socialism of Karl Marx."
>
> "But," said Wittgenstein, "when Lenin intervened in 1917 his move was not scientific, it was tragic." With the "necessity" of the hero's move in a tragedy.

Rhees connects these ideas with the following remark from 1947, which he says expresses things Wittgenstein "had said for years": "Someone reacts *like this*: he says 'Not that!'—and resists it. Out of this situation perhaps develop situations which are equally intolerable; and perhaps by then strength for any further revolt is exhausted. We say 'If *he* hadn't done *that*, the evil would not have come about.' But with what justification? Who knows the laws according to which society unfolds? I am sure even the cleverest has no idea. If you fight, you fight. If you hope, you hope. Someone can fight, hope, and even believe without believing *scientifically*." Rhees, *Personal Recollections*, 223. The translation used here appears at Wittgenstein, *Culture and Value*, 69.

81. Given the weight that McDowell places on the ideas of tradition and *Bildung* in *Mind and World*, it is perhaps not surprising to find him addressing the question of conservatism at the close of the book. Of course, while it's possible that the mere occurrence of certain words like "tradition" is anathema to some, that is not a reaction that should be taken very seriously. As Sabina Lovibond writes, "The language of 'decline,' 'disappearance,' 'threat' and so forth, with all its conservationist connotations, may suggest that the 'politics of significance' (for it does not seem altogether satisfactory to speak here of an *ethics*, since it is the very possibility of ethics that is at stake) will be, at least in a loose sense, a 'conservative' one. However, we should remember that the defence of 'practices,' and of the values internal to them, against the encroachments of instrumental rationality is a project in which the left has at least as much of an investment as the right." Lovibond, "The Late Seriousness of Cora Diamond," 54.

6. THE FATE OF METAPHYSICS

1. The source of the epigraph for this chapter is Wittgenstein, *Wittgenstein's Nachlass*, 132 8 11 (September 1946; my translation).

2. For a discussion of some differences between Cavell and McDowell on this issue, see Martin Gustafsson, "Perfect Pitch and Austinian Examples," 356–389.

3. Even if one doesn't read Cavell and McDowell as making knowledge claims, however, it should be possible in some way to make their interpretations accountable to the phenomena of which they purport to make sense. While this is not a debate I can enter into here, I doubt very much whether McDowell's and Cavell's views stand up against a philosophically adequate assessment of the historical and ethnological record. Nor do I find that they have made compelling cases on purely conceptual grounds for seeing the drive for metaphysical explanation as inherently human.

4. I mention the *Investigations* here only because, so far as I can tell, the interpretations of Wittgenstein offered by Cavell and McDowell seem to be based on their readings of this work and do not really take up the relevance that the *Tractatus* or other sources such as manuscripts, typescripts, letters, diaries, recorded conversations, and transcribed lectures may have for the question I address in this chapter.

5. So that I am not misunderstood here, I want to stress three things. First, in claiming that Wittgenstein thought it possible to abandon metaphysics, I should not be understood as endorsing Richard Rorty's specific understanding of the route to, or the nature of, a postmetaphysical culture. Second, I am not claiming that Wittgenstein thinks philosophy can be brought to an end through one of its own maneuvers. In particular, I am not suggesting

that it may be brought to a close either by a constructive account of what makes meaning possible, an account that would thus provide a solution to any philosophical problem that could arise, or by the discovery of a method that dissolves all possible philosophical problems once and for all. (This is to say that my discussion here is meant to be neutral regarding debates between what have been termed "Pyrrhonian" and "non-Pyrrhonian" readers of Wittgenstein.) Rather, I mean to make it doubtful that Wittgenstein believed in a particular etiology of metaphysical problems attributed to him by Cavell and McDowell. Third, despite seeing the potentially endless variety of specific ways that philosophical puzzlement can take shape, McDowell and Cavell are themselves committed to the idea that this puzzlement can be designated, even if not dissolved, in general terms. Cavell is content to use the term "skepticism" to refer to various ways in which we lose faith in our criteria, however much the content of the specific problems thereby engendered may vary. He writes, "What challenges one's humanity in philosophy, tempts one to excessive despair or to false hope, is named skepticism. It is the scene of a struggle of philosophy with itself, for itself.... Then why can't [skepticism] be ignored? For Wittgenstein that would amount to ignoring philosophy, and surely nothing could be more easily ignored—unless false hope and excessive despair are signs or effects of unobserved philosophy." Cavell, "Declining Decline," 40. See also *The Claim of Reason*, 46. McDowell's own diagnosis rests on the general idea that philosophical problems arise from our overlooking the role played by *Bildung* in our acquiring a second nature. Consequently, if it is coherent for Cavell and McDowell to give a general description of the philosophical problematics they believe Wittgenstein thought are inescapable, then it is also coherent for me to use a general description, for instance, "metaphysics," in arguing that some things Wittgenstein actually says stand in conflict with their belief. See also Stern, "How Many Wittgensteins?"

6. McDowell, *Mind and World*, 177–178.

7. Wittgenstein, *Blue and Brown Books*, 18. Lest it seem that Wittgenstein's many remarks attacking the influence of scientific thinking in philosophy don't really hit modern naturalism per se, the latter being a general metaphysical position that is, strictly speaking, separable from a specifically scientific metaphysics like physicalism, I would reply that the rise of modern naturalism in its various forms is unthinkable apart from the prestige of modern science and the pressure this exerts on philosophers to be "scientific."

8. While it should be mentioned that what Wittgenstein says in his descriptions of the other three tendencies is not put as forcefully as his claim that the "real source of metaphysics" is the attraction that scientific method exerts on philosophers, this claim itself appears to conflict with this remark from 1947 that I have already quoted (chapter 5, p. 133): "Philosophical investigations: conceptual investigations. The essence of metaphysics: that the difference between factual and conceptual investigations is unclear to it. The metaphysical question always has the appearance of being a factual one, although the problem is a conceptual one." In fact, there need be no genuine conflict. The error named in this remark is the more fundamental of the two for Wittgenstein, the fascination with scientific method being merely the most common form that this confusion takes today. It results from a failure to distinguish between grammatical remarks that give the causal *Betrachtungsform* and ordinary empirical statements of causal relations made on the basis of that way of seeing things.

9. See Cavell, "The Availability of the Later Wittgenstein," in *Must We Mean What We Say?*, 61–62. See also, for example, *Must We Mean What We Say?*, 154, 158–160, 263, 338–339, 351; Cavell, *The World Viewed*, 21–23, 126–127, 146–147, 205–206, 213.

10. Cavell, *The Claim of Reason*, 108–109.

11. Ibid., 110.

12. Cavell, "Declining Decline," 41. Note that it is important to distinguish between Cavell's use of "conventionalist" in this passage from his use of "convention" in the prior quotation. "Conventionalist" is meant to correspond to only one of the senses (or levels) of "convention," the one that is traditionally opposed to logical necessity.

13. Cavell, "Declining Decline," 54.

14. Ibid., 57. We read in *The Claim of Reason* (109): "Nothing is more human than the wish to deny one's humanity, or to assert it at the expense of others. But if that is what skepticism entails, it cannot be combated through simple 'refutations.'"

15. Cavell, "Declining Decline," 55.

16. I mean to point to a distinction here between the role that this view of philosophical confusion plays in Cavell's own thought and in his work on Wittgenstein. It does seem to me to be absolutely central to the former.

17. Cavell, *The Claim of Reason*, 44.

18. Cavell, "Declining Decline," 54.

19. Cavell, "The Argument of the Ordinary," 66, 92.

20. See Bourdieu, *Outline of a Theory of Practice*, 93–94.

21. Cavell, *The Claim of Reason*, 111.

22. Cavell, "The Argument of the Ordinary," 94.

23. Wittgenstein, *Wittgenstein's Nachlass*, 174 0 24 (April 1950). A slightly different translation of this passage is in Wittgenstein, *Last Writings on the Philosophy of Psychology*, 2:89. Drury relates an episode from 1929 when he and Wittgenstein were looking at a carving on the outside of Ely Cathedral described in the guidebook as being a humorous scene of two peasants: "That must be wrong. They would never have meant this to be funny. It is the case that we forget the meaning of certain facial expressions and misinterpret their reproduction. What does it mean to us if a Chinaman smiles?" Rhees, *Recollections of Wittgenstein*, 119.

24. Von Wright, "Wittgenstein in Relation to His Times," in his *Wittgenstein*, 216.

25. Cavell, "Declining Decline," 52–53.

26. Ibid., 43.

27. Ibid., 44.

28. Ibid., 42.

29. While not intending to insinuate anything about Cavell himself, I will point out that his concern can be reframed in a way that redistributes the suspicion about oppression. Say if you like that "'Skepticism is part of the human condition' is a grammatical remark" and so can't be confirmed or discomfirmed by experience. How many peoples thereby become (have already been made out to be) nonhuman because they don't partake in various modern obsessions like skepticism? How recalcitrant will we allow our grammar to be in the face of such experience?

30. And to "accuse" me of giving an "antihumanist" reading of Wittgenstein is a red herring. Even if true, it is irrelevant to ethical and political criticism, and at any rate it can be

transposed if necessary into a question about what *kind* of humanism Wittgenstein's thought expresses.

31.   Wittgenstein wrote in 1940 (MS 162b 67r): "If we use the ethnological approach does that mean we are saying philosophy is ethnology? No it only means we are taking up our position far outside, in order to see *the* things *more objectively*." Wittgenstein, *Culture and Value*, 45.

32.   Wittgenstein, *Philosophical Investigations*, §109, §115, §122, p. 224. See also Wittgenstein, *Culture and Value*, 19 (MS 154 25v), 22 (MS 111 133).

33.   Kant, *Critique of Pure Reason*, 7.

34.   Wittgenstein, *Philosophical Investigations*, §66.

35.   Hilmy, in *The Later Wittgenstein*, has attempted to provide an account of the later Wittgenstein's struggle against modern intellectual currents mainly in terms of his rejection of explanations in philosophy, especially empirical psychological explanations. These excerpts give a sense of Hilmy's conclusions: "The scope of his conception of metaphysics was such that it encompassed not only traditional metaphysics, but also, and especially, the dominant mode of reflection of our own epoch; and it is primarily the latter, the 'metaphysics' of our own epoch that constituted the intellectual current against which he was struggling" (225). "For Wittgenstein, scientific reflection, instead of being free of metaphysics, is itself often a *form* of metaphysics, a *source* of the metaphysics of our epoch" (225). So far, so good. But difficulties in Hilmy's position become apparent a bit later: "It would seem that the intellectual tendency toward a 'scientific way of thinking,' which Wittgenstein considered characteristic of our age, *itself* was viewed by him as stemming from language, from the misleading expressions of language. He would thus seem to have viewed the ultimate source of the metaphysics of our times as lying in language itself" (226). "Thus the *Kampf* which was his later philosophy, a *Kampf* against the scientific intellectual fashions of the day, seems to have been perceived by him within the even broader horizon of a *Kampf* against language" (226). Hilmy's view, then, seems to be the familiar one that Wittgenstein thought of language itself as the real underlying culprit, whether one is fighting against modern naturalism or various forms of rationalism. Presumably, the idea is that intellectual fashions, like the prestige of natural science, will, combined with certain misleading features of language and our natural inclinations to misunderstand them, lead us into confusion in certain ways, while different fashions, perhaps the prestige of mathematics and computer science, will combine with misleading features of language and our natural inclinations to misunderstand *them* to produce confusion in different ways. This means, in either case, that Wittgenstein saw his struggle against metaphysics as a never-ending part of human life and so puts Hilmy's position close to the one advanced by McDowell and Cavell, at least on this question. As will be apparent below, I think there are good reasons for reading Wittgenstein's *Kampf* as one with people and their culturally and historically inflected relation to language and not as one with language itself.

36.   Von Wright, "Wittgenstein in Relation to His Times," 206.

37.   Ibid., 207.

38.   Wittgenstein, *Culture and Value*, 55.

39.   Ibid., 70.

40.   Cf. Wittgenstein, *Philosophical Investigations*, §221. While not exactly self-evident, when Wittgenstein writes of "the way of life" (*die Lebensweise*) in the above quotation, I take it

to be fairly clear that he means something like historically situated groups of people, not humanity in general.

41. Ibid., §20, §24, §48, §52, §73, §139, §140.

42. Ibid., §39, §143, §159, §254, §334, §402, §588, and p. 191.

43. James Klagge grudgingly agrees with the basic point that it is "quite unlikely that an a priori case could be made for the inevitable need for philosophy." But he adds that "Still, short of (what would seem to us to be) significant mental deterioration, it is hard to imagine what changes "would make all these questions superfluous." Klagge, "Wittgenstein in Exile," 318.

44. See Rhees, *Recollections of Wittgenstein*, 95, where Kant and Berkeley are praised as "deep"; and 120, where Wittgenstein calls Leibniz a "great man."

45. Ibid., 120.

46. When Drury told Wittgenstein what A. E. Taylor had said of Hume, that he wasn't sure whether he was a great philosopher or just a very clever man, Wittgenstein remarked that while he couldn't comment on Hume, the distinction between a real philosopher and a very clever man is a real one and of great importance. Rhees, *Personal Recollections*, 95.

47. Von Wright, "Wittgenstein in Relation to His Times," 209. Malcolm writes, "With regard to the question of what the future would hold for his work—whether it would disappear without leaving a mark, or whether, if it continued to live, it would prove any help to mankind—he was in doubt." Malcolm, *Ludwig Wittgenstein, a Memoir*, 60.

48. Wittgenstein, *Culture and Value*, 69.

49. Wittgenstein, "Remarks on Frazer's *Golden Bough*," 133.

50. Ibid.

51. Wittgenstein, *Philosophical Investigations*, §18.

52. Wittgenstein, *Culture and Value*, 68–69. Rhees recalls a conversation that seems to date from the late 1930s or early 1940s and that touches on the same themes: "Once when we were sitting in Trafalgar Square he spoke of the architecture of the buildings and especially of Canada House. We had been talking of music and of how hard it is to play Brahms at the present day. Myra Hess played Brahms exactly in the way which had been right during Brahms's lifetime. But to play him that way *now*—with just the emotional emphasis to fit the emotional reactions of people then—this made the music meaningless for us. There was only one man he had heard in recent years, a pianist who really did know what the music meant and played it—'and that was the *great* Brahms.' A nose for what was music and what was rhetoric. The way Myra Hess played it would have been music in Brahms's day, but now it's just rhetoric; and whatever it gives us, it isn't Brahms. Wittgenstein pointed to Canada House, which the builders were just finishing. This architecture has followed a tradition by taking over certain rhetorical forms, but it says nothing in them. Large scale, meant to fit within a great culture. But—waving his hand towards it—'that's *bombast*; that's Hitler and Mussolini.' He would not have said that another architect might have built one that *wasn't*. Not today, and not here. And Canada House helped to show why Hitler and Mussolini *had* to work with bombast. As it showed how truly they were one in spirit with us." Rhees, *Personal Recollections*, 225–226.

53. Wittgenstein, *Wittgenstein's Nachlass*, 120 145r 23 (April 1938). We read elsewhere: "I believe I summed up where I stand in relation to philosophy when I said: really one should write philosophy only as one *writes a poem*. That, it seems to me, must reveal how far my

thinking belongs to the present, the future, or the past. For I was acknowledging myself, with these words, to be someone who cannot quite do what he would like to be able to do." Wittgenstein, *Culture and Value*, 28.

54. Wittgenstein, *Culture and Value*, 70–71. Malcolm recalls, "He once concluded a year's lectures with this sentence: 'The only seed that I am likely to sow is a certain jargon.' " Malcolm, *Ludwig Wittgenstein, a Memoir*, 63.

55. Wittgenstein, *Remarks on the Foundations of Mathematics*, 132. Besides his point about the sickness of philosophical problems requiring a change of life that is more fundamental than anything philosophy itself can effect, what Wittgenstein says here harmonizes well with the passages I cite on page 164 in support of my contention that he believed it possible to abandon metaphysics.

56. Cavell certainly recognizes the hope for cultural change permeating Wittgenstein's work. In fact, in one of the many places in "Declining Decline" where he appears to want to point out a kinship between Heidegger and Wittgenstein, he writes: "[Heidegger's] reconception implies that the recuperation or recoupment or redemption of the thing (in itself)— a process essential to the redemption of the human—will come about only by a shift of Western culture; a shift, now only in preparation, that will alter Western man's process of judgment. . . . However opposite in other respects Wittgenstein's intellectual taste is from Heidegger's, in linking the comprehension of the objective and the cultural they are closer together than each is to any other major philosopher of their age" (49). Nevertheless, for Cavell, Wittgenstein does not share Heidegger's conviction that a profound enough change in these cultural factors may bring with it a genuine release from the problems that constitute the metaphysical tradition. Cavell thinks instead that the sought after cultural transformation comes when we acknowledge and embrace our tendency to repudiate our humanity. Wittgenstein may at one point have seen in the Russian revolution a possibility for cultural rejuvenation of the sort that I am mentioning here. That he was anything but a doctrinaire Marxist, however, can easily be seen from his remarks on Frazer's work. He would never have accepted a Marxist account of the development of history, culture, and religion, since such reductive accounts are exactly what so many of the remarks on Frazer are intended to call into question. Ray Monk writes, in this vein, "His perception of the decline of the countries of Western Europe was always more Spenglerian than Marxian, and as we have remarked earlier, it is likely that he was extremely attracted to the portrait of life in the Soviet Union drawn by Keynes in his *Short View of Russia*—a portrait which, while deprecating Marxism as an economic theory, applauded its practice in Russia as a new religion, in which there were no supernatural beliefs but, rather, deeply held religious attitudes." Monk, *Duty of Genius*, 348. See also Janik and Toulmin, *Wittgenstein's Vienna*, 142.

57. Wittgenstein, *Culture and Value*, 5.

58. Wittgenstein, *Wittgenstein's Nachlass*, 183 46 (my translation). See also Wittgenstein, *Private and Public Occasions*, 54. Wittgenstein continued to employ Spenglerian tropes well into his later phase of philosophizing, as seen in this remark from 1947 (quoted earlier in chapter 4, note 46): "Perhaps one day a culture will arise out of this civilization. Then there will be a real history of the discoveries of the 18th, 19th, and 20th centuries, which will be of profound interest."

BIBLIOGRAPHY

Allison, Henry. *Kant's Transcendental Idealism.* New Haven, Conn.: Yale University Press, 1983.

Anscombe, G. E. M. *An Introduction to Wittgenstein's Tractatus.* London: Hutchison University Library, 1959.

———. "Critical Notice of Saul A. Kripke, *Wittgenstein on Rules and Private Language.*" *Canadian Journal of Philosophy* 15: 103–109.

———. "Wittgenstein on Rules and Private Language." *Ethics* 95: 342–352.

Augustine. *City of God.* Trans. H. Bettenson. London: Penguin, 1984.

———. *Confessions.* Trans. R. S. Pine-Coffin. London: Penguin, 1961.

Ayer, A. J. *Language, Truth, and Logic.* New York: Dover, 1952.

———, ed. *Logical Positivism.* New York: The Free Press, 1959.

Baker, G. P., and P. M. S. Hacker. *An Analytical Commentary on Wittgenstein's* Philosophical Investigations. Oxford: Blackwell, 1980.

———. *Wittgenstein: Rules, Grammar, and Necessity: An Analytic Commentary on the Philosophical Investigations.* Oxford: Blackwell, 1985.

Black, Max. *A Companion to Wittgenstein's "Tractatus."* Cambridge: Cambridge University Press, 1964.

Blattner, William. "Remarks on Iain Thomson's *Heidegger on Ontotheology.*" Paper presented at the Pacific Division of the American Philosophical Association, March 23, 2006.

Bloor, David. *Wittgenstein, Rules, and Institutions.* New York: Routledge, 1997.

Bourdieu, Pierre. *Outline of a Theory of Practice.* Cambridge: Cambridge University Press, 1977.

Bouveresse, Jacques. "'The Darkness of This Time': Wittgenstein and the Modern World." In *Wittgenstein Centenary Essays,* ed. A. P. Griffiths, 11–39. Cambridge: Cambridge University Press, 1992.

Bouwsma, O. K. *Wittgenstein: Conversations, 1949–1951.* Ed. J. L. Craft and Ronald E. Hustwit. Indianapolis, Ind.: Hackett, 1986.

Brenner, William H. *Wittgenstein's* Philosophical Investigations. Albany, N.Y.: SUNY Press, 1999.

Britton, K. "Portrait of a Philosopher." *The Listener* 53: 1071–1072.

Carman, Taylor. *Heidegger's Analytic: Interpretation, Discourse, and Authenticity in* Being and Time. Cambridge: Cambridge University Press, 2003.

Carnap, Rudolph. "The Elimination of Metaphysics Through Logical Analysis of Language." In *Logical Positivism*, ed. A. J. Ayer, 60–81. Glencoe, Ill.: The Free Press, 1959.

——. *The Logical Syntax of Language*. Peru, Ill.: Open Court, 2002.

Carruthers, Peter. *The Metaphysics of the* Tractatus: Cambridge: Cambridge University Press, 1990.

Cavell, Stanley. "The Argument of the Ordinary." In *Conditions Handsome and Unhandsome: The Constitution of Emersonian Perfectionism*. Chicago: University of Chicago Press, 1990.

——. *The Claim of Reason: Wittgenstein, Skepticism, Morality, and Tragedy*. Oxford: Clarendon Press, 1979.

——. "Declining Decline." In *This New Yet Unapproachable America: Lectures After Emerson After Wittgenstein*. Albuquerque: Living Batch Press, 1989.

——. "Existentialism and Analytic Philosophy." *Daedalus* 93 (1964): 946–974.

——. *Must We Mean What We Say? A Book of Essays*. New York: Scribner, 1969.

——. *The World Viewed: Reflections on the Ontology of Film*. New York: Viking, 1971.

Conant, James. "Kierkegaard, Wittgenstein, and Nonsense." In *Pursuits of Reason*, ed. Ted Cohen, Paul Guyer, and Hilary Putnam, 195–224. Lubbock: Texas Tech University Press, 1982.

——. "The Method of the *Tractatus*." In *From Frege to Wittgenstein: Perspectives on Early Analytic Philosophy*, ed. Erich Reck, 374–462. Oxford: Oxford University Press, 2002.

——. "Must We Show What We Cannot Say?" In *The Senses of Stanley Cavell*, ed. Richard Fleming and Michael Payne, 242–283. Lewisburg, Penn.: Bucknell University Press, 1989.

——. "Putting Two and Two Together: Kierkegaard, Wittgenstein, and the Point of View for Their Work as Authors." In *Philosophy and the Grammar of Religious Belief*, ed. Timothy Tessin and Mario von der Ruhr, 248–331. New York: St. Martin's Press, 1995.

——. "The Search for Logically Alien Thought: Descartes, Kant, Frege, and the *Tractatus*." *Philosophical Topics* 20, no. 1 (Fall 1991): 115–180.

——. "Throwing Away the Top of the Ladder." *Yale Review* 79 (1989–1990): 328–364.

——. "Two Conceptions of *Die Überwindung der Metaphysik*." In *Wittgenstein in America*, ed. Timothy McCarthy and Sean C. Stidd, 13–61. Oxford: Oxford University Press, 2001.

Conant, James, and Cora Diamond. "On Reading the *Tractatus* Resolutely." In *The Lasting Significance of Wittgenstein's Philosophy*, ed. Max Kölbel and Bernhard Weiss, 46–99. London: Routledge, 2004.

Cooper, David E. *Existentialism: A Reconstruction*. Oxford: Blackwell, 1990.

——. *Heidegger*. London: The Claridge Press, 1996.

——. "Wittgenstein, Heidegger, and Humility." *Philosophy* 72 (1997): 105–123.

Costello, Diarmuid. "'Making Sense' of Nonsense: Conant and Diamond Read Wittgenstein's *Tractatus*." In *Post-Analytic* Tractatus: *A Reader*, ed. Barry Stocker, 99–125. Aldershot: Ashgate, 2004.

Crary, Alice, and Read, Rupert, eds. *The New Wittgenstein*. London: Routledge, 2000.

——. "Wittgenstein's Philosophy in Relation to Political Thought." In *The New Wittgenstein*, ed. Alice Crary and Rupert Read, 118–145. London: Routledge, 2000.

Diamond, Cora. "Criss-cross Philosophy." In *Wittgenstein at Work: Method in the Philosophical Investigations*, ed. Erich Ammereller and Eugen Fischer, 201–220. London: Routledge, 2004.

——. "Does Bismarck Have a Beetle in His Box?" In *The New Wittgenstein*, ed. Alice Crary and Rupert Read, 262–292. London: Routledge, 2000.

——. "Ethics, Imagination, and the Method of the *Tractatus.*" In *The New Wittgenstein*, ed. Alice Crary and Rupert Read, 149–173. London: Routledge, 2000.

——. "Frege and Nonsense." In *The Realistic Spirit: Wittgenstein, Philosophy, and the Mind.* Cambridge: The MIT Press, 1991.

——. "How Long Is the Standard Metre in Paris." In *Wittgenstein in America*, ed. Timothy G. McCarthy and Sean C. Stidd, 104–139. Oxford: Clarendon Press, 2001.

——. "Logical Syntax in Wittgenstein's *Tractatus.*" *Philosophical Quarterly* 55, no. 218 (January 2005): 78–89.

——. *The Realistic Spirit: Wittgenstein, Philosophy, and the Mind.* Cambridge, Mass.: The MIT Press, 1991.

——. "Rules: Looking in the Right Place." In *Attention to Particulars: Essays in Honor of Rush Rhees*, ed. D. Z. Phillips and Peter Winch, 12–34. New York: St. Martin's Press, 1989.

——. "Throwing Away the Ladder: How to Read the *Tractatus.*" In *The Realistic Spirit: Wittgenstein, Philosophy, and the Mind.* Cambridge, Mass.: The MIT Press, 1991.

——. "What Does a Concept Script Do?" In *The Realistic Spirit: Wittgenstein, Philosophy, and the Mind*, 115–144. Cambridge, Mass.: The MIT Press, 1991.

——. "What Nonsense Might Be." In *The Realistic Spirit: Wittgenstein, Philosophy, and the Mind.* Cambridge, Mass.: The MIT Press, 1991.

——. "Wittgenstein, Mathematics, and Ethics: Resisting the Attractions of Realism." In *The Cambridge Companion to Wittgenstein*, ed. David Stern and Hans Sluga, 226–260. Cambridge: Cambridge University Press, 1996.

Dreyfus, Hubert L. *Being-in-the-World: A Commentary on Heidegger's* Being and Time, *Division I.* Cambridge, Mass.: The MIT Press, 1991.

——. "Could Anything Be More Intelligible Than Everyday Intelligibility? Reinterpreting Division I of *Being and Time* in the light of Division II." In *Appropriating Heidegger*, ed. James E. Faulconer and Mark A. Wrathall. Cambridge: Cambridge University Press, 2000.

——. "Heidegger on the Connection Between Nihilism, Art, Technology, and Politics." In *The Cambridge Companion to Heidegger*, ed. Charles Guignon, 289–316. Cambridge: Cambridge University Press, 1993.

——. "Overcoming the Myth of the Mental: How Philosophers Can Profit from the Phenomenology of Everyday Expertise." APA Pacific Division Presidential Address, 2005. *Proceedings and Addresses of the American Philosophical Association* 79, no. 2 (November 2005).

——. "Response to McDowell." *Inquiry* 50, no. 4 (August 2007): 371–377.

——. "The Return of the Myth of the Mental." *Inquiry* 50, no. 4 (August 2007): 352–365.

Dreyfus, Stuart, and Hubert Dreyfus. *Mind Over Machine.* New York: The Free Press, 1986.

Drury, Maurice O'Connor. *The Danger of Words.* Bristol: Thoemmes Press, 1996.

Edwards, James C. *Ethics Without Philosophy: Wittgenstein and the Moral Life.* Gainesville: University of Florida, 1982.

Engel, S. M. "Schopenhauer's Impact on Wittgenstein." *Journal of the History of Philosophy* 7: 285–302.

Engelmann, Paul. *Letters from Ludwig Wittgenstein, with a Memoir.* Ed. B. F. McGuinness. Trans. L. Furtmüller. New York: Horizon Press, 1968.

Fogelin, Robert J. *Wittgenstein.* 2nd ed. London: Routledge & Kegan Paul, 1987.

Frege, Gottlob. *The Basic Laws of Arithmetic; Exposition of the System*. Ed. and trans. Montgomery Furth. Berkeley: University of California Press, 1964.

——. *The Foundations of Arithmetic: A Logico-Mathematical Enquiry Into the Concept of Number*. Trans. J. L. Austin. 2nd rev. ed. Evanston, Ill.: Northwestern University Press, 1978.

——. *The Frege Reader*. Ed. Michael Beaney. Oxford: Blackwell, 1997.

——. *Posthumous Writings*. Ed. Hans Hermes, Friedrich Kambartel, and Friedrich Kaulbach. Trans. Peter Long and Roger White. Oxford: Blackwell, 1979.

——. *Translations from the Philosophical Writings of Gottlob Frege*. Ed. Peter Geach and Max Black. Oxford: Blackwell, 1980.

Friedman, Michael. *A Parting of the Ways: Carnap, Cassirer, and Heidegger*. Peru, Ill.: Open Court, 2000.

Friedlander, Eli. *Signs of Sense: Reading Wittgenstein's Tractatus*. Cambridge, Mass.: Harvard University Press, 2001.

Gardiner, P. *Schopenhauer*. Harmondsworth: Penguin, 1963.

Gasking, D. A. T., and A. C. Jackson. "Ludwig Wittgenstein." *American Journal of Philosophy* 29: 73–80.

Geach, Peter. "Saying and Showing in Frege and Wittgenstein." In *Essays in Honour of G. H. von Wright*, ed. J. Hintikka, 56–70. Originally published in *Acta Philosophica Fennica* 28 (1976).

Genette, Gérard. *Paratexts*. Cambridge: Cambridge University Press, 1987.

Glock, Hans-Johann. "*Philosophical Investigations*: Principles of Interpretation." In *Wittgenstein: Towards a Re-Evaluation*, ed. Rudolf Haller and Johannes Brandl. Vienna: Hölder-Pichler-Tempsky, 1992.

Goldfarb, Warren. "I Want You to Hand Me a Slab." *Synthese* 56, no. 3: 265–282.

——. "Kripke on Wittgenstein on Rules." *Journal of Philosophy* 82: 471–488.

——. "Metaphysics and Nonsense: On Cora Diamond's *The Realistic Spirit*." *Journal of Philosophical Research* 22 (1997): 57–73.

——. "Wittgenstein, Mind, and Scientism." *Journal of Philosophy* 86 (1989): 635–642.

——. "Wittgenstein on Fixity of Meaning." In *Early Analytic Philosophy*, ed. William W. Tait, 75–89. Chicago: Open Court, 1997.

——. "Wittgenstein on Mind and Meaning." In *The Wittgenstein Legacy*, ed. Peter A. French, Theodore E. Uehling, and Howard K. Wettsetin, 109–122. South Bend, Ind.: University of Notre Dame Press, 1992.

Goodman, R. B. "How a Thing Is Said and Heard: Wittgenstein and Kierkegaard." *History of Philosophy Quarterly* 3: 335–353.

——. "Schopenhauer and Wittgenstein on Ethics." *Journal of the History of Philosophy* 17: 437–447.

——. *Wittgenstein and William James*. Cambridge: Cambridge University Press, 2002.

Griffiths, A. Phillips. "Wittgenstein and the Four-Fold Root of the Principle of Sufficient Reason." *Proceedings of the Aristotelian Society (Supplementary Volume)* 50: 1–20.

Guignon, Charles. *Heidegger and the Problem of Knowledge*. Indianapolis, Ind.: Hackett, 1983.

Guignon, Charles, and Derek Pereboom, eds. *Existentialism: Basic Writings*. Indianapolis, Ind.: Hackett, 1995.

Gustafsson, Martin. "Perfect Pitch and Austinian Examples: Cavell, McDowell, Wittgenstein, and the Philosophical Significance of Ordinary Language." *Inquiry* 48, no. 4 (August 2005): 356–389.

Hacker, P. M. S. *Insight and Illusion*. Rev. ed. Oxford: Clarendon Press, 1986.

——. "Was He Trying to Whistle it?" In *The New Wittgenstein*, ed. Alice Crary and Rupert Read, 353–388. London: Routledge, 2000.

——. "Wittgenstein, Carnap, and the New American Wittgensteinians." *The Philosophical Quarterly* 53, no. 210 (January 2003): 1–23.

Haller, Rudolf. *Questions on Wittgenstein*. Lincoln: University of Nebraska Press, 1988.

Hänsel, Ludwig. *Ludwig Wittgenstein. Eine Freundschaft: Briefe, Aufsätze, Kommentar*. Innsbruck: Haymon Verlag, 1994.

Heidegger, Martin. *Basic Problems of Phenomenology*. Trans. Albert Hofstadter. Bloomington: University of Indiana Press, 1982.

——. *Basic Questions in Philosophy: Selected "Problems" of "Logic."* Bloomington: Indiana University Press, 1994; *Gesamtausgabe*. Band 45. Frankfurt am Main: Vittorio Klostermann, 1992.

——. *Basic Writings*. Ed. David Farrell Krell. New York: Harper & Row, 1977.

——. *Being and Time*. Trans. John Macquarrie and Edward Robinson. New York: Harper & Row, 1962.

——. *Being and Time*. Trans. Joan Stambaugh. Albany, N.Y.: SUNY Press, 1996.

——. *Discourse on Thinking*. Trans. John M. Andersen and E. Hans Freund. New York: Harper, 1969.

——. *Introduction to Metaphysics*. Trans. Ralph Manheim. New Haven, Conn.: Yale University Press, 1959.

——. *Poetry, Language, Thought*. Trans. Albert Hofstadter. New York: Harper & Row, 1975.

——. *The Question Concerning Technology and Other Essays*. Trans. William Lovitt. New York: Harper & Row, 1977.

——. "The Way Back Into the Ground of Metaphysics." In *Existentialism from Dostoyevsky to Sartre*, ed. Walter Kaufmann. New York: New American Library, 1975.

——. *What Is Called Thinking?* Trans. J. Glenn Gray. New York: Harper & Row, 1972.

——. "What Is Metaphysics?" In *Basic Writings*, ed. David Farrell Krell. New York: Harper & Row, 1977.

Heller, Erich. "Ludwig Wittgenstein: Unphilosophische Betrachtungen." *Merkur* 13, no. 142: 1101–1120.

Hertz, Heinrich. *The Principles of Mechanics*. New York: Dover, 1956.

Hilmy, S. Stephen. *The Later Wittgenstein: The Emergence of a New Philosophical Method*. Oxford: Blackwell, 1987.

Hintikka, Jaakko, and Merrill B. Hintikka. *Investigating Wittgenstein*. Oxford: Blackwell, 1986.

Hylton, Peter. "Functions, Operations, and Sense in Wittgenstein's *Tractatus*." In *Early Analytic Philosophy*, ed. William W. Tait, 91–105. Chicago: Open Court, 1997.

——. "The Nature of the Proposition and the Revolt Against Idealism." In *Philosophy in History*, ed. R. Rorty and J. Schneewind, 375–397. Cambridge: Cambridge University Press, 1984.

——. *Russell, Idealism, and the Emergence of Analytic Philosophy*. Oxford: Clarendon Press, 1990.

Ishiguro, Hide. "Use and Reference of Names." In *Studies in the Philosophy of Wittgenstein*, ed. Peter Winch, 20–50. London: Routledge & K. Paul, 1969.

James, William. *The Varieties of Religious Experience*. New York: Vintage, 1990.

Janik, Allan. *Essays on Wittgenstein and Weininger*. Amsterdam: Rodopi, 1985.

——. "Schopenhauer and the Early Wittgenstein." *Philosophical Studies* (Ireland) 15: 76–95.

Janik, Allan, and Stephen Toulmin. *Wittgenstein's Vienna*. New York: Simon and Schuster, 1973.

Kant, Immanuel. *Critique of Pure Reason*. Trans. Norman Kemp Smith. New York: St. Martin's Press, 1965.

Kanterian, Edward. *Wittgenstein*. London: Reaktion Books, 2007.

Keicher, Peter. "*Untersuchungen zu* Wittgenstein's '*Diktat für Schlick.*'" In *Skriftserie fra Wittgensteinarkivet ved Universitetet i Bergen* 15 (1998): 43–90.

Kenny, Anthony. *Frege*. London: Penguin, 1995.

——. *Wittgenstein*. Harmondsworth: Penguin, 1975.

Kierkegaard, Søren. *Concluding Unscientific Postscript to Philosophical Fragments*. Ed. and trans. Howard V. Hong and Edna H. Hong. Princeton, N.J.: Princeton University Press, 1992.

——. *Fear and Trembling: A Dialectical Lyric*. Trans. Alastair Hannay. Harmondsworth: Penguin, 1985.

——. *Philosophical Fragments*. Trans. Howard V. Hong and Edna Hong. Princeton, N.J.: Princeton University Press, 1985.

——. *The Point of View for My Work as an Author*. Trans. Walter Lowrie. New York: Harper and Brothers, 1962.

——. *The Present Age*. Trans. Alexander Dru. New York: Harper & Row, 1962.

——. *The Sickness Unto Death: A Christian Psychological Exposition for Edification and Awakening by Anti-Climacus*. Trans. Alastair Hannay. London: Penguin, 1989.

Kisiel, Theodore. *The Genesis of Heidegger's* Being and Time. Berkeley: University of California Press, 1993.

Klagge, James. "Wittgenstein in Exile." In *Religion and Wittgenstein's Legacy*, ed. D. Z. Phillips and Mario von der Ruhr, 311–324. Ashgate: Aldershot, 2004.

——. "Wittgenstein on Non-Mediative Causality." *Journal of the History of Philosophy* (October 1999): 653–667.

Kremer, Michael. "The Argument of 'On Denoting.'" *Philosophical Review* 103, no. 2: 249–297.

——. "The Cardinal Problem of Philosophy." In *Wittgenstein and the Moral Life: Essays in Honor of Cora Diamond*, ed. Alice Crary, 143–176. Cambridge, Mass.: The MIT Press, 2007.

——. "Contextualism and Holism in the Early Wittgenstein: From *Prototractatus* to *Tractatus*." *Philosophical Topics* 25, no. 2 (1997): 87–120.

——. "Mathematics and Meaning in the *Tractatus*." *Philosophical Investigations* 25 (2002): 272–303.

——. "The Purpose of Tractarian Nonsense." *Nous* 35, no. 1 (March 2001): 39–73.

——. "To What Extent Is Solipsism a Truth?" In *Post-Analytic* Tractatus, ed. Barry Stocker, 59–84. Aldershot: Ashgate, 2004.

Kripke, Saul A. *Wittgenstein on Rules and Private Language: An Elementary Exposition*. Oxford: Blackwell, 1982.

Kuusela, Oskari. *The Struggle Against Dogmatism: Wittgenstein and the Concept of Philosophy*. Cambridge, Mass.: Harvard University Press, 2008.

Lovibond, Sabina. "The Late Seriousness of Cora Diamond." *Journal of Philosophical Research* 22 (1997): 43–55.

——. *Realism and Imagination in Ethics*. Oxford: Blackwell, 1983.

Malcolm, Norman. *Ludwig Wittgenstein, a Memoir*. London: Oxford University Press, 1962.

——. *Nothing Is Hidden*. Oxford: Blackwell, 1986.

——. *Wittgenstein: A Religious Point of View?* Ed. Peter Winch. Ithaca, N.Y.: Cornell University Press, 1994.

Maslow, Alexander. *A Study in Wittgenstein's Tractatus.* Berkeley: University of California Press, 1961.

McDowell, John. "Can We Conceive Meaning, Understanding, etc. as States of Mind?" Lecture in Skjolden, Norway, June 3, 2005. http://wab.aksis.uib.no/wab_contrib-audio-mcd-sk05.page.

——. "How Not to Read *Philosophical Investigations*: Brandom's Wittgenstein." In *Proceedings of the 24th International Wittgenstein-Symposium*, ed. Rudolph Haller and Klaus Puhl, 245–256. Wien: Hölder-Pichler-Tempsky, 2001.

——. "Meaning and Intentionality in Wittgenstein's Later Philosophy." In *The Wittgenstein Legacy*, ed. Peter A. French, Theodore E. Uehling, and Howard K. Wettstein, 40–52. South Bend, Ind.: University of Notre Dame Press, 1992.

——. *Mind and World.* Cambridge, Mass.: Harvard University Press, 1994.

——. "Non-Cognitivism and Rule-Following." In *Wittgenstein: To Follow a Rule*, ed. S. H. Holtzman and C. M. Leich, 141–162. London: Routledge and Kegan Paul, 1981.

——. "Response to Dreyfus." *Inquiry* 50, no. 4 (August 2007): 366–370.

——. "What Myth?" *Inquiry* 50, no. 4 (August 2007): 338–351.

——. "Wittgenstein on Following a Rule." In *Essays on Wittgenstein's Later Philosophy*, ed. Crispin Wright, 324–363. Dordrecht: Reidel, 1984.

McGinn, Marie. "Between Metaphysics and Nonsense: Elucidation in Wittgenstein's *Tractatus*." *The Philosophical Quarterly* 49, no. 197 (1999): 491–513.

McGuinness, Brian, "Freud and Wittgenstein." In *Wittgenstein and His Times*, ed. Brian McGuinness, 27–43. Oxford: Blackwell, 1982.

——. "The Mysticism of the *Tractatus*." *Philosophical Review* 75, no. 3 (1966): 305–328.

——. "Wittgenstein: Philosophy and Literature." In *Wittgenstein: The Philosopher and His Works*, ed. Alois Pichler and Simo Säätelä, 326–340. Bergen: Working Papers from the Wittgenstein Archives at the University of Bergen, No. 17, 2005.

——. *Young Ludwig: Wittgenstein's Life, 1889–1921.* Oxford: Oxford University Press, 2005.

McManus, Denis. "Rules, Regression and the 'Background': Dreyfus, Heidegger, and McDowell." *European Journal of Philosophy* 16, no. 3 (2008): 432–458.

Merleau-Ponty, Maurice. *The Phenomenology of Perception.* Trans. Colin Smith. London: Routledge & Kegan Paul, 2002.

Monk, Ray. *Ludwig Wittgenstein: The Duty of Genius.* New York: The Free Press, 1990.

Mounce, H. O. *Wittgenstein's Tractatus: An Introduction.* Chicago: University of Chicago Press, 1981.

Mulhall, Stephen. *Heidegger and Being and Time.* London: Routledge, 1996.

——. *Wittgenstein's Private Language: Grammar, Nonsense, and Imagination in Philosophical Investigations §§243–315.* Oxford: Oxford University Press, 2007.

Murray, Michael. "A Note on Wittgenstein and Heidegger." *The Philosophical Review* 83 (1974): 501–503.

Nedo, M. and M. Ranchetti, eds. *Ludwig Wittgenstein: Sein Leben in Bildern und Texten.* Frankfurt: Suhrkamp, 1983.

Nyíri, J. C. "Wittgenstein's Later Work in Relation to Conservatism." In *Wittgenstein and His Times*, ed. Brian McGuinness, 44–68. Oxford: Blackwell, 1982.

——. "Wittgenstein's New Traditionalism." In *Essays on Wittgenstein in Honour of G. H. von Wright*, ed. J. Hintikka. Originally published in *Acta Philosophica Fennica* 28 (1976).

Parks, Tim. "Description of a Struggle" *The Nation* (June 14, 2004): 42–43.

Pears, D. F. *The False Prison*. Oxford: Clarendon Press, 1987.

Polt, Richard. *Heidegger: An Introduction*. Ithaca, N.Y.: Cornell University Press, 1999.

Ramsey, Frank Plumpton. *The Foundations of Mathematics and Other Logical Essays*. London: Routledge & Kegan Paul, 1931.

Reid, Lynette. "Wittgenstein's Ladder: The *Tractatus* and Nonsense." *Philosophical Investigations* 21: 97–151.

Renan, Ernst. *History of the People of Israel*. Vol. 1. London: General Books, 2010.

Rentsch, Thomas. *Heidegger und Wittgenstein. Existential- und Sprachanalysen zu den Grundlagen philosophischer Anthropologie*. Stuttgart: Klett-Cota, 1985.

Rhees, Rush, ed. *Ludwig Wittgenstein: Personal Recollections*. Totowa, N.J.: Rowman and Littlefield, 1981.

——. "Wittgenstein on Language and Ritual." In *Wittgenstein and His Times*, ed. Brian McGuinness, 69–107. Oxford: Blackwell, 1982.

Ricketts, Thomas. "Pictures, Logic, and the Limits of Sense in Wittgenstein's *Tractatus*." In *The Cambridge Companion to Wittgenstein*, ed. David Stern and Hans Sluga, 59–99. Cambridge: Cambridge University Press, 1996.

——. "Frege, the *Tractatus*, and the Logocentric Predicament." *Nous* 19, no. 1: 3–15.

——. "Frege's 1906 Foray Into Metalogic." *Philosophical Topics* 25, no. 2 (1997): 69–188.

——. "Generality, Meaning, and Sense in Frege." *Pacific Philosophical Quarterly* 67, no. 3: 172–195.

——. "Logic and Truth in Frege." *Proceedings of the Aristotelian Society (Supplementary Volume)* 70 (1996): 141–175.

——. "Objectivity and Objecthood: Frege's Metaphysics of Judgement." In *Frege Synthesized: Essays on the Philosophical and Foundational Work of Gottlob Frege*, ed. L. Haaparanta and J. Hintikka, 65–95. Dordrecht: Reidel, 1986.

——. "Truth-Values and Courses-of-Value in Frege's *Grundgesetze*." In *Early Analytic Philosophy*, ed. William Tait, 187–211. Chicago: Open Court, 1997.

Rohatyn, D. A. "A Note on Heidegger and Wittgenstein." *Philosophy Today* 15: 69–71.

Rorty, Richard. *Essays on Heidegger and Others*. Cambridge: Cambridge University Press, 1991.

——. "Heidegger, Wittgenstein, and the Reification of Language." In *The Cambridge Companion to Heidegger*, ed. Charles Guignon, 337–357. Cambridge: Cambridge University Press, 1993.

Rowe, M. W. "Goethe and Wittgenstein." *Philosophy* 66 (1991): 283–303.

Rubin, Jane. *Too Much of Nothing: Modern Culture, The Self, and Salvation in Kierkegaard's Thought*. Ph.D. dissertation, University of California, Berkeley, 1984.

Russell, Bertrand. *Analysis of Mind*. London: Routledge, 1995.

——. *Introduction to Mathematical Philosophy*. London: G. Allen & Unwin, 1975.

——. *Logic and Knowledge: Essays 1901–1950*. Ed. Robert Charles Marsh. London: George Allen & Unwin, 1956.

——. *Mysticism and Logic, and Other Essays*. New York: Longmans, Green, 1921.

——. "On Denoting." In *Essays in Analysis*, ed. Douglas Lackey, 103–119. London: Allen and Unwin, 1973.

——. *Philosophical Essays*. London: Allen & Unwin, 1966.

———. *The Philosophy of Logical Atomism*. Ed. David Pears. Chicago: Open Court, 1985.

———. *The Principles of Mathematics*. New York: Norton, 1996.

———. *The Problems of Philosophy*. New York: Oxford University Press, 1959.

———. *Theory of Knowledge: The 1913 Manuscript*. London: George Allen and Unwin, 1984.

Russell, Bertrand, and Alfred North Whitehead. *Principia Mathematica to *56*. Cambridge: Cambridge University Press, 1962.

Ryle, Gilbert. "Ludwig Wittgenstein." *Analysis* 12: 1–9.

Schopenhauer, Arthur. *Essays and Aphorisms*. Ed. and trans. R. J. Hollingdale. London: Penguin, 1970.

———. *The Four-fold Root of the Principle of Sufficient Reason*. Trans. E. F. J. Payne. La Salle, Ill.: Open Court, 1974.

———. *The World as Will and Representation*. Vol. 1. Trans. E. F. J. Payne. New York: Dover, 1966.

Schulte, Joachim. "Chor und Gesetz: Zur 'morphologischen Methode' bei Goethe und Wittgenstein." In *Chor und Gesetz: Wittgenstein im Kontext*, 11–42. Frankfurt am Main: Surhkamp, 1990.

Sluga, Hans D. *Gottlob Frege*. London: Routledge and Kegan Paul, 1980.

Spengler, Oswald. *The Decline of the West*. New York: Alfred Knopf, 1926.

Stern, David G. "How Many Wittgensteins?" In *Wittgenstein: The Philosopher and His Works*, ed. Alois Pichler and Simo Säätelä, 164–188. Working Papers from the Wittgenstein Archives at the University of Bergen 17. Bergen: Wittgenstein Archives at the University of Bergen, 2005.

———. "The 'Middle Wittgenstein': From Logical Atomism to Practical Holism." *Synthese* 87 (1991): 203–226.

———. "Nestroy, Augustine, and the Opening of the *Philosophical Investigations*." In *Proceedings of the 24th International Wittgenstein-Symposium*, ed. Rudolf Haller and Klaus Puhl, 425–445. Wien: Hölder-Pichler-Tempsky, 2001.

Stone, Brad. "Curiosity as the Thief of Wonder: An Essay on Heidegger's Critique of the Ordinary Conception of Time." *Kronoscope* 6, no. 2 (2006): 205–229.

Sullivan, Peter M. "On Trying to Be Resolute: A Response to Kremer on the *Tractatus*." *European Journal of Philosophy* 10, no. 1 (2002): 43–78.

———. "What Is the *Tractatus* About?" In *The Lasting Significance of Wittgenstein's Philosophy*, ed. Max Kölbel and Bernhard Weiss, 32–45. London: Routledge, 2004.

Szabados, Bela. "Autobiography After Wittgenstein." *Journal of Aesthetics and Art Criticism* 50, no. 1 (1992): 1–12.

———. "Autobiography and Philosophy." *Metaphilosophy* 26, nos. 1–2 (1995): 63–80.

Taylor, Charles. *The Ethics of Authenticity*. Cambridge, Mass.: Harvard University Press, 1991.

———. *Modern Social Imaginaries*. Durham, N.C.: Duke University Press, 2004.

———. *Philosophical Arguments*. Cambridge, Mass.: Harvard University Press, 1995.

———. *Philosophical Papers*. Vol. 1: *Human Agency and Language*. Cambridge: Cambridge University Press, 1985.

———. *Philosophical Papers*. Vol. 2: *Philosophy and the Human Sciences*. Cambridge: Cambridge University Press, 1985.

———. *Sources of the Self: The Making of the Modern Identity*. Cambridge, Mass.: Harvard University Press, 1989.

——. "To Follow a Rule." In *Philosophical Arguments*. Cambridge, Mass.: Harvard University Press, 1995.

——. "Understanding and Explanation in the 'Geisteswissenschaften.'" In *Wittgenstein: To Follow a Rule*, ed. S. H. Holtzman and C. M. Leich, 191–210. London: Routledge and Kegan Paul, 1981.

Thompson, Caleb. "Wittgenstein's Confessions." *Philosophical Investigations* 23, no. 1 (2000): 1–25.

——. "Wittgenstein, Tolstoy, and the Meaning of Life." *Philosophical Investigations* 20, no. 2 (1997): 97–116.

Tilghman, Benjamin R. *Wittgenstein, Ethics, and Aesthetics: The View from Eternity*. Albany, N.Y.: SUNY Press, 1991.

Tolstoy, Leo. *Confession*. New York: Norton, 1996.

——. *My Confession, My Religion, the Gospel in Brief*. New York: Charles Scribner's Sons, 1922.

Toulmin, Stephen. "Ludwig Wittgenstein." *Encounter* 32 (January 1969): 58–71.

von Savigny, Eike. *Wittgenstein's "Philosophische Untersuchungen": Ein Buch für Leser*. Frankfurt am Main: Vittorio Klostermann, 1994.

von Wright, G. H. *Wittgenstein*. Oxford: Blackwell, 1982.

Waismann, Friedrich. *Wittgenstein and the Vienna Circle*. Ed. Brian McGuinness. Trans. Joachim Schulte and Brian McGuinness. Oxford: Blackwell, 1979.

Weiner, David Avraham. *Genius and Talent: Schopenhauer's Influence on Wittgenstein's Early Philosophy*. Rutherford, N.J.: Fairleigh Dickinson University Press, 1992.

Weiner, Joan. "Frege and the Linguistic Turn." *Philosophical Topics* 25, no. 2 (1997): 265–288.

——. *Frege in Perspective*. Ithaca, N.Y.: Cornell University Press, 1990.

——. "Has Frege a Philosophy of Language?" In *Early Analytic Philosophy*, ed. William Tait, 249–272. Chicago: Open Court, 1997.

Wiggins, David. "Truth, Invention, and the Meaning of Life." *Proceedings of the British Academy* (1976).

Williams, Meredith. "Nonsense and Cosmic Exhile." In *The Lasting Significance of Wittgenstein's Philosophy*, ed. Max Kölbel and Bernhard Weiss, 6–31. London: Routledge, 2004.

Williams, Meredith. *Wittgenstein, Mind and Meaning: Towards a Social Conception of Mind*. London: Routledge, 1999.

Wittgenstein, Ludwig. *Blue and Brown Books*. 2nd ed. Oxford: Blackwell, 1969.

——. *Culture and Value*. Rev. 2nd ed. Ed. G. H. von Wright. Trans. Peter Winch. Oxford: Blackwell, 1998.

——. *Cambridge Letters: Correspondence with Russell, Keynes, Moore, and Sraffa*. Ed. B. F. McGuinness and G. H. von Wright. Ithaca, N.Y.: Cornell University Press, 1997.

——. "Lecture on Ethics." In *Philosophical Occasions, 1912–1951*, ed. James C. Klagge and Alfred Nordmann. Indianapolis, Ind.: Hackett, 1993.

——. *Lectures and Conversations on Aesthetics, Psychology,, and Religious Belief*. Ed. Cyril Barrett. Berkeley: University of California Press, 1966.

——. *Letters to C. K. Ogden*. Ed. G. H. von Wright. Oxford: Blackwell, 1973.

——. *Ludwig Wittgenstein: Public and Private Occasions*. Ed. James C. Klagge and Alfred Nordmann. Lanham, Md.: Rowman and Littlefield, 2003.

——. *Ludwig Wittgenstein und der Wiener Kreis*. Ed. Friedrich Waismann. Frankfurt: Suhrkamp, 2001.

——. *Notebooks, 1914–1916*. Ed. G. E. M. Anscombe and G. H. von Wright. Trans. G. E. M. Anscombe. Chicago: University of Chicago Press, 1979.

——. *On Certainty*. Ed. G. E. M. Anscombe and G. H. von Wright. Trans. Denis Paul and G. E. M. Anscombe. New York: Harper, 1972.

——. *Philosophical Grammar*. Ed. Rush Rhees. Trans. Anthony Kenny. Oxford: Blackwell 1974.

——. *Philosophical Investigations*. 2nd ed. Ed. G. E. M Anscombe and Rush Rhees. Trans. G. E. M. Anscombe. Oxford: Blackwell, 1997.

——. *Philosophical Occasions, 1912–1951*. Ed. James C. Klagge and Alfred Nordmann. Indianapolis, Ind.: Hackett, 1993.

——. *Philosophical Remarks*. Ed. Rush Rhees. Trans. Raymond Hargreaves and Roger White. Oxford: Blackwell, 1975.

——. *Philosophische Untersuchungen. Kritisch-genetische Edition*. Ed. Joachim Schulte. Frankfurt am Main: Suhrkamp, 2001.

——. *Prototractatus: An Early Version of* Tractatus Logico-philosophicus. Ed. B. F. McGuinness, T. Nyberg, and G. H. von Wright. Trans. D. F. Pears and B. F. McGuinness. Ithaca, N.Y.: Cornell University Press, 1971.

——. "Remarks on Frazer's *Golden Bough*." In *Philosophical Occasions, 1912–1951*, ed. James C. Klagge and Alfred Normann. Indianapolis, Ind.: Hackett, 1993.

——. *Remarks on the Foundations of Mathematics*. Ed. G. H. von Wright, R. Rhees, and G. E. M. Anscombe. Trans. G. E. M. Anscombe. Cambridge, Mass.: The MIT Press, 1983.

——. *Remarks on the Philosophy of Psychology*. Ed. G. E. M. Anscombe and G. H. von Wright. Trans. G. E. M. Anscombe. Chicago: University of Chicago Press, 1980.

——. *Tractatus Logico-philosophicus*. Trans. C. K. Ogden. London: Routledge & K. Paul, 1922.

——. *Tractatus Logico-philosophicus*. Ed. D. F. Pears and B. F. McGuinness. London: Routledge & K. Paul, 1974 (1961).

——. *Wittgenstein's Lectures: Cambridge, 1932–1935*. Ed. Alice Ambrose. Amherst, N.Y.: Prometheus Books, 2001.

——. *Wittgenstein's Lectures: Cambridge, 1930–1932*. Ed. Desmond Lee. Oxford: Blackwell, 1980.

——. *Wittgenstein's Lectures on the Foundations of Mathematics, Cambridge, 1939*. Ed. Cora Diamond. Ithaca, N.Y.: Cornell University Press, 1976.

——. *Wittgenstein's Nachlass: The Bergen Electronic Edition. Text and Facsimile Version*. Oxford: Oxford University Press, 2000.

——. *Zettel*. Ed. G. E. M. Anscombe and G. H. von Wright. Trans. G. E. M. Anscombe. Berkeley: University of California Press, 1967.

Wolgast, Elizabeth. "A Religious Point of View." *Philosophical Investigations* 27, no. 2 (2004): 129–147.

Worthington, B. A. "Ethics and the Limits of Language in Wittgenstein's *Tractatus*." *Journal of the History of Philosophy* 19: 481–496.

Young, J. "Wittgenstein, Kant, Schopenhauer, and Critical Philosophy." *Theoria* 50: 73–105.

Zimmerman, Michael. *Heidegger's Confrontation with Modernity: Technology, Politics, Art*. Bloomington: Indiana University Press, 1990.

INDEX

on, 118–20, 121, 211n37, 211n38; Goethe
quoted in light of, 211n40; language function and, 210n38; philosophical questions
resulting from, 121–22; practices reciprocity
with, 115, 117–18, 121, 211n35; rules as rails,
116, 127, 137, 143, 212n43, 216n14, 219n43;
Taylor on, 117–18, 211n35, 212n43
Russell, Bertrand, 22, 52, 93, 175n9; criticism of,
96–97; letter to, 65
Russian revolution, 230n56

safety, experience of absolute, 28, 37, 59, 62–67,
187n60; guilt and, 64, 192n93
Saint Paul, 81, 84; faith writings by, 77, 82; Kremer on Wittgenstein, Augustine and, 83
Schlick, Moritz, 74; letter to, 110, 175n10
Schopenhauer, Arthur, 26–30, 177n24, 178n39,
214n7; Anscombe on influence of, 26, 29,
178n39; Hacker on, 26, 177n24; nature
insight of, 27, 66; *The World as Will and
Representation*, 27–28
Schulte, Joachim, 108
science: behavior and, 224n80; cultural context
of, 57–58, 189n73; ethical, 39, 40–41; language and, 228n35; meaning and, 141–42,
220n46; metaphysics and, 165; mythology
of rationality in, 216n14; over use of term,
98; philosophical problems as based in, 154;
progress and, 126, 214n4; wonder removed
by, 56–57, 137, 189n71
scientific rationality, 122–23, 213n46, 216n14
scientific thinking, 51, 98, 186n48, 228n35
self, they-, 46, 48, 62
self-justification, 83
self-understanding, 2, 143–44, 171n3; awakening reader's, 51, 61, 68, 81, 98, 194n103;
embodied, 212n43; truism acknowledgment as, 121
sentences: anyone, 60, 61, 66–67, 85; *Begriffsschrift* notation about, 94–95; Broad
on *Tractatus*, 207n29; declarative, later
remarks on, 97–98; Diamond on nonsensical, 59, 207n25; indicative, 102–3; use of, 96.
See also ordinary sentences

Situation, 49, 185n38
skepticism, 161–62, 225n5, 227n29; modern
naturalism and, 165
social conservatism, charge of political and,
148–50, 161, 223nn74–76, 224nn77–78,
224nn80–81
solipsism, 13, 26; Hacker on Transcendental,
29–30, 178n43
Spengler, Oswald: on completed systems,
99–100; *Decline of the West*, 132; Haller on
influence of, 128, 214n7; Heidegger's criticism of, 220n51; influence of, 127–34, 149,
214n7, 215n9, 216nn18–19, 230n58; political
conservatism and, 149
Sraffa, Piero, 127
Stern, David G., 108–10, 209n13, 209n16,
213n48
students. *See* readers
substantial nonsense, 30–31
surprise, Cavell on wonder and, 138,
219nn37–38

Taylor, Charles, 9–10, 114, 136, 138, 141; on
disengaged picture, 122, 212n43; on Heidegger, 8; on rule following, 117–18, 211n35,
212n43
theology, Wittgenstein's attitude toward religion and systematic, 146–47, 222n64
theory: against, 2, 3, 27, 67, 165; absence of
logic or language, 94–95; of deterioration,
135–36; disengaged, 114, 116–17, 120–22,
139, 212nn42–43; as having no value, 67,
165; magical practices as, Frazer's view of,
129–30; of meaning, 112, 113, 118, 210n20;
philosophy reliance on, 2, 3; *Tractatus* readings targeting, 112
therapeutic readings, *Tractatus* resolute and,
182n1
they (Das Man): Heidegger's concept of,
46–47, 49, 50, 71, 184nn19–20, 199n130;
tranquilized ways of, 63
they-self, 46, 48, 62
thinking: assimilation of Wittgenstein's, 1–2;
causal scientific modes of, 98; deliberate or

thinking (*continued*)
unconscious, 47, 184n23; new ways of, 164, 166; scientific, 51, 98, 186n48, 228n35; spirit *vs.* content of, 149
throwing away ladder, of elucidatory nonsense, 42–43, 86, 92–93, 95–96
"Throwing Away the Ladder" (Diamond), 205n12, 207n25
totality: contrasted with limited whole, 54; of language, 61–62; world as, 54
Toulmin, Stephen, 1, 30, 125–26, 172n13, 214n2; *Wittgenstein's Vienna*, 4
Tractatus (Wittgenstein), 6, 12–13; *Being and Time* contrasted with, 75, 89, 199n138; *Being and Time* resonances with, 59–71, 59–74, 72, 190n86, 191n87, 195n107, 199n128, 199n130; concluding remarks of, 20–21, 92; *Concluding Unscientific Postscript* compared to, 79–81; as cultural critique, 50–51, 55–56, 98, 185n45, 186n47, 189n73; Diamond on philosophy in, 42, 43, 182n1; *existentiale* of, 96; Friedlander on, 172n17; front matter of, 110; imagination employed in, 33–34; individualization in reader of, 86–87; ineffable truths in, 24, 30, 32, 40, 41, 77, 176n14, 181n81; interpretations of, 19–41; metaphysics in, 36, 95, 206n22; motto to, 209n14; notebooks for, 100; *Philosophical Investigations* as refuting, 90; *Philosophical Investigations* contrasted with, 99–103; preface to, 20, 21, 31, 69, 85–86, 91, 92, 94, 110, 206n14; progress between *Philosophical Investigations* and, 111, 112, 150; propositions discussion in, 21–24, 25; *Protractatus* and, 187n58; saying and showing in, 21–24, 176n18; theories in, readings on, 112; transformational aim of, 85–87; translation of passages in, 175n6, 176n19; Wittgenstein's criticism of, 90–91, 94, 96–98, 205n6, 207n29; "world" expressed in, 54. *See also* ethical aim, *Tractatus*; nonsense, *Tractatus* role of; resolute readings, *Tractatus*

tradition: *Bildung* and, 225n81; illusions as basis of philosophical, 32–33, 35, 86, 180n64; religion and, 147–48
Transcendental Solipsism, Hacker's, 29–30, 178n43
transformation: cultural, 152, 167–69, 230n56; philosopher's role in, 167–68; reader's, 84–85, 123–24; relationship to language, 2, 61, 70, 91, 98, 138; in thinking about progress, 123–24; *Tractatus* aim of, 85–87
translation: *Being and Time* terms, 185n28; *Culture and Value* passages, 189n71; *Nachlass* passages, 51, 186n49; *Tractatus* passages, 175n6, 176n19; Waismann's recordings, 197n120
transvaluation, of values, 168
truth: as agreement with reality, 69, 196n112; authenticity and, 69; historical, 146; ineffable, 24, 30, 32, 40, 41, 77, 176n14, 176n19, 181n81; subjectivity becoming, 79

understanding: embodied, 212n43; practices' background, 136–37, 218n34; urge to misunderstand, 163. *See also* self-understanding
Understanding-of-Being, Heidegger's, 46
urge: to confront limits of language, 44–45, 60, 71–72, 89, 194n105; to misunderstand, 163

values: later philosophy on wonder and, 134–44; transvaluation of, 168
Varieties of Religious Experience (James), 65, 193n97
Vienna Circle, 72
virtue: grammar of wonder with, 147–48; later philosophy on wonder and, 134–44; reverence as, 14, 141; as *Tractatus* ethical aim, 83–84, 204n163; transformation compared to, 204n163; wonder as meta-, 141
von Wright, G. H., 4, 11–12, 160–61, 166, 229n47; on unhealthy culture, 163–64

Waismann, Friedrich, recordings by, 3, 7, 64, 67, 71–72, 194n105, 197n120; on completed systems, 99, 207n2